U-Boat War
1914-1918

U-Boat War
1914-1918
Two Contrasting Accounts from
Both Sides of the Conflict at Sea
During the Great War

The U-Boat Hunters
by James B. Connolly

The Diary of a
U-Boat Commander
by Karl von Schenk

With an introduction and
explanatory notes by
Etienne

*U-Boat War 1914-1918: Two Contrasting Accounts from
Both Sides of the Conflict at Sea During the Great War*

The U-Boat Hunters
by James B. Connolly

The Diary of a U-Boat Commander
by Karl von Schenk

Published by Leonaur Ltd

Text in this form and material original to this edition
copyright © 2008 Leonaur Ltd

ISBN: 978-1-84677-458-4 (hardcover)
ISBN: 978-1-84677-457-7 (softcover)

http://www.leonaur.com

Publisher's Notes

The opinions expressed in this book are those of the author
and are not necessarily those of the publisher.

Contents

The U-Boat Hunters   7
  Foreword   9
  Navy Ships   11
  Navy Men   17
  Seeing Them Across   23
  The U-Boats Appear   31
  Crossing the Channel   41
  The Censors   50
  One They Didn't Get   58
  The Doctor Takes Charge   67
  The 343 Stays Up   77
  The Cargo Boats   84
  Flotilla Humour—At Sea   92
  Flotilla Humour—Ashore   100
  The Unquenchable Destroyer Boys   108
  The Marines Have Landed   117
  The Navy as a Career   126
  The Sea Babies   135

The Diary of a U-Boat Commander   **149**

The U-Boat Hunters

by James B. Connolly

"Where you-all going?... Can't you-all see where you're going? Keep off—keep off."

Foreword

What a great thing if we could do away with war!

But men are not cast in that mould. We shall continue to have wars; and some day the world is going to have a war to which the present will serve only as a try-out.

When that war comes our country will probably have to bear the burden for the western hemisphere. In that war our navy will be our first line of defence; and what we do for our navy now will have much to do with what our navy will be able to do for us then.

Our navy to-day is made up of good ships and capable, courageous, hard-working officers and men. There are some fuddy-duddies and politicians among them, but most of them are on the job every minute. Their highest hope is the chance to serve their country. The chapters in this book which tell of their U-boat hunting only prove once more their great qualities.

There are chapters in this book which have nothing to do with U-boat hunting, but have much to do with the navy. Such are the two opening chapters and the three closing chapters. The motive of four of those chapters will probably be obvious; the chapter on the workings of a submarine is included in the hope of interesting our young fellows in that type of craft.

The need of such a chapter? Take this illustration of what people do not know about submarines: Three years ago an admiral on the other side was called into conference on the U-boat problem. When it came his turn to speak he said: "Gentlemen, it is child's talk to say that the U-boats will ever amount to anything! Disregard them utterly!"

Only three years ago that was, and that naval officer was considered for commander-in-chief of the Grand Fleet! Three years ago, and last year the U-boats sank 6,600,000 tons of shipping!

Right now Germany probably contemplates, or is actually constructing, U-boats with armour and guns heavy enough to engage on the surface any war craft up to the battle-cruiser class. How far from that to fighting the heaviest of surface craft—even to the battleships?

In the event of invasion—we might as well face that; refusing to think about it certainly will not eliminate the possibility—in the event of invasion by a powerful foe our first line of defence will be our navy. The navy will always be our first line of defence; and so the need to-day of interesting in our navy young men—progressive young men, who will learn from the past but prefer to live in the future.

J. B. C.

Chapter 1

Navy Ships

More than one-third of our naval force was being reviewed by the President. A most impressive assembly of men-o'-war it was, in tonnage and weight of metal the greatest ever floated by the waters of the western hemisphere.

The last of the fleet had arrived on the night before. From the bluffs along the shore they might have been seen approaching with a mysterious play of lights across the shadowy waters. In the morning they were all there. Hardly a type was lacking—the last 16,000-ton double-turreted battleship, the protected and heavy-armoured cruisers, monitors, despatch-boats, gun-boats, destroyers, attendant transport, and supply ships. Fifty ships, 1,200 guns, 16,000 men: all were there, even to the fascinating little submarines with their round black backs just showing above the water.

It was that chromatic sort of a morning when the canvas of the sailing-boats stands out startlingly white against the drizzly sky and the smoke from the stacks of the steamers takes on an accented coal-black, and, drooping, trails low in a murky wake. Rather a dull setting at this early hour; but not sufficiently dull to check the vivacity of the actors in the scene.

The President comes up the side of the *Mayflower* and, arrived at the head of the gangway, stands rigid as any stanchion to attention while his colours are shot to the truck and the scarlet-coated band plays the national hymn. Then, ascending to the bridge, he takes station by the starboard rail with the Secretary of the Navy at his shoulder. The clouds roll away, the sun comes out, and all is as it should be while he prepares to review the fleet, which thereafter responds aboundingly to every burst of his own inexhaustible enthusiasm.

And this fleet, which is lying to anchor in three lines of four miles or so each in length, with a respectful margin of clear water all about, is, viewed merely as a marine pageant, magnificent; as a display of potential fighting power, most convincing. No man might look on it and his sensibilities—admiration, patriotism, respect, whatever they might be—remain unstirred. To witness it is to pass in mental review the great fleets of other days and inevitably to draw conclusions. Beside this armament the ill-destined Armada, Von Tromp's stubborn squadrons, Nelson's walls of oak, or Farragut's steam and sail would dissolve like the glucose squadrons that boys buy at Christmas time. Even Dewey's workman-like batteries (this to mark the onward rush of naval science) would be rated obsolete beside the latest of these!

It was first those impressive battleships; and bearing down on them one better saw what terrible war-engines they are. Big guns pointing forward, big guns pointing astern, long-reaching guns abeam, and little business-looking machine-guns in the tops—their mere appearance suggests their ponderous might. A single broadside from any of these, properly placed, and there would be an end to the most renowned flag-ships of wooden-fleet days. And that this frightful power need never wait on wind or tide, nor be hindered in execution by any weather much short of a hurricane, is assured when we note that to-day, while the largest of the excursion steamers are heaving to the whitecaps, these are lying as immovable almost as sea-walls.

It is, first, the flag-ship which thunders out her greeting—one, two, three—twenty-one smoke-wreathed guns—while her sailor-men, arm to shoulder, mark in unwavering blue the lines of deck and superstructure. Meantime the officers on the bridge, admiral in the foreground, are standing in salute; and in the intervals of gun-fire there are crashing out over the waters again the strains of the "Star Spangled Banner." And the flag-ship left astern, the guns of the next in line boom out, and on her also the band plays and men and officers stand to attention; and so the next, and next. And, the battleships passed, come the armoured cruisers, riding the waters almost as ponderously as the battleships and hardly less powerful, but much faster on the trail; and they may run or fight as they please. After examining them, long and swift-looking, with no more space between decks than is needed for machinery, stores, armament, and lung-play for live men, the inevitable reflection recurs that the advance of mechanical power must colour our dreams of romance in future. Surely the old ways are gone. Imagine one of the old three-deckers aiming to work to windward of one of these in a gale, and if by any special dispensation of Providence she was allowed to win the weather berth, imagine her trying, while she rolled down to her middle deck, to damage one of these belted brutes, who meantime would be leisurely picking out the particular plank by which she intended to introduce into her enemy's vitals a weight of explosive metal sufficient in all truth to blow her out of water.

After the cruisers passed the craft of comparatively small tonnage and power follow—the gun-boats, transports, and supply ships; and, almost forgotten, the monitors, riding undisturbedly, like squat little forts afloat, with freeboard so low that with a slightly undulating sea a turtle could swim aboard. And after them the destroyers, which look their name. Most wicked inventions; no shining brass-work nor holy-stoned quarter, no decorative and convenient companionway down the side—no anything that doesn't make for results. Ugly, wicked-looking, with hooded ports from under which peer the muzzles of long-barrelled weapons that look as if they were designed for the single business of boring, and boring quickly, holes in steel plate.

So the *Mayflower* steams down the four long lines in review; and always the batteries and bands in action, the immortal hymn echoing out like rolling thunder between the flame-lit broadsides. From shore to shore the cannon detonate and our fighting blood is stirred. On the pleasure craft skirting the line of pickets like vaguely outlined picture boats in the dim, perspective haze, the people seem also to be stirred. We dream of the glory of battle; but better than that, the hymn which has stirred men to some fine deeds in the past, and shall to just as brave in the future, mounts like a surging tide to our hearts: *"Oh, say, can you see?"* it is asking. And we can see—no need of the glass—ahead, astern, abeam, aloft, some thousands of them streaming in the fresh west wind, and within signal distance of their beautiful waving folds a multitude of men and women in whom the sense of patriotism must have become immeasurably deepened for being within call this day.

The vibration of brass and pipe, the music and the saluting, one ship and the next, and never the welcome of one died out before the tumult of the next began. It was like the ceaseless roar of the ever-rolling ocean, with never an instant when the ear-drum did not vibrate to the salute of cannon, the blood tingle to the call of the nation's hymn. One felt faith in ships and crews after it; and later, when in the cabin of the *Mayflower* the admirals and captains gathered, to meet them and to listen was to feel anew the assurance that this navy will be ready when the hour comes to do whatever may be deemed right and well by the people.

* * * * *

The admirals and the *attachés* having departed and dinner become a thing of the past, it was time to review the electric-light display.

We were almost abreast of the first in line, and she was like a ship from fairyland. Along her run the bulbed lights extended, and thence to her turrets, and, higher up, followed the outline of stacks and tops and masts, with floating strings of them suspended here and there between. Most striking of all, her name in gigantic, flaming letters faced forward from her bridge. Now one ship decked in a multiplicity of jewels on this clear calm night would have been a beautiful sight—but where there were forty-odd of them—!

It was a sailor of the fleet, lurking in the shifting shadows of the bridge, that he might enjoy his surreptitious cigarette and not suffer disratement therefore, who reviewed the illuminations most illuminingly. "Man, but they do blaze out, don't they? They make me think of the post-cards we used to buy in foreign ports. You held them up before the light and they came out shining like a Christmas-tree. But no ships of cards these—and that's the wonderful thing, too. Seeing them to-day, with their batteries in view, 'twas enough to put the fear o' God in a man's heart, and now look at them—like a child's dream of heaven—that is, if we don't sheer too close and see that the guns are still there. And, look now, the tricks they're at!"

Outlined in incandescents, the semaphores of a dozen ships were being worked most industriously. "Jerk up and down like the legs and arms of the mechanical dolls at the theatre, don't they? But these here could be dancing for something more than the people's amusement if 'twas necessary. And what are they saying? Oh, most likely it's 'The compliments of the admiral, and will you come aboard the flag-ship and try a taste of punch?' And 'With pleasure,' that other one is saying. And they'll be lowering away the launch and no doubt be having a pleasant chat presently. And they could just as easily be saying (if 'twas the right time), 'Pipe to quarters and load with shell'—just as easy; and they could revolve the near turret of that one, and ten seconds after they cut loose you and me, if we weren't already killed by rush of air, would be brushing the salt water from our eyes and clawing around for a stray piece of wreckage to hang on to. Just as easy—but look at 'em now again!"

The search-lights were paralleling and intersecting, now revealing the perpendicular depths beside the vessel, and now flooding the sky. Twenty of them, simultaneously flashing, were sweeping the surface of the Sound, one instant outlining the arboured Long Island shore, the next betraying the beaches of Connecticut. One, beaming westerly, disclosed a loaded excursion steamer half-way to Hell Gate, and, a moment later, turning a hand-spring, picked up in its diverging path the Fall River steamer miles away to the eastward.

"The torpedo-boats'd have the devil's own time trying to lay aboard to-night, wouldn't they? And yet if 'twas cloudy 'twould be the submarines! Did you see them to-day? Weren't they cute—like little whale pups setting on the water—yes. They say they've got them where they turn somersaults now. Great, yes—but terrible, too, when you think they're liable to come your way some fine day. Imagine yourself, all at once, some night when you ought to be sound asleep in your hammock, finding yourself, afore you're yet fair awake, so high in the sky that you can almost reach out and take hold of the handle of the Dipper! And when you come down and get the official report, learning that one of those cute little playthings had been making a sub-aqueous call.

"It's ninety-odd years since the American navy proved it could do a good job; for, of course, none of us count Spain, who wasn't ready to begin with, and wasn't our size, anyway. And yet, we mightn't make out so bad 'gainst a bigger enemy at that. Our fellows can shoot, that's sure. There's a gun crew in this ship we're breasting now, and I saw them awhile ago put eight 12-inch shot in succession through that regulation floating target we use, and it was as far away as the farther end of that line of cruisers there, and the target was bobbing up and down, and we steaming by at 10 knots an hour. Not too bad—hah? And a hundred crews like 'em in the navy. That's for the shooting."

He flicked the end of another fleeting cigarette over the rail. "Yes, the American navy has fought pretty well, and this navy, no fear, will fight too. There's more different kinds of people in it than ever before, they say—though as to that I guess there were always more kinds of people in the navy than the historians ever gave credit for. Now it's all kinds like the nation itself, I suppose. And that ought to make for good fighting, don't you think?"

CHAPTER 2

Navy Men

The foregoing occasion was the first of several naval spectacles staged by Theodore Roosevelt during his presidency to show the public that we had a growing navy, and not too small a navy, and a navy that, ship for ship, need ask for no odds in its equipment at least.

More than any President we ever had did Theodore Roosevelt work for a big navy. To no President before him in our country did the prospect of a great European war loom so near; a war which meant our participation, not so much through any will of our people as by the pressure of happenings from the other side. Hence, the need of the country for as large a navy as we could get together. With an eye for this future need President Roosevelt asked for 4 battleships a year. There were men in Congress who believed that to talk of war was foolish; there would be no more war; so, instead of 4, Congress gave him 2, and the famous "big stick" had to come into play before they gave him even the two.

During these years I had the privilege from President Roosevelt of cruising on United States war-ships—gun-boats, destroyers, cruisers, battleships (later, through the good offices of Secretary Daniels, I became acquainted with submarines and navy airplanes).

The war-ships were an interesting study, and the life aboard a war-ship then was even more interesting, for after all, men, not materials, were the chief thing. Almost any fairly well-trained bunch of mechanics will turn out a pretty good machine to order. But there is no turning out good men to order; only good-living generations can do that.

If it was a matter of machinery alone, then the Prussian idea would have this war already won. But that alone cannot prevail, can never prevail for the long run. It is the spirit which must win.

The personnel of the navy, officers and men, seemed always so much more interesting to me, that for one hour I spent in looking over ship equipment, I probably spent forty in observing the men; and when you are locked up in ships for weeks or months with a lot of men you must, where your heart and mind are not closed, come away in time with some sort of knowledge of them.

And what sort are they?

Well, they are nearly all young—average age about twenty-one years; and they come from anywhere and everywhere—from the farms, the prairies, the corners of city streets; and they have been many things—farm-hands, carpenters, mechanics, barbers, trolley-car men, clerks, street loafers, college boys. Some are terribly sophisticated in worldly ways and some so green, of course, that the wags have frequent chances to keep their wits on edge. Some have come with the plain notion that if a fellow has got to fight, why then the navy offers the most comfortable outlook for a fellow— during this war it especially offers it—dry hammock every night, no mud, no cooties, and three hot meals at regular intervals—but many are there with the bright hope of some day pointing a 14-inch gun and sending a relay of 1,400-pound shells where they will blow something foreign and opposing high as the flying clouds.

Blowing up ships and people may have once seemed a terrible idea, but a few weeks in the community of a war-ship with its matter-of-fact, professional manner of discussing such subjects soon brings them around to common, seagoing notions of the matter.

Four years ago at Vera Cruz our modern navy had its first taste of war. It was only a light touch of war, and there was no doubt of the outcome; but in little affairs men may be tried out, too. Through somebody's blunder, for which somebody should have been jacked-up, our blue-jackets were sent up in solid sections to occupy a large open area on the Vera Cruz water-front. Standing there in solid columns, not knowing just what was going to happen, but feeling to a certainty that something stirring was going to happen, and to happen soon, they stood there grinning widely and waiting for the ball to open. It may have been their childish innocence, it may have been their untutored ignorance, but when that sheeted rifle fire first burst from the roof of the Naval College, and a solid squad or two of our lads went down, and following that the snipers began to get them in ones and twos and threes—when that happened there was no distressing confusion in their ranks. When, later, it became necessary for the *Prairie* and *Chester* to fire just over their heads to batter the walls of that same War College, it made no difference. The ships' gunnery was rapid and excellent—they knew it would be—and when the shells went whistling through the walls of the second story, the marines and blue-jackets stood under the first story and let them whistle. Plaster and bricks from the shaken walls came tumbling down upon them. They ducked beneath the falling mortar, some of them, but they all took their shells standing.

They are not the sailors of classic tradition, these battleship lads of the twentieth century. Every man to the age he lives in—it must be so. The old phrase, "Drunk as a sailor," meant, in most men's minds, drunk as a man-o'-war's man. I was born and brought up in a great seaport—Boston—and my earliest memories are of loafing days along the harbour front and the husky-voiced, roaring fellows coming ashore in the pulling boats from the men-o'-war; fine, rolling-gaited fellows, in from long cruises and flamingly eager to make the most of their short liberty. Great-hearted men, who gave truth to the phrase—"and spending his money like a drunken sailor"—and knowing, usually, but two inescapable obligations—to do his duty aboard ship and to stand by a shipmate in trouble ashore. Almost any of the old-time policemen of the large seaports can tell you many fine tales of the riotous hours along the waterfront in the old days.

Such is the passing tradition. The present lad of the navy is creating a new one. For one thing, he no longer gets drunk—that is, he does not get drunk by divisions. To illustrate:

During that greatest steaming stunt in all maritime history—the cruise of our sixteen battleships with their auxiliaries around the world—all naval records were broken in the number of enlisted men allowed ashore. Every day in large foreign ports saw 4,000 of our blue-jackets and marines allowed shore liberty. Now consider the case of the first foreign port where liberty was granted, Rio de Janeiro in South America; and what happened in Rio was what happened in other ports.

It was five weeks or more since leaving home, and during that five weeks they had been for twelve days steaming along one of the hottest coasts (Brazil) in all the world—the tropics—and it was summer-time once they were south of the line; and in all that time no chance for an enlisted man to get a drink of any kind of liquor—no beer or light wine even—no matter what the intensity of the thirst which may have possessed him.

Now he is suddenly thrown ashore with his pockets full of money. He has only to go to the paymaster and draw pretty much all he pleases. By actual figures the men of the battle fleet—about 13,000—drew $200,000 in gold to spend ashore in Rio—about $15 a man. For five or six weeks not a drop to drink, and all at once 4,000 of them thrown daily to roam into the midst of 500 grog shops with their pockets full of money, and no restrictions placed upon them, except one: they must be back to their ship that same night!

I was a passenger with that battle fleet, and night after night I stood on the great stone quay in Rio and watched them returning to their ships. On no night did I see more than forty or fifty who might be said to be "soused"; on no night did I see more than a dozen or fifteen who had to be thrown into the accommodation barge with the "dead ones," the helpless ones who were so far gone that they had to be carried up the sides of their ships from the barge which made the last rounds of the fleet.

Now I would like to make an observation; gratuitous, but perhaps of human interest and pertinent right here: I think if we took 4,000 lawyers or doctors or authors or car-drivers or clerks—4,000 of almost any sort from civil life—and locked them up so that for five or six weeks in a warm or a cold climate they could not get a drink of any kind of liquor, no matter how great their fancied or real need; and at the end of that five or six weeks took the whole 4,000 of them, with their pockets full of money, and suddenly threw them into the middle of all the grog-shops of a great city—I do think that more than forty—that is, one per cent of them—would be found "soused"—that is, if we had means of locating them all at the end of the day.

The heroic sailor of tradition has passed—a sailor of another kind, but just as efficient and just as heroic in another way—the way of his day—is rapidly creating another tradition. The lad who in the lusty days of his youth can thus hold himself in check is a pretty good product of American development. He pretty generally passes up the grog-shop, but he visits the art galleries, the museums, the cathedrals, the K. of C.'s, and Y. M. C. A.'s ashore, takes books from the library on shipboard, buys post-cards and mails them home to let his friends know of the great things in the world. On that world cruise referred to the men cleaned Rio de Janeiro out of 250,000 post-cards.

I doubt if many of them, on the first try, could lay out on a topsail-yard in a gale of wind without immediately falling overboard; but they don't have to lay out on topsail-yards nowadays. They do have to shoot, however; and they can shoot. Lay a gun's crew of them behind a big turret-gun and watch them make lacework of a target at 11,000 yards.

*****

The main question is, Have we the spirit to-day? As to that, no man having yet devised any apparatus wherewith to measure energy of soul and mind, it is difficult to prove to whoever will not believe, or does not in himself possess the germ, the existence of this thing that may not be measured by foot-rule or bushel basket. The belching of powder and the roll of drumhead do not prove it. We can always hire men to do that, and to do it well. And yet, to be present at the review described in the preceding chapter was to experience the thrill that may not be measured, to note how the enthusiasm of the occasion seemed to be animating the crews, to share in the feeling of pride which mantled all cheeks, and, ship after ship slipping past, to feel that pride of fleet intensify, until we echoed the cry of the Commander-in-Chief, whose enthusiasm for all that is good for the nation is unquenchable. As the President said, it was a glorious day.

No doubt of it. Men had met and there was kinship in the meeting. From that auspicious opening in the morning when the clouds seemed to dissolve for the express purpose of allowing a fresh-washed sky to enter into the colour scheme of the beautiful picture—blue dome, chalk-white and sea-green war-ships, green and blue and white-edged little seas—until that last moment at night when the last call on the last ship was blown and to its lingering cadence the last unwinking incandescent of the fairy-like illumination was switched off, leaving the hushed and darkened fleet riding to only the necessary anchor lights on the motionless, moon-lit sound—who witnessed it all might not doubt the existence of that spirit which in conflict makes for more than thickness of armour or weight of shell.

* * * * *

We went to war; and it was with an immense confidence in what they would do that I heard of the sailing of our first group of destroyers for the business of convoying ships and hunting U-boats on the other side. Ships were up to date and officers and men knew their business; and there was something more than knowing their business.

Other groups of destroyers followed that first one, and a lot of us were wondering how they were making out. They had sailed out into the Atlantic—that we knew; but what were they doing? We who knew them believed they were doing well. But how well?

I thought it worth-while finding out. I went to Washington and from Secretary Daniels and Chief Censor George Creel secured necessary credentials, and through the War Department the word which would put me aboard a troop-ship.

It is only justice to Secretary Daniels to say that he granted me all aid even though I told him I would probably work for *Collier's* on the trip—for *Collier's* which had been pounding him editorially.

What I learned of this game of escorting ships and hunting U-boats is in the chapters which follow.

CHAPTER 3

Seeing Them Across

He had been on what most anybody would agree was pretty trying sort of work; and so, having an idea that a furlough was coming to him, he applied for it, but did not get it. The department had other things in view. Instead of going home, he took time to write a few letters, printing the one to his little girl in big capitals, so that—being six going on seven—she might, with mama's help, be able to read it.

They sent him to a ship that had been running between north and south ports on our own coast, shifting in winter-time to tropical waters. She was one of a group of thirty or forty that the department had on its little list to be made over into transports. She was the handsomest boat, but war makes nothing of beauty. Our officer ordered all her gleaming black under-paint off, also her pure white topside enamelling with the gold decorations here and there; then he swabbed her top and bottom with that dull blue-grey which the naval sharps say does blend best with a deep-sea background.

She had the prettiest little lounging-room. Our officers retained that—for even in war officers must have some place aboard ship to gather for a smoke and gossip—but they threw out the large, lovely fat pieces of furniture. In case of submarine attack or an order to abandon ship, the men might want to make a passage of that room in a hurry and no time there—in the dark it might be—to be falling over chairs and tables.

There was a sun-parlour, a large, splendid room with wide windows and the deck on three sides. There were thick draperies, filmy laces, and many easy chairs. In the old days cabin passengers used to sit there and absorb the soft tropic breezes while digesting their breakfasts. An army quartermaster-captain surveyed it with our naval officer. "Swell," said the Q. M. C. "We'll haul down that plush and fluffy stuff, dump those chairs and rugs over the side, plant my desk here, my chief clerk's there, my other clerks' desks over there, open those fine wide windows and let the north Atlantic breezes blow on our beaded brows while we're doing our paper work. Fine!"

Our naval officer did that and a hundred other things to the inside and outside of the beautiful ship and reported her fit for transport service, or as fit as ever a made-over ship could be made to be, whereupon he was ordered to take her to such and such a dock in such and such a port—which he did. Then many large, heavy cases were lowered into her hold, and troops and troops and more troops filed aboard and took up what was left of the spaces between decks with themselves and their war gear.

She lay then with her water-line a foot deeper than anybody around there ever remembered seeing her in her swell passenger days; then she shoved out into the stream and kicked her way down the harbour, and as she did so, though there was not a single trooper's head showing above her rail, everybody seemed to know. Passing tugs, motor-boats, ferry-boats blew their whistles—every kind of a boat that had a whistle blew it—and there was an excursion boat loaded down with women and children. Her band had been playing ragtime, but it suddenly stopped and broke into *Goodbye, Good Luck, God Bless You*, to the troop-ship bound for France.

There was a war-ship waiting below—not the biggest by a good deal in our fleet, but big enough to have hope one day of firing her broadside on the battle-line. But the great duty of a war-ship is to be immediately useful. She was there, and smaller war-ships with her, to see that the troop-ships got protection on the run across.

Our troop-ship, other troop-ships, every one in turn, steamed up, reported her presence, and tucked into a berth under the wings of the big war-ship; and there they stayed until night, until the signal came to get under way. When it did, one after the other they up-anchored and kicked into line. They had been warned to make no fuss in going, and they made none. From somewhere ashore a great search-light swept our top structure, swept every top structure as we filed out. Some one on each top structure must have given the proper sign, for that was all.

SHE SHOVED OUT INTO THE STREAM AND KICKED HER WAY DOWN THE HARBOUR, AND AS SHE DID SO. . . . EVERYBODY SEEMED TO KNOW.

All that night, and next day, for days and days thereafter, with shifting formations and varying speeds, we steamed. All were good, seaworthy ships, but little things will happen. There was one that was always lagging. The flag-ship, meaning the war-ship of most tonnage, inquired why. The answer came, whereat the war-ship of most tonnage showed right there that she was fit to do something more than furnish long-reaching guns for the fleet's protection.

The next thing the fleet knew they were ordered to shut off steam. They did so. It was a perfect, calm day, and the ships lay, still as paint between a clear blue sky and a deep-blue sea while a boat-load of blue-jackets from the big fighting ship rowed across a swell so gentle that it seemed to be only serving to put life into a picture. The lagging steamer had been short a few oilers or firemen or water-tenders. The big ship had them to spare. After that the slow one picked right up. Soon it was standard speed with everybody in proper alignment again.

Not often do seagoing people get the chance to see a fleet of merchant steamers cruising the wide ocean. A full-rigged sailing-ship, a steam-collier, a tramp steamer, all came out of their way in one day to view the strange sight. As they did so, one of our smaller and faster war-ships would trot over to have a closer peek in turn at the curious ones; to ask them questions; probably also to tell them to keep their wireless mouths shut, if they had any.

One day one big freighter did not answer signals promptly. Perhaps she could not read them. In these war times it is not too easy to get crews who are sea-wise in every detail—the expert signal-man among the officers might have been off watch and having a nap. Anyway, one of our little fighting fellows went bounding after her. It was like watching a sheep-dog at work. The war-ship moved up from behind, drew up, and then, showing her teeth, headed the freighter the other way and held her headed that way while she put an officer aboard and asked an explanation, which was probably given and doubtless all right, for the officer came back and the freighter resumed her regular course. Day in and day out that was the way of it, every passing ship being viewed as suspect and our own ships, of varying speeds and tonnage, trying to keep a good alignment.

The weather generally was fine, but one morning we ran into a fog. A fog has its virtues; a submarine cannot see you in a fog. But neither can you see a submarine. And somewhere handy to you is a bunch of your own ships, and no telling when one of them may come riding out of the mist and climb aboard by way of your port or starboard quarter!

A whistle by day or a search-light by night would have been a great help to our naval officer on the bridge during that fog, but he was denied that. So he made out (as did every other commander on every other bridge during the fog) with whatever other means he could devise. Nothing happened to us.

The fog passed on, and then one day came a slatey grey sea and a slatey sky. Gray seas look hard; white crests moving across grey seas look hard too. Our naval officer took time to look around on them. Gray hulls were smashing high bows into them, making boiling white water of the hard grey sea and throwing it to either side in fine, high-rolling billows as they pressed on. They were a fine sight then, with the smoke pouring out and trailing low from some of them. They were not trying to make smoke, but if a ship must make smoke, it will not be seen so far on a grey day.

Our naval officer held the bridge from early that morning to nine o'clock that night. He had an idea that he might be able to sneak in a couple of hours' sleep against the strain of the later night. It was not bad weather when he left—a good breeze blowing and plenty of white showing. It was dirty, but not bad weather. He got in one hour in his bunk, turning in with his clothes on, when he was called to go on the bridge again. Something had happened. He could feel the increasing wind before he was fairly rolled out of his bunk.

As he stepped out on deck he could see that the lookouts had adopted life-belts for the night. The lookouts were men from among the troops, and now each man as he went off watch was handing over his life-belt to the next coming on. They had had to use the soldiers for lookouts. In these war days no merchant ship can supply from her regular crew one-tenth of the men needed for lookout work in the war zone. The soldiers were all right, but just then our naval officer felt sorry for them. He had been having them up before him afternoons, lecturing them on their duties as lookouts. That very afternoon he had had a bunch of them before him while he explained a few new things. He had spent extra time on the men who were to be on forward watch this very night, with the men who were to go into the bow or into the forward crow's nest. And now they were there, buried as the bow went smash into it, or—those of them who had drawn the crow's nest—swinging a hundred feet in the air. All right for old sea-goers, but most of these boys had never in their lives before been on an ocean-going ship. Some had never even seen a big ship until they came to the seacoast for their trip. They had great eyesight, some of these young fellows—men who had lain on the bull's-eye at a thousand yards regularly were bound to have that—and they made good lookouts once they got the idea, but climbing the last twenty feet of that ladder to the crow's nest, leaning back under part of the time with life-belt stuffed under their overcoats—they surely must have been thinking that a soldier's duties were difficult as well as various in these days of war.

A ship on tossing seas and the wind blowing a dirge through the rigging—well, a man may be brave enough to fight all the Germans this side the Russian line, but if he is new to sea life he is apt to see things. Two soldiers were standing on deck when our naval officer came out of his room. They were not on guard. They did not have to be there—they were staying awake on their own account. One said to the other: "There, there—look! Ain't that a submarine?"

It was a shadow as high as a house. "If that is a submarine," thinks our officer, "then it is good night to us, for she's a whale of a one!"

It was no submarine. It was the shadow of one of their own ships which had been driven out of column.

It was blowing hard when our officer made the bridge. He could not see far, but far enough to see that the ocean was black, and that across the black of it the white patches were flying—dead white patches leaping high in the night.

The fleet was in direct column ahead, or should have been. Some were surely having their troubles staying there. This steaming close behind a ship, with another ship close behind you—and you have to be close up to see from one to the other on such a night—made me think as I stood under the bridge that night: "Give me all the submarines in the world before this with a fleet that has not had a chance to practise evolutions."

There was not a steaming light of any kind, not even one shaded little one in the stern, which an enemy might see and, seeing, swing in behind it. Rather than show even the smallest little guiding light, our fellows preferred to steam this way in the night.

The glad morning came, glad for the reason that an almost warm, bright sun came with it. The sun showed three ships gone from the column. There was more than one of us who wished that we too had gone from the column about six hours ago. We would have slept better. Still, it was a good experience to have—behind you. Wind and sea went down; all hands felt better—especially the lookouts. Those who came down from the crow's nest looked as if the grace of God had suddenly fallen on them.

By and by we picked up the drifters. They were looking just as hard for us as we were for them; and later that day we ran into our escorts from the other side. Everybody at once felt as if the trip was as good as over. The fact was that the worst part of the war zone was ahead of us. All hands were still turning in with life-belts handy, and most of them with clothes on, but there was a feeling that now it was up to these new escorts.

Before we reached France on this run we were in a U-boat fight, which I shall tell of later. What I want to say now is that the submarine fight had an enjoyable side to it, but as for that night run of our troop-ships in gale and sea—a big ship just ahead, a big ship just behind, big high-bowed ships plunging down at fourteen knots an hour from roaring waters in the dark—there was no fun in that!

Of the scores of devices the fleet used to beat the U-boats on that run across, a man can say nothing here. But to get back: our naval officer stuck to his bridge until one most beautiful morning he took his ship into a most beautiful port on a most beautiful shore. I never before heard anybody so describe that same port, but the general verdict says it did look pretty good.

This story of our troop-ship's run across is given from the view-point of the naval officer in charge. It could just as well have been written from the view-point of the merchant captain or his officers aboard—all on the job; or the chief engineer or his assistants—all on the job, and who put in more than one hour guessing at what was going on above; or from the view-point of the quartermaster captain, or his clerks, or the oilers, or the firemen, or the water-tenders, or the cooks, or anybody else, high or low, in the ship's regular service.

This transport service is one tough game. It is well enough for us who have but one trip to make. But one trip after another! They had good right to look a bit younger when they made the other side. But before we can win this war we've got to get the million or two or three million men across; and the millions of tons of supplies. Somebody has got to see them across. These men on the troop-ships are doing it. May nothing happen to them!

Chapter 4

The U-Boats Appear

The soldier lookouts in the forward crow's nest had been especially advised to have an eye out for the convoys which were to pick us up as we neared the other side; and they were very much on the job.

One bright morning came: "Smoke three points off the port bow.... Smoke broad off the starboard bow.... Smoke dead ahead. ... One point off the.... Broad off the...." and so on. Their excited calls rattled down like rapid fire to the bridge; the thrill in their voices rolled like a wave through the ship. That smoke, incidentally, meant that the strangers, whoever they were, had already identified us and so were not afraid to let us see them.

Everybody that was not already on deck came running up to have a look for himself. It was our escort. Darting across our bows they came—low-riding, slim, grey bodies. The ranking one reported to our flag-ship; and all, without any fuss or extra foam, took position and went to work as though they had been there for weeks. And as they did our big war-ship and the little ones which had come across with her wheeled about and went off. There was no ceremonious leave-taking. They simply turned on their heels and flew. They might as well have said: "We are glad to have met you and been with you, but we can do no more for you, so goodbye and good luck; we're going back home as fast as we can get there."

A soldier watched them going and said: "The night before we left home I went to a show, and a fellow sang *Goodbye, Broadway! Hello, France!* I thought it was great. I know what they're saying aboard those ships there now. 'Hello, Broadway! Goodbye, France!' is what they're saying. And I betcher it'll be a straight line with no time wasted zigzagging for them on the way back!"

He had it about right. They carried the most eloquent sterns that any of us had seen on ships for a long time. The big one in the middle, the others like chickens under either wing—away they went, belting it for about sixteen knots good. In one half-hour all we could see of them was a cloud of smoke to the west'ard. Just how far off the French coast we were at this time does not matter here, or from what direction we were approaching; but we were far enough off for that group of destroyers to show how they went about their work of guarding the troop-ships. To comb the sea about us was their mission; and they were attending to it every minute. The fleet steamed on.

We proceeded under advices not to fall asleep with too much clothes on, and never to get too far away from our life-belts. It may have been true that some men slept with their life-belts on, but it is probably not true that one man took his to the bathroom with him—not true because about the time we got that far along the steward refused to prepare any more baths. He had enough on his mind, he said, without fussing with baths.

There was one place we looked forward to passing with lively feelings. We may not name the place here, but here is how it was described: "Ever been to that big aquarium in Naples? Yes? Well, remember those devil-fish hiding behind the rock on the bottom? Along comes an innocent young fish who is a stranger to those waters. Mr. Devilfish, hiding behind, has a peek at it coming. He waits. Mr. Young Fish drifts by his hiding-place, and then—Good night, young fishie."

That kind of talk in the watches of the night sounded like lively action before us. We waited for—call it the Devilfish's Cave—and waited; and the first thing we knew when we came to inquire further about it, we were safely past it, with never a sign of any devilfish, unless it would be the one torpedo which went by the bow of one of us from some distance one noontime. Some distance it must have been because it was a clear day with a smooth sea, and under such weather conditions, with the hundreds of wide-awake lookouts in the fleet, no U-boat could have put up a periscope within any near distance and not be seen by somebody. As for long-distance shots from submarines—there is small need to worry about them. Subs like to get within a thousand yards or less. Those three and four mile shots—it is like trying to hit a sea-gull with a rifle. Amateurs try that kind of shooting, but the professional, who has to reckon the cost of powder and shot, lets it pass. Not that the Germans are sparing of the cost of war, but a sub which has to make a voyage of three thousand miles to take on a fresh load of torpedoes is not firing too many for the mere practice.

We drew near the coast of France, and still nothing had happened. We were getting hails, of course, from the lookouts. There was one who called it a dull watch when he did not see at least one periscope. He had never seen a periscope in his life, but he had read about periscopes. One night just at dark he stood us all on our heads by reporting one just alongside. We all got a flash at it then, an ominous object, bobbing under our port quarter, and then it went down into our wake. It bobbed up again, and we all had another look. It was a beer-keg. The ship's first officer, the one who had a gold medal as big as a saucer for saving life at sea, eyed the keg, and then he eyed the lookout, saying: "An empty one too! If you'd only report a full one, we might gaff it aboard."

When that same first officer was one day asked if he intended taking his big medal with him in case we had to take to the boats, he replied: "With twenty-eight persons in the boat! Good Lord, don't you think she'll be carrying enough freight?"

We steamed along, dark night astern this time and the white morning above our bow. The bridge—three naval and two ship's officers—had for some time been using the glasses. From aloft forward came the sudden yell: "Land ho!"

The bridge nodded that it heard. "Land ho!" repeated the lookout stentoriously. "Two points off the port bow," and then, peering doubtfully down at the bridge: "Am I right?"

"You are," said the bridge sweetly; "we've been looking at it for half an hour." Which was rather rough, for to shore-going eyes land does at first look like a low cloud on the horizon and, naturally, a fellow wants to make sure.

Pretty soon we could most of us see it from the deck, and it did look good. I once saw the flat, bleak Atlantic coast of Patagonia after ten days at sea, and the high iron wintry coast of Newfoundland after another period at sea, and I clearly recall that even they both looked like fine countries. And the coast of France was neither bleak nor icy, so you may guess that it was a pleasing sight on this summer morning. It was a dream of a day, the sea like a green-tinted mirror, the sky blue as paint, and the softest little breath of air floating off the land to us. We were perhaps ten miles offshore.

The enchanted land lay before us and our troubles behind us—or so we thought—and yet we were many of us disappointed. After our more than three thousand miles we had not even caught sight of a U-boat.

Now, we probably did not want to see one, but we sort of had an idea that we were entitled to have one pop up and then disappear. Something to talk about, without anybody coming to harm through it—that was about our composite idea.

However, there are compensations for all things; we could now prepare peacefully for going ashore. I was in the lounge-room below sharpening a pencil, and, there being no waste-basket handy, carefully shunting the shavings into a writing-desk drawer.

The fire-alarm rang. That was the signal to hurry on deck with your life-belt, take your station by your boat, and prepare to abandon ship. But we had been doing that every day since we left home. The first time we heard that call we had gone jumping, but after the third or fourth time we moved more leisurely.

Some took their life-belts from their rooms and started up. Every soldier, of course, grabbed one from where they were piled up in the passageways and went at once. They had no option. Their officers would get after them if they did not.

I thought I would finish sharpening my pencil. I thought I heard a blast from a ship's whistle somewhere outside; but I was not sure. Then I heard a blast from our own ship's whistle. *Wugh-wugh-wugh!* I did not wait for any more. I did not finish sharpening the pencil. I did not wait to shut the desk drawer. I did not do anything but move. There were six blasts from the whistle, and six blasts meant U-boats.

There was a heavy-set officer coming down the passageway. He was heavier by twenty pounds than I was, but I had more speed. I know I had. Not since the winter's day on George's Bank a quartering sea chased me down the cabin companionway of the *Charles W. Parker* of Gloucester have I moved so fast on a ship, and I was fifteen years younger then. We bounced off each other. We did not stop to talk when we straightened out. He went his way and I went mine, and if I looked anything like him, then my jaw was thrust out and my eyes had an earnest look in them.

My life-belt was under my bunk. It did not stay there long. I went back down the passageway jumping. There was a fine crush going up to the boat-deck. Only a seagoing man knows how to take a ship's ladder with speed. You just got to have practice at it. There were some fine athletic boys among the troopers, but "Sweet mother," wailed a ship's man, "are those new army shoes made of leather, or are they lead that they move so slow?" And that comment did not have to travel a lonesome road.

While scooting up the ladder we heard a gun; and another gun. As we made the boat-deck there was another ship barking out six short blasts.

The ships of the fleet, when we got to where we could see them, were headed every which way. We could feel our own ship heel over—she turned so sharply. Every ship in the fleet was going it—right angles, quarter angles, all degrees of angles. But what impressed us most—we almost laughed to see her—was the lubber of the fleet. She was twice the tonnage of most of us, and early in the run across she had brought anguish to our souls by the way she lagged. "You bum, you loafer, you old cart-horse, why don't you move up?" our soldiers used to yell across at her. She had not then enough men in her steam department to keep her engines warm, so she reported. But now she had steam enough. She was wide and high, a huge hulk of a ship, and here she was now charging—charging was the word—like a motor-boat at where somebody said the U-boat had just submerged. Whether she got her U-boat, I don't know; but she certainly did cut through the water for about a mile.

The ship next behind us went after something; and the ship next ahead went tearing away after something else, and another ship—but, man, a battalion of eyes could not follow them all. A destroyer went—*zizz-sh zizz*—a thirty-odd knot clip—and the next thing we saw was a ten-foot column of solid white water shooting straight up beside that destroyer.

And then came the terrific *Bo-o-om!* Our ship shook from one end to the other. I thought it came from inside of us—that it was a loading-port door let drop by some careless ship's man below. The ship's officer in charge of our life-boat thought so, too. He stepped to the ship's side to look down. "That one, he should be put in the brig—scaring us all like that!"

I agreed with him heartily, only I thought he should be put in a second brig after he got out of the first one. Some time later we learned that it was the shock from the bomb dropped by the destroyer, from which you can gauge what chance the submarine will have which happens to catch one of those bombs on its back.

We carried two 5-inch guns in our bow and two astern. Those gun crews had been standing by those guns from the first day out. For the last three days they had been sleeping near them in their life-jackets and taking their meals standing beside them. They were not going to be left out of it. About a thousand yards away some one reported a floating torpedo. Whether it was a live or a spent one made no matter. It was too soft a target; besides, some ship in the hurry of manoeuvring might run into it. Bang! went two of our 5-inch fellows, one from each end of the ship and both together.

That was when we heard from our chief engineer. He had been below from the beginning, and knew from the way the bells were coming down from the bridge that there was something doing topside. When the destroyer dropped her first bomb he wondered if the ship was torpedoed. He waited, and his men, with their shovels and slice-bars and oil-cans—they waited, every one of them, with one sharp eye to the nearest ash-hoist, which reminded the chief that he would never leave home again—and this time he meant it—without installing those four more ladders leading up from the engine and fire-room quarters to the decks. No, sir, he would not.

But nothing happened! And then those two 5-inch guns went off together. War-ships are built to withstand impact, but merchant-ships—no. This time the chief was sure she was torpedoed. His fire-room force were mostly Spaniards. He used to talk at table about his fire-room gang. "You would think, with your ship coming through the war zone and your watch down in the bottom of her, that you would want to go up topside when your watch was done, for, of course, if any U-boat got the ship, it would be the fellows below who would first get the full benefit." But that gang of his! "Doggone, they'd sit there when their watch was over, six or eight of 'em, and play some cross-eyed Spanish card-game for a peseta a corner. What d'y' know about them?"

The chief's gang could not talk English, but they had speaking eyes. They now looked at the chief, and he went up to have a peek. He came back soon. "They are having target practice," he told them. He had been running the Caribbean ports long enough to be able to say that much in Spanish; but more than all he smiled as he said it. You want to smile to get away with anything like that in the fire-room of a troop-ship in the U-boat country.

Every ship in the fleet was now having something to say with her guns; and with their incessant manoeuvring at such close quarters the sea was all torn up by their wakes. Two or three wakes or bow waves would cross each other, and the sea would roll up with a bounding white crest. There were also the wakes of hidden submarines. You could tell them if you saw any by the way they did not stop in one place; they moved on. When a gunner saw a submarine wake he fired; where he wasn't sure he fired anyway. What was he there for? Bang! Boom! Solid shot were ricocheting, piling up little white splashes, and the shrapnel were making little holes and bursting into little white smoke puffs all over the place.

You must not forget that it was a beautiful day and a perfectly calm sea with the shore of France looming like a blue mirage on the horizon. It lasted about forty minutes altogether, and through it all the little destroyers—don't forget them—were weaving in and out among the big ships; and on the big ships were thousands of troopers, white life-belts around their olive-drab uniforms, standing steadily by life-boats and rafts.

Our fellows on the destroyers did handle their little ships well. And the troop-ships were handled well—no collisions and no gun-shells going aboard anybody else. A few went across other people's bows and sterns, but not too near to worry. And in the middle of it all, our guns made so much noise that before we heard them we saw them—two airplanes, whirring and cavorting about and above us. Whenever they saw a destroyer turn and shoot, they would turn and shoot after the destroyer. They could move about three times as fast as a destroyer, and so quite often beat the destroyer to it.

Later the airplanes escorted us into port. They were big, powerful biplanes, and carried a sky-pointing gun mounted forward and the colours of France painted on their little wings aft. They kept circling about us until we made our harbour. Whenever they swooped low enough our troopers gave them a fine cheer.

My job being to tell what I saw and heard, I want to say here that throughout the entire mêlée I never saw one periscope! And there were thousands like me who never saw a periscope. But there were hundreds of others—cool, sensible people—who are ready to make affidavits that they did see periscopes.

Why did not more of us see any? Well, a submarine commander needs to turn up his periscope for only four, five, six, or seven seconds to have a look. If you do not happen to be gazing directly at the spot, you do not see it or the white bone which it makes going through the water.

On my ship the ranking officer was a regular army colonel who had seen active and dangerous service in the Philippines and elsewhere. He is given rather to understatement than overstatement of facts—a cool, level-headed observer. He saw a periscope. We had another officer who had been in the service in the Spanish War, had got out and was now back. He was probably the best lookout of all the army officers in the ship—a solid, substantial man with a keen eye. He could see what anybody else could see, but further than that you had to show him. Several of us had already christened him "Show me." He reported two periscopes. Now he had never seen a submarine operating in his life. I asked him to describe the action of the periscope. He described it perfectly as I had noticed it in trial trips of submarines off Cape Cod, which is where the Electric Boat Company used to try theirs out before turning them over to purchasers.

My own notion of it is that the U-boats have many of us bluffed. They must be capable men who go in submarines; of good nerve, quick wit, and the power to withstand long nervous strain. Such men in a submarine are going to throw great scares into people of less capacity on surface ships. Put such men somewhere else than in a submarine and they will outwit men not so well equipped for the war game.

But these men, no men, can make the submarine do impossible things. Before firing a torpedo the submarine must come near enough to the surface to stick out her periscope, to have a look around to locate her target. In sticking out the periscope, lookouts on ships are likely to see it. On merchant ships they do not keep a lookout which combs the sea thoroughly; they do not carry men enough for that. The strain of such a lookout is great. Men cannot stand to it as to an ordinary watch; they have to be relieved frequently; and so submarines may have an advantage over merchant ships, especially if the merchant ships are slow-moving freighters. But a war-ship, or a troop-ship in convoy is something else. Troop-ships carry an immense number of lookouts, not overworked men who are liable to go to sleep on watch, but keen-eyed young fellows of high vitality, surrounded by other young fellows of high vitality, and all competing to see who can see something first.

They will spot a periscope, under normal conditions, at a pretty good distance; which does not mean that that periscope is at once going to be blown out of the water. Hitting a piece of 4-inch pipe at any distance is not easy; the pipe moving and the ship moving does not make it any easier.

But the submarine has shown herself. To get her torpedo home she will have to move nearer. With a thousand eyes looking for her and five, six, a dozen ships with four guns or more apiece waiting to have a crack at her, she is not going to have a pleasant time after she moves nearer. She must show her periscope again to locate her target. To show her periscope she must get her hull somewhere near the surface; it takes a little time—not so much, but a little time to get her hull safely below again; and while she is doing that who can say that not one of our five, six, or a dozen ships will be handy to the spot? And if one of our ships should happen to be handy enough, what can save the submarine from being rammed? And if she is rammed there is no hope for her—she is gone.

I am pretty much of one mind with our first officer in this submarine matter. In the middle of the combat off the French coast he was making the rounds, cutting away the lashings which held the life-boats to the davits—this in case we had to leave the ship. He had a squint at the banging guns, the charging troop-ships, the flying destroyers; and then he looked up long enough to say: "A fat chance a U-boat would have if she so much as stuck her nose out. In four seconds she'd be like a rabbit among a pack of hunting-dogs. She might get away, but I bet you no bookmaker would take her end of it."

This argument does not apply to a slow-steaming freighter going it alone; it is for the matter of troop-ships moving at a fairly good speed. For myself that time the fleet steamed in direct column ahead, one ship jam up behind another, in a rough sea and on a black night, at high speed without lights of any kind, they did a more difficult thing than to evade or stand off half a dozen U-boat attacks. No fleet of ships can be put beyond all danger of submarine attack, but the danger to the subs can be made so great that it won't be worth the price the attacking force will pay.

I do not know how many U-boats were in that attack. The official figures will no doubt be given out in time. Our moderate estimators here put it down as three, with one transport ramming and sinking one U-boat. Two honest lads of one of our own forward gun crews say that our ship bumped over another. They felt the bump. Perhaps they did, but blue-jackets at twenty years of age are apt to be optimistic, as witness:

The day after that U-boat fight the skipper, first officer, chief engineer, and myself were trying our French on a waiter in a café ashore, but not quite putting it over; we had to resort to a little English to get action for one important item of our meal. A party of American blue-jackets—gun crews—were at another table. They heard us speak English, whereat one of them called over: "Say, you guys comprong English? Wee, wee? Then you oughter been where we were yesterday. Yuh'd seen something. Fighting U-boats we were. Comprong? U-boats—wee, wee, U-boats. Thirty-six of 'em came after us an' we sunk twelve. Whaddyer know about that?" We did not know, so we opened up a bottle of the ordinary red wine of the country, price *deux* francs, and drank to their enthusiastic health.

Chapter 5
Crossing the Channel

To get out of France after getting in, a man has to go to Paris, see the prefect of police, various consuls, and so on. It was all interesting—the life in Paris—but it had nothing to do with U-boats. I had to go to England, and to make England, I had to go to Havre.

And I was in Havre. Looking out the window at a roof across the narrow street was a sign which read Hotel of the Six Allies. The Six looked as though it had been painted over. The head waiter told me later that it had. It had begun at three, then it became four—five—now six. But there were more than six now—did not the great United States count? Oh, yes, truly yes—but the paint and painters! They were growing more scarce. The war—yes. Everything was the war.

The head waiter was a little old fellow with a round back, a quizzical eye, and the hair of a first violin. After I beat my way by main strength through three *table-d'hôte* meals with him he let me know that he could talk English. Why hadn't he told me so before? Oh! Did I not wish to practise my French? So many did, and if they made him understand, the tips were sometimes more inspiring.

The steamer for England had been scheduled to leave the night of the day our train arrived, but she did not leave. We did not learn whether it was the full moon or the U-boats shifting their hunting-grounds or the late air-raids on the south coast of England. Whatever the cause, no one growled much. The steamship people and the government were doing their best with a difficult service. The delay gave us another day to look the port over. I had been there years before. Then it was all French; now it seemed to be mostly British. The streets, the shops, the cafés, were crowded with

English, Canadian, and Australian soldiers. British soldiers were running the tram-cars. In the country outside was a large British camp. The French owners of the ships and of the cafés in the narrow streets near the jetties catered especially to the British soldier and sailor. English tobacco, English *rosbif*—they advertised these in quaintly worded signs.

Ships lay between the jetties and the breakwater, coasting and deep-water steamers, and the little fishing-cutters with the tanned sails. There was a fleet (or a flock) of seaplanes all ready to take to either the water or the air. They took to both while we looked, hurdling the breakwater from the basin to get more quickly to some smoke on the horizon. They were brand-new planes all, with the most beautiful polished maple pontoons and bright varnish over paint that still smelled fresh.

Soldiers not so worn and weary as those on the hospital veranda came down to the jetty promenade. Priests, nursing sisters, other soldiers and sailors came also. What interested them most was the sun shining on the bright new wood of the planes flying out to see what the smoke meant. It was a ship from across the ocean somewhere, and the planes circled it into the basin—one more ship which had beat the U-boat game and brought home something needed. There was some noise along the jetty and yet more noise in the wide and narrow streets of the town—clanging trams, whip-cracking fiacres, yelling newsboys, honking taxis, and soldiers and sailors tramping the pavements. Noise enough, and of the kind befitting a Channel port in war time; but for a time at least we heard the noise let down, and the bustle softened.

In a wide street of shops appeared a white-haired priest with a white crucifix held high before him. Behind him was another priest reading from a book of prayer. Two laymen came next, bearing a little white-painted table with a little white coffin—a cheap board coffin—resting on it. There was a canopy of plain white boards over the little coffin. There were a few white blossoms on the canopy and beside the coffin a few lilies of the valley—only a few.

Two other laymen followed the coffin bearers. All the men were bareheaded. Three women—young women and young mothers to look at—followed the two men. One of the young women was in deep black. A group of little girls followed the young woman. Two very old women came last. No more than that, walking through a crowded street at two o'clock of a bright day! It was on us almost before we saw it. Men took off their hats as it passed; women blessed themselves. Sometimes men's lips murmured a short prayer; always the women did. The soldiers and sailors, when they were French, saluted nearly always; the British sometimes. The officers, if anything, saluted more profoundly than the enlisted men, and, when they did not stop dead, held a hand to their caps for eight or ten paces in passing.

Two soldiers were talking with two girls of the streets. One of the soldiers took off his cap. One of the girls stopped talking to say a little word of prayer. Both soldiers faced about, and all four gazed in silence for long after the little cortège had passed on. Then the first soldier put on his cap, all faced about, and resumed their talk, but more slowly and not quite so loudly as before.

An English Tommy was driving a tram—a swearing Tommy that you could hear a block away. He came on the mourners from behind. He was in a hurry, and by clanging his bell he could have crowded by. But he held the tram in check, nursing it so as not to frighten the two old women in the rear—until they came to a wide square. Here there was room. He clanged his bell, not too loudly, turned on the juice, and hurried to make up for lost time. Men are being killed by the million over here, and other men who have been there—these very men on these streets—will tell you that they hardly turn their heads to see one more killed. But a little child is different.

Our steamer was to sail next night—at what hour no one could say, but it was well to be there in good time, we were told, so we went with the hotel bus. A little porter woman was there with my 70-pound bag before I even knew "things were ready"; and she said she did not roll it down the five flights from my room. She carried it every stair step of the way. Her husband was in the war, and she had five children and it required more than a few *sous* in the week for five children, the eldest fourteen. I agreed that it did.

Swinging on to the jetty, we had to take notice of a shop advertising to rent life-saving apparatus for the trip across the Channel. It was fine—a one-piece suit which came from the toes to the ears and a hood which you could turn in over your head! There was a painting of a torpedoed passenger ship going up in flames, topside and the hull settling down into the rolling billows. Men and women were jumping into the sea and drowning in agony. They had no life-saving, one-piece suits. But all were not so thoughtless. There were others floating along high out of water with the most beatific expressions on their faces. They had been thoughtful enough to buy one of the patent one-piece suits. The painting was in colours, red and black mostly.

The afternoon had closed in showers, and when we made the steamer landing we stood in pools of water in the hollows of the worn stone flags. We were in good time, but a hundred or more who had been in better time were already inside the shed. The hold-overs from three days were there, military people mostly. We waited—and waited—and waited. It was the eternal passport matter. One at a time they had to pass the tribunal inside. A pleasant-mannered young English soldier stood guard at the shed door. Every half-hour or so, at command of a voice from the inside, he would let another dozen or twenty slide by. When he did so, those of us in the rear would hurry to fill the void, picking up our baggage from our feet as we pushed on. I had hired a porter, an old man, to look after my 70-pound bag. He stood by patiently for two hours or so. Then, without warning, he ran off and did not come back. I had not paid him, so he must have grown very tired. After that, whenever I moved forward, I had to pick up my two bags myself—the other weighed 40 pounds. Sometimes I put the bags into a pool of water—sometimes I put my feet.

Not every one had to wait. An officer would be passed through immediately, which did not please two enlisted men near me, just back from what they called rough work at the front. The little one, called Scotty, had a fear that the boat might leave before he could get there. He wanted to "mak' a train oot o' Lunnon" at two of the next afternoon, "mak' a nicht train oot o' Glesgie" (Glasgow) and surprise his folk by walking in on 'em "afore brekkist." They would be glad to see him, be sure.

"Almost as glad to see you come as they was goin'?" asked the soldier with him, and then urged Scotty to stop over in London for a bit o' fun.

"I'll not," said Scotty. "I'll mak' the trains as I said an' surprise 'em afore brekkist. Besides, there's a football match on for the arternoon arter to-morrer, and an old pal o' mine is playin' for'ard for oor team. But let 'em allow all these officers aboord first—'ere's anither ane—listen tae 'im!"

But it was not an officer this time. It was a voice asking if any privileges were accorded a King's messenger. The guard at the door said certainly, but where was he? Everybody made way for the voice. He turned out to be a little man with a scraggy beard and large round spectacles. The guard eyed him doubtfully. The King's messenger stood on his toes and whispered up into the guard's ear.

The guard looked down on him. "King's messenger! Go on with yer!" He shoved him back.

"Yes, garn with yer!" said Scotty, "but he's gained a guid half oor wi' his King's-messenger talk. I think I'll hae tae be something important masel' sune."

The soldier with Scotty could speak French. He spoke it to a pretty young French girl and her mother who had been pressed up against them. The mother had a new hat in a big paper box. Whenever the rush threatened to crush the hat-box, she would hold it high over her head till she could hold it no longer, when she let it get crushed.

Whenever the girl spoke to the other soldier Scotty would want to know what she said. "She's sairtainly pretty. What did she say that time, Tid?"

Tid kept to himself what she said. "It's a cut above the likes of you we're discussin'," said Tid.

"She'll be goin' to England to marry an English officer," said Scotty.

The girl whirled on him. "No. No Engleesh *officier*—a French *officier*!"

"I had a notion you'd spoil it," said Tid.

"Ma Gud," groaned Scotty. "I wonder, Tid, did she hear a' I said this nicht o' her, and ma lips no two feet frae her ear!"

The night was growing cooler. The girl's fur neck-piece slipped down from her shoulders. The mother had passed her the hat-box, and the girl had no hand free for the neck-piece. Scotty put it back for her. She thanked him sweetly.

"You're no mad noo?" said Scotty. "I'll tak' a steady billet tae put it back." He took to slyly stroking the fur piece when he thought she could not see him.

A woman lost her passport, but did not know it until she was about to be passed through the door. Then she shrieked. She came back in the crowd to look for it. She had been standing in one spot for an hour—it must be there. She rushed to the spot, lit a match, and began to look under her feet. A man lit a match and began to look under his feet. Another man lit a match and began to look under his feet. We all lit matches and began to look under our feet.

She shrieked again. "Ma Gud, she's a dyin' woman!" said Scotty.

She was not. She had found her passport. The business of waiting was resumed by the rest of us.

The little cafés along the water-front were closing; loads of soldiers and sailors began to flow out on to the jetty. One began to sing, and another; others to whirl along in grotesque dance steps. Two began to talk loudly. They came to blows. A third one stepped in to stop it, whereupon one of the first two turned on him to inquire what he was interfering for.

"But he's a friend o' mine," explained the third man.

"Is he a better friend o' yours than o' me? Answer me that. Is he? Do you know him longer than I know him? No? Then mind your own and do not be interferin'." The third man felt properly rebuked. He withdrew his objections and the other two resumed their fight.

We were inside the shed at last; and by and by I came before a man in a little office inside the shed. He was a Frenchman, but spoke good English.

"Your passport, please."

I produced it. He took a look and passed it back.

"Any gold on your person?"

"Thirty dollars—American."

"Hand it over, please. Wait. Are you American?"

"I am."

"In that case keep it. That is all. Pass out. Next."

Next came a little house with a row of men sitting at a long, narrow pine-board table. The first had a quick look at my passport and handed it on to a man who sat on his left before a card index in boxes. That one dug into his boxes, found what he was looking for, and slid the passport along to the next on his left, who slid it along to the man on his left, and he to the man on his left, and he to the last one.

You chased that passport down the line, answering the questions which each one put in turn, as to where you last came from, where before that, and before that, and the date, your business, where you were going in England, why, for how long, and where you would stay. They were all pleasantly put, but you had the feeling that let you stumble and it would be God help you. Each asked a question or two that nobody else had thought of. The last one had the least of all to say. He probably thought that if, after all, you were a German spy, you had earned your exemption. He only made a note of your name, handed out a red card, said to give it to the soldier at the out-going door, claim your baggage, have the customs inspector pass it, and go aboard the steamer when you liked. All I saw liked to go aboard at once.

There was a man of many buttons behind a shining brass grill on the steamer—French, apparently, but also speaking plain English. I handed in my ticket and asked for a berth. He was snappy. "Have you one reserved?"

"Why, no. When I bought my steamer ticket I was told that there would be no need to reserve a berth—there would be plenty."

"He told you wrong. There are no berths."

"But is he not your agent—the man who sold me the ticket?"

"No."

"But you accept his ticket?"

"There is no berth."

"You mean that I pay for a first-class ticket on your steamer and then have to walk the deck?"

"There is no berth, I say." He talked like a machine-gun, and the marble Roman gods were not more impassive as he turned to the next. I saluted him. You just have to honour a man who knows exactly what he wants to say and says it, which did not prevent me from saying over the next one's shoulder what I thought of his manners, the ethics of his company, and the cheek of the well-known tourist agency which had sold me the ticket in Paris.

But it did not get me anything. He went right on about his business of turning more people away.

I had a look around. The smoking-room air was all blue, and all khaki as to chairs and tables. Also all khaki as to sleeping-quarters. They had been campaigning for a year or more on the western line, and had not lost any time here. And every blessed one of them had a whiskey and soda before him. They were talking, but not of the war. They were going home for a ten days' leave after a year at the front and were trying to forget the war. There was also a lounge-room and a dining-saloon, but bunks there were also already commandeered by the strategic military.

It could be a worse night to walk the deck. To see what was doing a man would want to walk the deck anyway.

There was a fine bright moon mounting above the housetops of the water-front when we slid away from our jetty berth. Slid is the word. She was all power, this Channel steamer of hardly 1,500 tons, yet with two great smoke-stacks, three propellers, turbine-engines, and burning oil for fuel. That last is a cheerful item when you have to walk the deck—it means no cinders in your eyes.

Fuss? A strange word to her. She slipped like running oil from the jetty, past the breakwater lights, out by the few craft anchored there—a fast one for sure. To get a line on her speed, you had but to watch the shore marks fall away or the water slide by her side as out into the Channel she went.

People without berths, but with a chair and a rug from the head steward, began now to tuck away. At first they sat mostly by the rail watching things. Later they sought snugger corners; but two o'clock of a September morning in 50° north is still two o'clock in the morning. They began to go inside. The lights were turned off inside the ship, so when you walked around in there and felt your foot come down on something soft, you needed to tread lightly— that would be somebody's neck or stomach. There were life-rafts on the top deck, of a homelike sort of model, in the form of two benches with the air-tanks under the benches. If anything happened to the ship, you could go floating off with all the comforts of a seat on a bench in the park—if too many did not try to have seats at the same time. It was a fine night for anybody to spot us, but just as fine a night for us to spot them. And a ship cutting out devious courses at twenty-one knots, or whatever she was logging—she is not too easy to hit. To lay out for the ten and eleven knot cargo boats is more economical. Still, who knows? We paid tribute to the U-boats by making detours. All the big stars of the night were out, and by them we could follow her shifting courses. But no harm; she had speed enough to sail the Channel sidewise and still bring us in by morning. The night grew older and cooler. The last of the people who had paid toll to the steward for a chair and rug went inside. Only one couple were left; and they had not hired any chair. He was a young officer, and they sat under his olive-drab blanket, on a life-raft bench athwart-ship. From there without moving they could get sidewise peeks at the climbing moon. At five o'clock in the morning they were still sitting there, heads together and arms across each other's shoulders.

When we grew tired of walking we sought little anchorages. By two o'clock any man on deck could have had his pick of abandoned chairs, but they were not good chairs—the extension part too short. One very young Canadian officer opened up his kit, made a bed and what lee he could of the forward smoke-stack. A round smoke-stack makes a poor lee, but once tucked in he stuck, and was there in the morning when clear light came.

The moon went behind clouds, and from the clouds little cold showers of rain came peppering down. Heavier clouds came, and heavier squalls with rain; and a mean little cross sea began to make. Straight ahead, above the little seas a light showed, and soon another—this a powerful one. We were still going at a great clip. We might know it anew by the way that big light jumped forward to meet us. Soon we had it off our bow, abeam, on our quarter; we were inshore.

A destroyer came out to meet us and blinked a message from screened lights. More ships met us. We passed other ships—all kinds of ships, of which in detail a man must not write here.

In good time and in smooth waters we made our landing. There was another long wait, the same passport grilling, but in a different way, and then a fast train to London. A taxi then, a room, a shave and bath, clean linen, and—oh boy!—the roast beef of old England and people you knew to talk to!

Chapter 6

The Censors

Before a visiting correspondent can do anything on the other side he has to report to a censor somewhere. In London the Chief Admiralty Censor was a retired Royal Navy captain and a Sir Knight, but not wearing his uniform or parading his knighthood. He was quartered in an old dark building where Nelson used to hang out in the days before Trafalgar. There was a sign on the door: *Don't knock. Come in.*

He was a good sort, with not a sign about him of that swank which so many of the military caste seem to think it necessary to adopt. He was perfectly willing to pass me on to our naval base and go right ahead with my work; but he did not have charge of the naval base. There was an admiral over there—not an American admiral—who had full charge of our war-ships there. Without his permission not one of them could tie up to a mooring in the harbour. I would have to get his permission even to visit the base. My very human censor in London said he would cable to him and let me know just as soon as word came.

Awaiting the pleasure of the naval base dictator held me two weeks in London. While waiting I had a look over the city. It was during a period when the moon was ripe for air-raids. There were seven of them in nine nights. My business in life being to see things and then to write about them, I walked the streets during two of them and viewed some of the others from club and hotel windows.

The underground railway stations did a great business while the raids were on; also bomb-proof basements. In a newspaper office, where I used to visit, were precise directions how to get to their bomb-proof cellar. And be sure to take the right one. They had two cellars, but only one was bomb-proof. Shops in the expensive shopping districts had signs up, advertising their bomb-proof cellars and inviting their patrons to make use of them; but the trouble with the shops was that most air-raids took place after they had shut up for the day.

There was a local regulation which said that when an air-raid was on any person at all might knock at the door of any house he pleased and claim admittance. If he were not admitted at once he could call a policeman, who would have to see that he was admitted. We used to speculate on what would happen if some hobo knocked at the front door of the town house of the Duke of Westminster, say, and demanded of the butler in plush knee-breeches that he be let in.

The chief defence against the Gotha was a barrage of guns mounted mostly on the roofs of buildings. An expected air-raid would be announced by policemen running through the streets on bicycles, on their chests and back were signs: *Air Raid On.* They also blew whistles.

The great search-lights would sweep the skies, and by and by there would be a great banging of barrage guns. Bang, bang, bang—that would be the defence guns. Boom! That would be a bomb. Bang, bang, bang, and *Boo-oom!* The guns fired 3-inch shrapnel. Three miles into the air the shrapnel shells would go! And what goes up has to come down. The next thing would be shrapnel showering into the streets. It seemed to me that I would rather take my chance with the bombs than with the shrapnel. A bomb came down, exploded, and had done with it; but the shrapnel fell all over the place.

You could see the shrapnel shells bursting high in the air—a beautiful sight—twinkling like big yellow stars, and then fading out. They would look more beautiful if only the pieces of them would stay up there after they burst. I was in Oxford Circus one night when a hatful of shrapnel fell about 20 feet away. One piece was about 5 inches long. Imagine that falling down from a height of 3 miles and hitting a fellow on the head. It would go clear on down through to your toes. Before any American city is raided I hope some chemist will invent a barrage shell which will dissipate all its energy and substance in the bursting. Surely an airplane can be wrecked by concussion.

An Australian soldier and a girl were standing in a doorway near me watching the shells burst. His was that common case—a soldier in London on leave, speculating on where the shrapnel would fall, and becoming peeved as he thought of it. "A hell of a place for a man to come on leave! I came here to get rest and quiet, and I run into this gory mess!"

While waiting the permission of the British authorities I learned that all a correspondent's troubles do not come from foreign censorship. An American newsman had cabled over something which did not please one of our admirals then in London. Meeting that same admiral, I put in a word for my trip to the naval base, thinking that he might warm up and hurry things along for me. He warmed up, but on the side away from me. He recounted the enormous villainy of that newsman, and in conclusion said: "Perhaps, after all, the best way to do is not to allow you newspaper men to send a word at all!"

Such an air of finality! He spoke as though he owned the navy; also the press.

One now and again grows up like that. By taking care not to die, and in the absence of plucking boards, they rise to be admirals. Then side-boys, the bosun's pipes, the 13 guns coming over the side—all this ritual goes to their heads. They get to thinking after a while that the whole business is a tribute to their genius, or valour, or something or other personal. Perhaps all this one needed was a little salve; but I thought it up to some writer to fire a shot across his bows. So I came back with: "That's all very well, sir, about your not allowing a word to be sent, but there may be another point of view. There are 110,000,000 people over in our country, and some of them may not look on our navy as the sole property of its officers. They may want to know what that navy of theirs is doing over here. And perhaps no harm in telling them—or some day they may decide to have no navy at all."

Imagination was not his long suit, so he had no card to follow with. But he did glare.

After two weeks of waiting I got word from my very human London censor that I might leave for the naval base. I left from Euston Station during an air-raid. The station had been darkened hours earlier, and it was a new kind of sport going around that big black place to locate the cloak-room, and after you got the cloak-room to identify your baggage from a big tumbled pile.

I lit a cigar, and as I did a policeman jumped me for showing a light. Stopping to light it under my hat, a tall, able woman, dragging a trunk by the strap, bowled into me. While we were in our compartments, the train all made up, there came a banging of barrage guns—bang, bang, bang—with now and then the *boo-oom!* of a bomb.

While we were waiting there we heard the crash of shrapnel coming through the glass roof. By and by another bunch of shrapnel fell with a fine ringing of metal on the concrete platform alongside the train. No harm done. The raiders passed, the banging and the booming stopped; but there was then no driver and stoker for the train. They had gone with the second load of shrapnel, and we had to wait two hours while they dug up a new crew.

After three and a half hours of deck-pacing on the steamer, and twenty-two hours of sitting up straight in third-class wooden seats, I made the naval base; and late at night though it was, there was a British naval officer at the hotel to let me know I was to report next morning to the British admiral in charge.

This admiral had a reputation in London for having no use for newspaper men. When this staff-officer asked me if I had heard of his admiral before, I told him what I heard in London. "He eats 'em alive," I was told by a big London journalist, and I repeated that now, of course without naming the journalist.

"And what do you think of that?" asked this staff-officer.

"If he tries to eat me alive I hope he chokes," I answered to that. I figured he would tell his chief that, but there had been so much boot-licking done by a couple of writers over there that, for the honour of the craft, I thought somebody ought to have a wallop at these press crushers once in a while.

This admiral is worth a paragraph, because he was a type. He was a capable man up to his limitations; a good executive, a devotee to duty; but he should have lived before printing-presses were invented. Also he, too, lacked imagination.

He was a man who acted as if priding himself on his brusqueness of language. He sat at his flat desk like a pagan image, never looked up, never said aye, no, or go to the devil when I stepped in and wished him "Good morning!"

I told him what I wanted. I wished to cruise with the American destroyers in their U-boat operations.

His answer was a No! Bing! No, sir!

"Whoops!" I said to myself. "I've come more than 4,000 miles, with a fine expense account to *Collier's*, and I'm turned down before I get going."

I spread before him my credentials—from the department and elsewhere. I spread before him a letter from Colonel Roosevelt, the same in his own handwriting. In France I could have lost my passport and yet got along on that letter. Batteries of inspectors used to sit up and come to life at the sight of a letter in the colonel's own handwriting.

This man did not turn his head to look at what I might have. All the credentials in the world were going to have no influence with him. He repeated his *no*, putting about seventeen n's in the *no*!

Then, mildly, I told him that I thought I ought to have something more than a No; that I should have a reason to go with the No. He intimated that he didn't have to give reasons unless he wished to.

I asked him why he should not wish to? Was it not right and fair that he should give a reason? I had come more than 4,000 miles at great expense to *Collier's*, for one thing. For another—and this more important—there was an anxiety among Americans to know something of the doings of our little destroyer flotilla. They had sailed out into the East, been swallowed up in the mists of the Atlantic—that was the last we had seen of them. They were the first of our forces to come in contact with the enemy. Were they doing good work over here, or were they tied up to a dock in some port and their officers and crews roistering ashore?

Still he said No.

Then I went on to tell him what I had told our own archaic type of admiral in London—with additions: that it was possible that we had in the United States a different idea of the navy from what the British public held; that in our own country a lot of people held the notion that the navy was not the property of the officers, not quite so much as it was the property of the people; and that holding that view, these same people thought themselves entitled to know what that navy was doing to back their faith in it. And perhaps it was not the worst policy in the world to tell them what that navy was doing.

Still he said *no*.

But why?

Well, for one thing (he was disintegrating a little), in the British service they did not allow civilians of any kind to go to sea with their ships in war time. That further—they allowed no reports of their work at sea to appear in the press.

I pointed out that reports of fine deeds were, nevertheless, appearing in the press; that from the London dailies of the week past I had made clippings of such, and if he cared to see them I would show them to him.

"But we allow no civilians to go cruising with ships at sea in war time. And I will not establish a precedent now."

It was the old *fetich*—precedent. I thought of judges who used to hang men on precedent. He surely had what is called the medieval mind, with apologies to that same medieval age.

I pointed out that conditions in our country and his were not the same. That there were hundreds of thousands of officers and men in the British navy; that those officers and men were regularly ashore on liberty or leave; that they gossiped, and that hundreds of thousands of officers and men gossiping could pass the word pretty far, especially in a country where there was not a single little hamlet more than 40 miles from tide-water. With us it was different. Our nearest Atlantic port was 3,000 miles from this very naval base; and 3,000 miles farther to the Pacific coast, with no hundreds of thousands of men on liberty ashore. If men like myself were not allowed to tell them something, how were they ever to learn what was doing?

I wound up by telling him he was an autocrat; which disturbed his graven serenity. Autocrat and autocracy were not pleasant-sounding words just then. He snapped his head up, and for the first time looked as if he might be human.

"We have to be autocratic in war time," he barked.

"Not in everything," I barked back.

Then, and not till then, did he soften. We had a little more conversation, and then he said he wanted that night to think over the unprecedented request. He would let me know next day.

A perfect bigot; and yet there were worse than he. He dared to say what he thought about the rights of his station. Some of his judgments may have been childish, but his convictions were deep and honest. I respected him, and later came to have almost a liking for him.

I have expended many paragraphs in telling of this interview, but it is meant to be more than a statement of one American correspondent. It is meant to explain a point of view which Americans may find it hard work to understand. That admiral in charge of our naval base can be multiplied all the world over. We have them in our own departments.

While waiting the admiral's pleasure I had a look at the port. A fine harbour, a beautiful harbour, but disfigured now by big, ugly war-buildings. The houses of the port set mostly up on terraces. There were several streets, but only one real one in the place, and that ran along the waterside. All the pubs of the port were naturally located on this waterside street, and so no tired seafarer had to walk far to get a drink. Not many of our fellows were to be seen on the streets in daylight; but at night they were plentiful. A couple of movie theatres took care of about three hundred of them; the rest walked the waterside street. There was a port order there that no sailor of ours could stay in a pub after eight in the evening, so at one minute past eight that waterside street looked like a naval parade. For the rest the port offered little or nothing to tempt a man. It was as rainy a place as ever I was in, and the back streets were crowded with children playing. Barefooted, healthy children! If they had not been healthy the weather would surely have killed them off. It was a most moral port, too; too moral for some people, who thought to put a little life into the place by making nightly calls there, and made the nightly calls till a local clergyman protested from the altar, whereupon some muscular young Christians ran the visitors back aboard their train and out of the port's history.

Next day the admiral gave me permission to make a cruise with our destroyers. He seemed to be giving it in the same stubborn fashion that he had at first refused it—as though he saw his duty in so doing. I was told that he said he did not think much of my manners; which, of course, worried me.

I knew quite a few officers in the navy who were commanding destroyers over there. Any one of them, known or unknown to me, was good enough for me as a skipper. No man not ready to take a chance puts in for command of a destroyer over there; and no man not fit is given a command. But I took passage with one that I had cruised with before—the alert, resourceful kind with plenty of nerve. If anything should happen, I knew he would be there with all his crew and his ship had.

What happened while with him and at the naval base I have tried to tell as separate incidents when I can, in the chapters which follow.

Chapter 7

One They Didn't Get

We were one of a group of American destroyers convoying a fleet of inbound British merchant steamers.

The messenger handed a radio in to the bridge.

"We are being shelled," said the radio; latitude and longitude followed, as did the name of the ship, *J. L. Luckenbach*. One of us knew her; an American ship of 6,000 tons or so.

Another radio came: "Shell burst in engine-room. Engineer crippled." S O S signals were no rare thing in those waters, but even so they were never passed up as lacking interest; the skipper waited for action. Pretty soon it came, a signal from the senior officer of our group. The 352—let us give that as the number of our ship—was to proceed at once to the assistance of the *Luckenbach*.

The skipper's first act was to shake up the second watch-officer, who also happened to be acting as chief engineer of the ship, and to pass him the word to speed the ship up to twenty-five knots. We were steaming at the head of the convoy column at eighteen knots at the time. The first watch-officer, having finished his breakfast and a morning watch, was just then taking a little nap on the port ward-room transom with his clothes and sea-boots still on. The active messenger shook him up too. The two officers made the deck together, one buttoning his blouse over a heavy sweater, the other a sheepskin coat over his blouse.

Word was sent to the *Luckenbach* that we were on the way. Within three minutes the radio came back: "Our steam is cut off. How soon can you get here?"

Up through the speaking-tube came a voice just then to say that we were making twenty-five knots. At the same moment our executive officer, who also happened to be the navigator, handed the skipper a slip of paper with the course and distance to the *Luckenbach*, saying: "That was at nine-fifteen."

It was then nine-seventeen. Down the tube to the engine-room went the order to make what speed she could. Also the skipper said: "She ought to be tearing off twenty-eight soon as she warms up. And she's how far now? Eighty-two miles? Send this radio: 'Stick to it—will be with you within three hours.'"

By this time all hands had an idea of what was doing and all began to brighten up. Men off watch, supposed to be asleep in their cots below, began to stroll up and have a look around decks. Some lingered near the wireless door, and every time the messenger passed they sort of stuck their ears up at him. He was a long-legged lad in rubber boots who took the deck in big strides. His lips never opened, but his eyes talked. The men turned from him with pleased expressions on their faces.

There was a little steel shelter built on to the chart house to port. It was for the protection of the forward gun crew, who had to be ready for action at any minute. Men standing by for action and not getting it legitimately, try to get it in some other way. So they used to burn up their spare energy in arguing. It did not matter what the argument was about—the President, Roosevelt, the Kaiser, the world series—any subject would do so long as it would grow into an argument. The rest of the crew could hear them—threatening to bust each other's eyes out—clear to the skid deck sometimes. But now all quiet here, and soon they were edging out of their igloo and calling down to the fellows on the main deck: "That right about a ship being shelled by a sub? Yes. Well!" They went down to their shelter smiling at one another.

Ship's cooks, who rarely wander far from their cosy galley stoves, began to show on deck; ward-room stewards came out on deck; a gang black-painting a tank hatch—they all slipped over to the rail and, leaning as far out as they could and not fall overboard, had long looks ahead. And then they all turned to see what 352's smoke-stacks were doing. There was great hope there.

The black smoke was getting blacker and heavier. They were sure feeding the oil to her. The chief came up the engine-room ladder. An old petty officer waylaid him. Doing well, was she, sir?—

She was. Hem! About how well, sir?—Damn' well. She was kicking out twenty-eight—twenty-eight good—and picking up.

Twenty-eight and picking up? And the best she showed in her builders' trial was twenty-nine-one! What d'y' know about her? Some little old packet, hah?

It was a fine day, the one fine day of the trip, a rarely fine day for this part of the northern ocean at this time of year. It was cloudy, but it was calm. There was a long, easy swell on, but no sea to make her dive or pitch. The swell, when she got going in good shape, set her to swinging a little, but that did not hurt. A destroyer just naturally likes to swing a little.

Swinging along she went, rolling one rail down and then the other, but not making it hard to stand almost anywhere around deck, except that when you went aft there was a drive of air that lifted you maybe a little faster than you started out to go. Swinging along she went, a long, easy swing, carrying a long white swash to either side of her, vibrating a thousand to the minute on her fantail, streaming out a long white and pale-blue wake for as far as we could see, and just clear of her taffrail piling up the finest little hill of clear white boiling water.

Twenty-nine, they say, she was making, and still picking up. What! Thirty? And a little more left in her? What d'y' know—some little baby, hah?

Another radio came to the bridge: "A shell below our waterline. Settling, but still afloat and still fighting."

"Good work. Stick to it," they said on the bridge, and wondered whether it was the skipper or the radio man who was framing the messages. He had the dramatic instinct, whoever he was.

Perhaps twenty minutes later came: "Water in our engine-room."

And then: "Fire in our fore-hold, but will not surrender. Look for our boats."

And: "They are now shooting at our antenna."

Radios to the bridge are not posted up for the crew to gossip over, but there was no keeping that last one under cover.

"Shelling their attenay? Well, the mortifying dogs! Whatever you do, don't let 'em get your attenay, old bucket."

Our thirty-knot clip was eating up the road. We were getting near the spot. The canvas caps came off the guns, and the gun crews

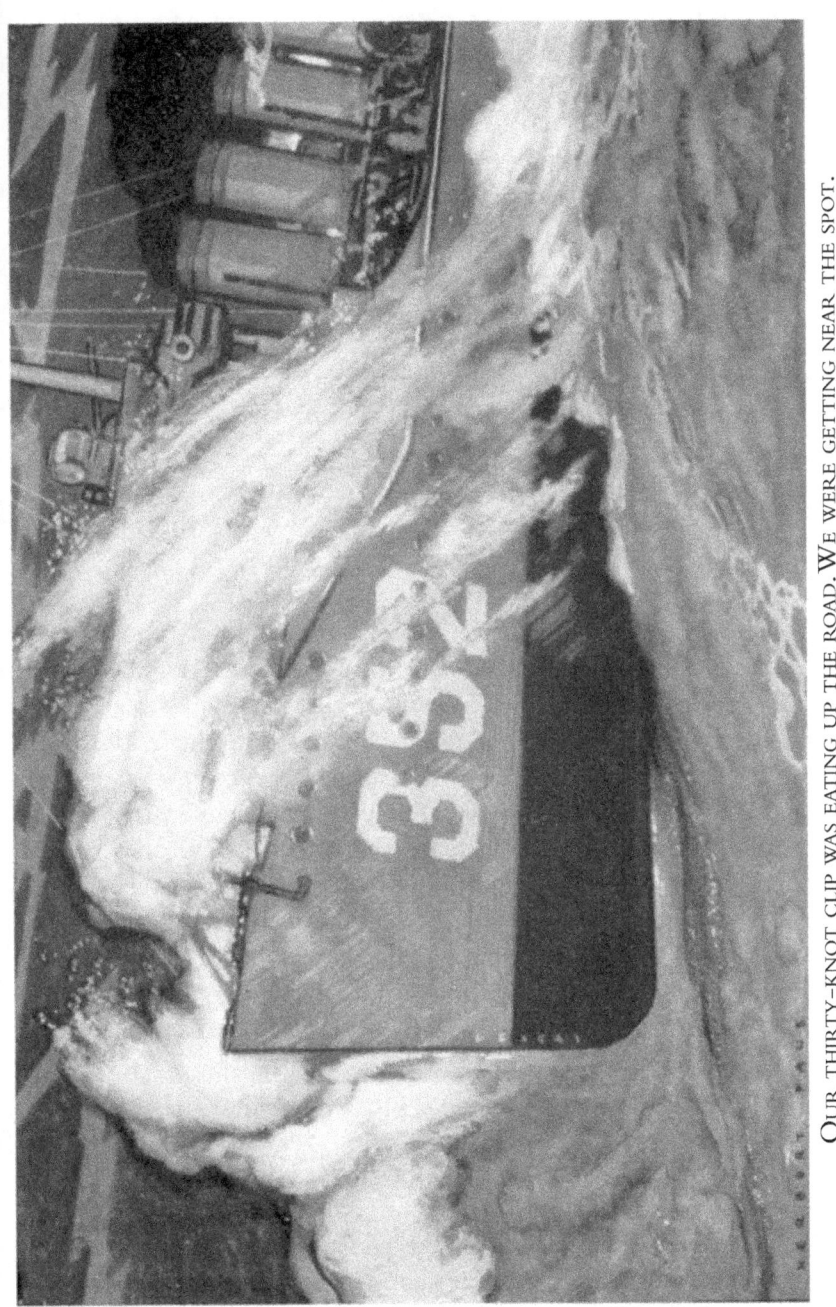

Our thirty-knot clip was eating up the road. We were getting near the spot.

were told to load and stand by. A chief gunner's mate was told to make ready his torpedo-tubes. He was a famous torpedo-man. He would stay up all night with an ailing gyro or hydrostatic piston and not even ask to sleep in next morning for a reward, and he had a record of making nothing but hits at torpedo-practice. But he had been glum all the trip. He had stayed past the legal hour on liberty the last time in, and the shore patrol had come along and scooped him up. A court-martial was coming to him and so he had been glum; but not now. He went around decks smiling, with a little steel thing that looked like a wrist-bag but wasn't. It held the keys to the magazines.

Pretty soon he had torpedo-tubes swinging inboard and outboard, and between every pair of tubes a man sitting up in an iron seat that looked like the kind that goes with a McCormick reaper, which all helped the gunner's mate to feel better. He stopped ten seconds to tell the story of the new gun-crew man who was sent up the yard to the storekeeper for a pair of spurs to ride the torpedo-tubes with.

There were four guns, one forward, one aft, and two in the waist. They had been slushed down with Vaseline to keep the saltwater rust off; now they were swabbing the grease off. Grease on the outside of a gun does not affect the shooting of the inside, but a gun ought naturally to look slick going into action.

Trainers and pointers stood beside their loaded guns, and other members of the gun crew held up shells, the noses of the shells stuck into the deck mat and the butts resting against the young chests of the gun crews as they stood in line. There was a nineteen-year-old lad who, when I knew him two years before, was doing boy's work in the Collier bookbindery. Now he was a gun-captain standing handy to his little pet and trying not to look too proud when he peeked up toward where I was.

The foretop reported smoke on the horizon ahead. That would be on the *Luckenbach*. And where she was the U-boat was. The forward gun was trained a point to right of the smoke.

One senior watch-officer, now in the foretop, called down that he could now see the ship. Smoke was coming out of her hull. Soon he reported shells splashing alongside of her. Those would be from the U-boat. Soon we all could see the ship from the bridge.

The foretop then reported the U-boat. She was almost dead ahead. She could not be seen from the bridge, but, directed by the foretop, the gun was trained on the horizon dead ahead; 11,000 yards was the range. The gun was one of the latest type—only a 4-inch—but a great little gun just the same.

"Train and fire," said the skipper. Bo-o-m! it went, flame and smoke. We could not see the splash from the bridge, nor could they in the foretop. It probably dropped beyond the submarine, which soon we could see—a pretty big fellow she looked with two guns. She had been shelling the ship even while we were running up, and as our first shot boomed out she let go another shell. We expected her to send a couple our way—she probably carried bigger guns than we did—but she did not; she let go another at the steamer. "Maybe at the antenna," said a chief quartermaster on the bridge.

We shortened our range. The gun was trained and ready for firing when a sea rolled up on us. The ocean was smooth enough, but the swell was still on—a long swell of the kind that does not sputter, but walk right up and announce their arrival by arriving. This long blue swell rolled up to our bow.

We were doing thirty knots and at thirty knots a little ship doesn't need a masthead sea to get action. We went into it head first. It came right on over our bow, over our foc'sle head, over the forward gun. The shield to the forward gun stood probably six feet above the foc'sle deck. That wave rolled right over the gun-shield.

There was a C. P. O. standing quite close to the shield. He grabbed a vertical rod on the outside of the shield, and just managed to hook in the fingers of one hand. The sea, all white and solid, rolled over the gun and the shield. The C. P. O. was swept off his feet, but he was a stubborn one and hung on. Behind him was the officer in charge of the firing. When he saw that sea rolling up there was nothing near but the C. P. O., so he grabbed the C. P. O. with both hands around the waist. He too was swept off his feet, but he hung on—to the C. P. O. They both floated flat out on the white roller, and the white roller went smash-o! up against the chart house.

The chart house was just under the bridge, and the glass windows had been taken out from the bridge railing so that they would not be smashed by the concussion of the forward gun. We were leaning out of these open spaces, just getting ready to laugh at the people below when, *swabbo!* up the side of the chart house and through the open spaces and into our open mouths came the wash of the sea.

Another wave followed that one, but not quite so high. As soon as it passed the forward gun was trained and fired. We had been making great leaps ahead all this time—the range now was under 9,000 yards. The foretop reported it short.

The U-boat was still there. We still expected her to send one our way. But nothing doing for us. She sent another shell toward the steamer. The steamer had quit firing. No use. The U-boat had simply taken position beyond range of the steamer's guns and leisurely as she pleased was shelling her. Our third shell landed close to the sub. And then down she went and wasted no time at it. Before we could train and fire again she was gone.

The sub, as we learned later, had landed fifteen shells into the steamer and wounded nine of her people, of whom three were of the blue-jacket gun crew.

One young blue-jacket had been hit twice. He was carrying a shell to the gun when he caught the second one—a piece of flying shell in his shoulder. He laid his own shell on the deck to see how about it, and got hit again; this time in what our navy calls the stern sheets. That made him mad. He shook his fist toward the sub. "No damn' German's going to hit me three times and get away with it." He grabbed his shell off the deck and slammed it into the gun-breech. "Hand it to 'em, Joe!" he yelled to the gun-pointer. Joe did his best, but he didn't have the gun—the shot splashed where most of them had, about half a mile short of the sub.

Still pouring the black smoke out of our funnels, we leaped toward the *Luckenbach* and hailed her through the megaphone when we breasted her. She hailed back that she had water in her afterhold and fire in her fore-hold, and gave us the number of her wounded. Two of the three wounded blue-jackets were injured seriously. We could see them stretched out under the gun.

We were steaming around the *Luckenbach* at twenty knots while we were hailing: this in case the sub took it in her head to pop up again and catch us slowed down. We did slow down and stop when it came time to clear away a whale-boat and send it over to the steamer with our senior watch-officer and the surgeon, with the needful surgical supplies.

We continued to steam circles around the steamer all the time they were aboard, with our lookouts keeping eyes skinned for the U-boat. By her manner of shelling the steamer after he had opened fire our skipper judged she was a tough one. She did show once while we were circling the *Luckenbach*. Her periscope popped up about a mile abeam of us. It may have popped up again—it was getting to be a nice little choppy sea good for sub work and no saying that it was not—but we only sighted it once, and then it did not linger.

The sea was growing lumpy when the whale-boat came bouncing back with our senior officer. It was right about the *Luckenbach* having nine injured, but all would get well. The doctor was looking after them. She was a cotton steamer. The kid who had been hit twice was all right. He was walking around deck with his cap over his port ear and proud as Billy-be-Damn'—three times wounded by German shell fire and got away with it!

The fire in the fore-hold? Most of it was from two old mattresses—at least that was all he found.

"Did you put the fire out?"

"Yes, sir. The steamer's crew were too tired to do any more hustling around to put any fire out, so we got out a hose and put it out."

"How about that bulkhead?" asked the skipper. "He hailed that he didn't think it would stand the strain of steaming."

"Maybe so, sir, but I don't agree with him. I don't see how that bulkhead's going to cave in with all those bales of cotton jammed up against it. What the most of them over there are suffering from is the reaction from that three hours of shelling—everything was looking pretty blue to them, sir."

"Can he make steam?"

"Yes, sir. Their engineer has two ribs busted in and a piece of shrapnel in his neck and part of his foot shot away. But he's all right. He was lying down when I first saw him, cursing the Germans blue. Then he says: 'Put me on my feet, men.' A couple of oilers put him on his feet. I thought he was going to give orders to make steam, but he only wanted to be stood up so as he could curse the

Germans a little better. Lying down interfered with his wind. He rolled it out in one steady stream for ten minutes. He was an Italian, or maybe a Spaniard, and his English wasn't perfect, but he could talk like hell. He's all right. He'll get steam up, sir."

By and by they did make steam and begin to move on a course our skipper wigwagged to them. The skipper left the surgeon aboard, and at twenty knots the 352 steamed more circles around the steamer, all lookouts meanwhile skinning their eyes afresh for signs of the sub. We could make out a lot of smoke on the southern horizon. It was the convoy we had left in the morning. An hour later the *Luckenbach* found her legs.

Our cripple broke no records for speed, but she was making revolutions, and by five o'clock we rejoined the convoy with her alongside.

So here is an eight hours' log for the 352: At nine in the morning she was responding to SOS-ing ninety miles away; at five in the afternoon we had her tucked away for the night in the column.

The tall quartermaster came up on the bridge to stand his watch. We were in our regular position, at the head of the column at twenty knots. He looked back at the fleet. "There you are, Lucky Bag. They must have had you checked up and counted in, a big ship and a three-million-dollar cargo, this morning, and here you are to-night—one they didn't get."

Chapter 8

The Doctor Takes Charge

Every American destroyer over here rates a young surgeon. What some of these surgeons don't know about seagoing can be found in about six hundred pages of Knight's "Modern Seamanship," but that does not matter much. Let them look after the casualties; there are capable young naval officers to look after the seagoing end.

Most of these young surgeons have a taste for adventure. If they had not, they would not be over here. The 352 drew one, born and raised in a Southern State. Before coming over here he had viewed the Atlantic once or twice from a distance, which did not quite content him. His ancestors must have crossed that same Atlantic to get to America, and somewhere within him was a high-pitched string that vibrated to every thrill of that same ocean now.

He used to speak of these things in the smoking-room of the King's Hotel here, which is where every destroyer officer comes at least once between cruises to get a—cup of coffee. He would have liked to make a few sea voyages when he was a little younger, but if a fellow is ever going to amount to anything he has to settle down sometime and become a respectable member of society—so his folks were always saying, and so he took up medicine. He liked his profession. A doctor can do a heap of good in a suffering world—especially if people will only let him. But so many people want a young doctor to be experienced before they ever will call him in! "Get experience," they say; and not a doggone one in a dozen'll ever give a fellow any chance to get the experience. "What the most of 'em want is for some one else to give us the experience."

He did as well as the next young doctor, but at times he would grow almost melancholy sitting before the smoking-room fire telling of his waiting for business in his home town.

He was not at all melancholy by nature. He could keep the ward-room mess ringing with darky stories on a quiet night in port. His messmates called him Doc; and when the ship was at sea they were all glad to see him on the bridge studying things out. He had plenty of time for that. In two cruises his only cases were one quartermaster, who got hove across the bridge and broke his nose, and a gunner's mate who broke his leg by being bounced out of his bunk one windy night. They were a disgustingly healthy lot, these destroyer crews.

But he felt pleased just to be out to sea. These high hills of moving water sure did give a little ship heaps of action sometimes. He would watch them from the bridge. He would watch the officer of the watch too, and the man at the wheel, and the lookouts with their eyes skinned for U-boats, and the signal quartermasters balanced on the flying bridge and sending their messages in a jumping sea-way. He would go down to the chart house with the navigator and stand by to pass him dividers and parallels. He would stop to sigh when he thought that if somebody had only tipped him off in time he might have gone to Annapolis and right now be a young naval officer dashing around on one of these same destroyers. Still, being a surgeon on one of them wasn't too bad. If they had a battle or anything, a ship's doctor wasn't going to be too far away.

It was in his third cruise that the 352 got the S O S which resulted in the rescue of the big steamer spoken of. There had been other S O S's—any number of them—but this time there was something doing for our young doctor. When she signalled that nine of her people had been wounded by shell and shrapnel fire, and the 352's skipper ordered a deck officer and a whale-boat away, he also told Doc to break out his medical gear and go along. Doc already had his surgical gear ready; from the first word of the shelling he had gone below, and now everything was laid out ready for action on the ward-room transom.

Over to the ship they went, all hands in life-vests, and while the deck officer of the 352 was cross-questioning the captain and engineer, and looking around to see how much damage had been done and so on, Doc was rigging up an operating-table between the chart house and the chart deck rail, slinging the table in sort of hammock style so that when the ship rolled she would not roll his patients overboard.

Doc was no mean little operator. The great danger to most of the wounded men was of infection. One after the other, he had his cases up, asked about four questions, had about four looks, and went to it. No knowing that the U-boat might pop up again and try a few more shells, or that a bulkhead would not give way, or a boiler blow up when they tried to make steam below. No knowing; no.

Up they came to his swinging table, where Doc took a probe, poked into the wound, wrapped cotton around the probe, soaked it in iodine, jabbed it in, twisted it around, swabbed it out, dressed it down, slapped the patient on the chest, said "Next," and did it all over again.

"Next! You'd think it was a blessed barber's shop," Doc heard one of them say. Only he was an officer—by the back of his head Doc knew it—some of them would have told him what they thought of his rapid-fire action. But it was no time for canoodling—it was war, and they were all rated as grown men and so able to stand a few little painful touches.

One terribly wounded patient gave him worry. On him Doc worked with great care. He was working on him, all the others being attended to, when the 352's deck officer came to say that he was going back to the destroyer to report. "The captain of this ship wants to abandon her," said the deck officer.

"Abandon ship and we will never be able to get this man I got here now off her—not in this sea, sir," said Doc. "And if he's left alone for two hours, he'll sure die."

"I'll signal what the skipper says." The officer went off with his crew in the whale-boat, leaving a hospital steward and a signal quartermaster to stay with the doctor.

Doc was working away on his hard case when his quartermaster came to say that the 352 had signalled that they were to stay aboard and that the steamer was to get under way and steer a course south half east magnetic.

The doctor, without looking up, said: "All right."

"Shall I tell the steamer's captain, sir?"

This time Doc looked up. "Why, of course, tell him. Why not? Why do you ask me that?"

"You are the ranking naval officer aboard here, sir. I take orders from you now, sir."

For about four seconds Doc neglected his patient. That was so; so he was.

"Yes, tell the captain."

The quartermaster ran up the bridge ladder. Doc gazed over the chart-rail down to the deck, up and around on the ship. "Doggone!" he breathed. "I am the ranking—I'm the only naval officer present." Then he shook his head and bent to his patient. He might have the rank, but the last thing he was going to do was to butt in on any regular ship's officers.

The disabled ship went on to her new course, south half east magnetic, with the destroyer steaming twenty-knot circles around her. And late in the afternoon they made the convoy. By night she was tucked in the rear of twenty other ships, the doctor and his emergency staff still aboard. They were to remain aboard until the steamer made port.

That same night something happened. On the steamer they did not know just what it was. They saw a column of white, a column of black—those who happened to be looking—another column of white, from the big ship of the fleet. And then dark came. There were radios flying about, but they were code messages and the radio man could not decode them because the first thing the steamer captain had done that morning when it looked as though the U-boat was going to make them take to the boats was to heave the code-books overboard. In the morning they would know.

Morning came, but with it not a ship in sight. Of twenty ships and a group of destroyers the night before, not one now. It was his signal-officer who thought it out first. "U-boats thick last night, sir, and the convoy must 'a' got orders to disperse or else change course," he said to the doctor.

"That sounds like good dope to me too." He turned to the steamer's captain. "Where were you bound, sir?"

"To Havre."

The doctor could see nothing else but to proceed to Havre, and on a zigzag course. The old captain did not know about the zigzagging; he had never done any zigzagging and did not know why he should now—besides, it mixed his reckoning all up.

The doctor said he would fix the zigzagging part of it, and, telling his hospital steward to have a special eye out for the very sick man, went into the chart house and proceeded to explain the zigzagging stuff. He paused to recall all he had ever learned while elbowing the 352's navigator over the chart-table; also the answers he had got to his questions while so doing.

You steer 45 degrees off the course you really want to make for so many minutes and then you steer 90 degrees from that for the same number of minutes back toward the course you really want to make—see, so—and that gives so many minutes to the good—see. That was one way.

"How many minutes?" asked the captain.

Doc had to stop and think that over. "Twice the square of the total minutes—no, no. Take twice the sum of the squares of the minutes on the two legs—and get the square root and then you have the hypotenuse of the two sides of the triangle; that is, you have the number of minutes' steaming you make good on your real course."

The old skipper knew nothing of square roots or hypotenuses or anything that looked like 'em, and he had always laid his course out by compass points.

"All right," said Doc, and after a while laid out the zigzag courses in compass points.

The old fellow did not quite like it, so all that day Doc alternated between his bad patient and the bridge to keep the skipper reassured about the zigzagging. Also he urged the crew to have a special watch out for U-boats.

That night Doc and the seasoned signal quartermaster stood alternate watches on the bridge. Doc would take a nap; the quartermaster would take a nap; between them they were figuring to keep a sort of official navy lookout. There were ship's crew men on the lookout too, but the reaction from the shelling had set in. Doc used to find them asleep in the bridge wings.

Just before dawn of the second morning Doc saw a shadow looming on their starboard bow. He had another look. It was another steamer—a big one. She was drawing nearer. "See that?" he called to the man at the wheel.

"See what?" sort of drowsed out the man at the wheel.

The trusty quartermaster from the 352 was getting a wink under the bridge-rail. Doc yelled to him, at the same time grabbing up the megaphone and roaring into the night air: "Where you-all going? Where the devil you-all going? Can't you-all see where you're going? Keep off—keep off."

"Can't *you* see where you're going?—keep off yourself."

By that time the signal quartermaster was awake and bounding across the bridge. He grabbed the wheel and began to spin it around. The ship's bow turned. Doc saw the big hulk go by him in the dark.

"Good work," said Doc. "How'd you spot him so quick?"

"I didn't spot him, sir. I don't see him yet. I went by the sound of his voice."

"Special little angel perched up aloft to look out for Jack when at sea—" sang Doc. "I thought that was a nursery rhyme. Now I know it's true. Between you and me, quartermaster, we'll get this ship to port yet."

They finished that night and the next day without seeing anything or having anything happen. Nothing except the argument about the forward compartment.

Among the shells which had come aboard the steamer was one which had punched a fine big hole in her bow. The ship's crew had put a plug there which worked all right till the ship took to rolling, which it did this day. The hole was just at the water-line. Before they knew anything about it there was the plug gone and the water up to a man's knees in the forward compartment. Doc said it should be stopped.

The old skipper wanted to know who was going to stop it. His crew? No, sir. He wouldn't ask any of 'em to go down there—besides, they wouldn't go. They were all used up since the battle with the U-boat. It made no difference if the ship sank. He'd had so much trouble that trip anyway that he wasn't too sure he wouldn't just as soon see her sink. He wasn't too sure they wouldn't all be better off in the boats. The U-boat had ordered them into the boats, and, only the destroyer had come along when it did, they would 'a' taken to the boats, and then they'd 'a' been picked up and no more watches or ships or holes in the for'ard compartment to worry about.

There was nothing left but for Doc to call for volunteers from among the gun crew. They were blue-jackets, and their only complaint on the trip had been that the U-boat's guns had outranged their guns. They volunteered in a body—even the three wounded members. Doc took all the sound ones and went down into the forward compartment with a mattress and some scantling he found in the hold. The water was by then about up to the men's waists. It was hard, cold work, but they got it done—the mattress stuffed into the hole and the scantling shoring it up. It still leaked, but not much—a little auxiliary steam in there at intervals did not quite keep her dried out, but it kept her head above water, so that was all right. All that day she was a lone steamer plugging her halting way over a wide sea. Seven knots was her speed, and all hands tickled to be making that because of weak places showing from time to time in her steam department—damages by shell fire which they did not appreciate properly at first.

They were nearing the coast of France. They would have to make a landfall soon, and running without lights, as they were, made things hard, so the old skipper began to talk to Doc. If the doctor didn't mind, he would take full charge of the ship himself. She was a big ship with a three-million-dollar cargo, and if anything happened her, the owners would naturally look to him, the master, for it.

Doc thought it was a pretty cool way to wash out all record of what his little force had done, but he also recognized the old fellow's position. "It sounds reasonable," said Doc, "but I think you ought to give me an idea of what you're going to do."

"There's been no sun for a sight these two days, but we were here"—he made a new dot over an old one on the chart—"and logging so many knots to-day noon we ought to be"—he made another dot—"about here now."

"How about the tides?"

"The tides? Oh, yes! Well, I don't know about the tides. You see, I never made a port in France before."

"You didn't?"

There was a coast chart-book in the rack. Doc took it down and began to read it. He made regular trips down to see how his wounded patient was getting on, but always hurried back to his coast chart-book. Interesting things in chart-books—he used to read them aboard the destroyer.

That night the first mate came up on the bridge. Doc asked him what kind of a light he expected to pick up. The mate told him. Doc thought he was wrong, and said so.

Well, that was the light the old man had said they would make. Where was he now? Asleep, and Lord knows he needed it.

Doc did not wake him up. He had argued enough with him, but he didn't think the old man had allowed for the tides, and if anything happened there would be no more arguments—he would just assert his rank and take charge of the ship.

Doc went below, gave his worst wounded patient a night potion and saw him to sleep. He also went down to see the chief engineer, who had been wounded three times—once in the head. The Doc talked to him awhile—he was inclined to rave—gave him a half-grain jolt of morphine and saw him to sleep. He told the signal quartermaster that he had better have a nap before he dropped in his tracks.

"But the night-watches, sir?"

"We'll leave the night-watches to the ship's crew and Providence. The watch may sleep on the job, but the Lord won't—at least I hope not. Anyway, I know I'm doggone tired," said Doc, and turned in.

Doc could have slept longer—about twenty-four hours longer, he thought, when he found himself awake. It was a sort of grinding under the ship which had wakened him.

By his illuminated wrist-watch he saw that it was three o'clock—three in the afternoon, he hoped. But it wasn't. It was three in the morning. He had been asleep two hours.

He went on deck just as his signal-officer came to tell him the ship was ashore.

Doc found the old man and the mate looking over charts under a hand-light in the chart house. "I could 'a' bet we'd 'a' picked up that other light," the old man was saying.

"The bettin' part don't explain it," said the mate. "A fine place to be high and dry and a U-boat come along in the morning and plunk us another few shells between our livers and lights. I'm tired of keeping my mind on U-boats."

That was when Doc horned in on the old skipper. "I been pretty easy with you-all. You ought to been twenty miles farther east. You listened to me and you-all would have been. Look here"—he hauled down the chart-book and showed them. "And now I'll take charge."

It was low tide when she ran on to the beach. With the flood-tide and the engines kicking back they had her off at daylight. After that, with Doc on the bridge, everything seemed to go all right. The mate said he must have come over the side with a medicine-chest full of horseshoes. By eleven o'clock next morning they were taking on a pilot outside Havre.

Havre is a regular French port with jetties leading down from the heart of the residential places almost. The people, seeing her coming, she bearing the evident marks of her late battle, crowded down to greet her. About five minutes was enough for her story to circulate. The blue-jacket gun crew, being in uniform, caught their eyes first. They cheered them, the *brav' Américains*. And then the wounded came. Oh, the pity! Three or four of the wounded, who had all that day been cavorting around deck, saw the dramatic values and assumed most languid poses. Oh, the great pity! Whereat two more almost fainted.

The worst wounded one—there was no pretence about him—had to be carried down the gang-plank. Doc went with him. Good nursing was what he needed; and he was going to see that he got it.

He got it in the port hospital; and then Doc and his two assistants turned in and slept sixteen hours by Doc's illuminated wrist-watch.

After cabling and getting his orders, Doc headed for his base. Their journey back by train and steamer—the two men in dungarees and life-vests, and Doc in sea-boots and one of those sheepskin coats they wear on destroyers—was noteworthy but not seagoing, so it is passed up here.

Doc made his port. We met him in the King's Hotel smoke-room, and he told us all about it. We had had it already from the quartermaster and the hospital steward, but Doc was to have a little touch of his own.

"There she was, a little down by the head, but safe in port," concluded Doc; "and while I was waiting for my orders I had a look around the place. There was a little square there with little cafés all around the square, and I sat in front of one of them and had my coffee."

"So this was France," I kept saying to myself. All my life I had been reading more or less about France, and it used to be a sort of dream to me to be thinking I might some day get there. And there I was—only a little corner of France, but it was France, and a pretty sunny little place after our week to sea.

"And while I sat there people came up and looked me over. I thought it was my needing a shave, but it wasn't. I had my cap on, and by my cap they knew me for the officer of the heroes of the ship. After a while they came up and spoke to me. I didn't get quite what they were all saying, but I was one brave man—we were all brave men, there was no doubt about that part. When they all got through one little girl came up and gave me a bunch of flowers."

He pulled out some kind of a faded flower and sighed. "She was about eight years old."

"No use talking," I said, "it's a great life." And the quartermaster—he stood with his signal-flags sticking out under his armpit—said:

"Yes, sir, a great life if we don't weaken."

"What's there to weaken about? Something doing every dog-gone minute since we left our ship."

CHAPTER 9

The 343 Stays Up

Most shore-going people, after a look at a fleet of our destroyers, would not mark them high up for safe ships. They are too long and slim and floppety-like. But no one can tell their officers and crews anything like that. They have tried them out and know. You take a destroyer in a ninety-mile breeze of wind, put her stern to it, give her five or six knots' headway, and there she'll lay till the North Atlantic blows dry. And that is not their only quality. Speed, of course; but not that either. They have a way of staying up after being cut up. There was that one which was of the first to cross over for the U-boat hunting game. One dark night she was struck amidships by a 2,000-ton British sloop-of-war. In crowded quarters and steaming without lights those little collisions are bound to occur.

This one was hit amidships—*bam!*—and amidships is a bad place for a destroyer to be hit—her big engine and boiler-room compartment lie amidships.

This one of ours was hit so hard that nobody aboard ever thought she would stay up. She did go down till her deck was flush with the water's edge, but there she stayed; and her crew, climbing back aboard, took a hawser from the sloop-of-war, which towed her back to port. She was a fine heartening sight coming in. If she could come back, why worry about minor mishaps?

One of them—the 343 say—had performed her duty, which was to see a small convoy to a point well on toward a large port, and was returning to the naval base.

She was in no great rush, and, it happening to be smooth water, which is a rare thing up this way at this time of the year, she stopped for a little needed gun practice.

There was no more thought than usual of U-boats. Nobody would have been surprised if one popped up—it was a coast where they had been regularly operating—but no one was particularly expecting one.

Destroyers are bad medicine if you do not get to them quickly, and lately the U-boats seemed to care more to get merchant ships; but this day the lookouts were not loafing on their job on that account.

The 343 got through with her target practice, and, except for a few gunners' mates still coddling their pet guns, the crew were taking it easy around deck; and also, because of the smooth sea, the ship was making easy weather of it toward port.

Seeing a periscope is oftentimes a matter of luck. When they stay up it is easy enough, but when they are porpoising, shooting it up for just a look around, you have to be looking right at one. What they first saw on the 343 was the wake of this torpedo, coming on at a forty-knot clip for the waist of the ship.

The commander of the 343 was on the bridge at the time and saw the wake almost with the cry of the lookout. The wake was then pretty handy to the ship, and the torpedo itself would be fifty feet or so ahead of the wake.

There was no getting away from it then. The only hope was to take it somewhere else than amidships. Engine and boiler compartments were amidships. If it struck her there they might as well call it taps for all hands. So the commander put the wheel hard over—to take it on his quarter, where there was also a chance that it would pass under her.

Torpedoes generally strike twelve to fifteen feet under water, but just before this one could make the 343 it broached—came to the surface of the water—but without slacking her forty-knot speed. It was unusual and spectacular. The sun shone on the polished sides of her as she leaped from the sea.

She struck the 343 above her water-line and pretty well aft. Those on her deck who saw her make that last leap out of water hoped for the best, though waiting for the worst. But the resulting explosion was nothing tremendous—so officers and men say, and so adding a little more data to U-boat history. The bark of one of their own little 4-inch guns was more impressive. There was a flame and an up-shooting cloud of black smoke, followed instantly by another explosion, that of their own depth charges, of which there were two of 300 pounds each in the stern. Those who had any thoughts about it at the time were sure that if the torpedo did not get them the depth charges would.

When they went to look they found that thirty-odd feet of the after end of their ship had been blown clean off. The torpedo had hit them on the port side, and the wreckage was hanging from the starboard quarter. Of the after gun only the base was left; they never did see any of the rest of it. The gunner's mate, one of those men who love to keep a gun in shape, was swabbing it out at the time, and they never saw anything of him again.

The chief petty officers' quarters were farthest aft on the 343. The after bulkhead to their compartment was blown in, leaving the inside of the ship open to sea and sun. Fourteen men were in there at the time, lounging around or in their bunks. Many of them were bruised and all were shook up, but they all made the deck. They do not know how they made it, but they did. The after hatchway to the deck was closed with tumbling wreckage, so they must have gone up the midships hatch.

One man taking a nap in the cot bunk farthest aft had a part of the bulkhead blown past him. It cut off a corner of his cot and broke one of his legs, and blew him into the passageway in passing. Landing in the passageway he sprained his other ankle. He is not quite sure how he made the deck without help, but he did make it, and he says he beat some of them to it at that.

The man who was working on the after gun with the gunner's mate who was blown up, saw the shining torpedo leaping in the sun and heading straight for his part of the ship. If he did not do something he knew he was in for it, so he began to take long high leaps forward. The explosion came while he was in the air on his third long high jump. All he remembers happening to him after that was of an ocean of water flowing over him, and he not minding it at all. When he came to, the doctor was looking him over for broken bones, but did not find any. After the doctor left him he sat up and said: "I bet I've been as near to a torpedo exploding and getting away with it as anybody in the world, hah?" And "Yes," said one of his shipmates, "and I bet you made a world's record for three long high jumps, without a run, too. You sure did travel, boy."

When it was all over the two propeller shafts were still sticking out astern, one naked and shining in the sun; the other also shining and naked, but with a propeller still in place on it. Spotting that, the skipper ordered the engines turned. To their delight the shaft revolved, the ship began to move. No record-breaking pace, but—God love the builder of a good little ship—she was making revolutions. The wreckage hanging from her starboard quarter acted as a rudder, and so, instead of going straight ahead, she began to go round in circles.

She continued to make circles, and her officers and men stood to stations and waited for what next would happen. Destroyer people have it that there are grades of U-boat commanders—some of nerve, some only ordinary. The U-boat man with nerve enough to attack a destroyer is a good one. He will bear watching; so what they expected was to see this U-boat come up and finish the job. If she did come up and at the right place to get another torpedo in, then the 343 was in for a bad time. So they waited, some thinking one thing, and some another, but all agreeing that the odds were against them.

The U-boat did show again. They saw her conning-tower slipping through the water at about 1,500 yards. The skipper of the 343 was ready in so far as he could be ready with his poor little cripple. Crews were at gun stations, and that conning-tower had hardly got above the surface when two of the 343's guns cut loose at it. They got in four shots, the fourth one pretty handy. But no more. She submerged to the discouragement of one earnest gun-pointer. He leaned against the breech of his little 4-inch to say: "One more and I'd 'ave got her. Bet you me next month's pay that I get her if she shows for two shots again."

She did not show again, but her not showing did not end the 343's troubles. They could steam in circles, but it was not getting them anywhere. A few miles away was one of the roughest shores in the world, the kind where green seas piled up against rocky cliffs—and a tide that was already setting them toward it. A bad enough place in any kind of weather, but with wind and sea making, and this time of year!

It was about two in the afternoon they were torpedoed. By dark they were being driven by the tide and white-capped seas to the shore. They had one hope left. Their radio operator had managed to keep the radio gear in commission, and through all their troubles he had been sending out S O S calls, though not with too great hope that anybody would come in time. The U-boats had been pretty active thereabout, and it was not on any main sea route. There was always the chance, of course, that some war-ships would be somewhere near.

For one hour, two hours, three, four, five, six hours they drifted. Their wireless kept going out of commission, and their radio operator kept patching it up and getting it going again. S O S—he never let up with that call. It was midnight when a British minesweeper bore down and hailed. By then they could hear the high seas breaking on the rocks abeam. The Britisher got the word across the wind, and tried to pass a messenger—a light line, that is—across to the 343. They did not make it. They tried again and again, but no use. The 343 was then within a few hundred yards of the breakers.

The skipper of the Britisher then hailed that he would try to get a boat to them. They could hear him calling for volunteers to man the boat. He got the volunteers, and without being able to see every detail of it in the dark, the 343's people knew what was happening. They were making a lee of the trawler so as to get the boat over. But the boat was swashing in and out against the side of the ship—up on a sea and then bang! in against the side of the ship. Merely as a sporting proposition, their own lives not depending on it, the 343's people would have been praying for that boat to get safely away.

The boat managed at last to get away from the side of the minesweeper, and in time, pitching down on the rollers, they made out to heave a line aboard the 343. And on the deck of the 343 they were right there to grab it and bend it on to a hawser. Fine. Off went the mine-sweeper after she had taken her boat aboard, tugging heartily. She tugged too heartily for the length and size of the hawser. It parted.

They did it all over again—the lowering the boat in the rough sea, the passing the line, the bending on of the bigger line, the attempt to tow. And again it parted. Wouldn't that test men's faith in their good luck? The 343 thought so. Once more tried it, and once more it parted, but this time not parting until they were far enough off the beach to be safe till daylight.

At daylight a British sloop-of-war came along with a real big hawser and gave them a real tow to our naval base. A group of us were steaming out with a fleet of merchantmen to sea as she was being towed in. Our fellows would have liked to turn out to give her a little cheer, also to inquire into the details of her mishap, but we had to keep on going, and wait until our return to port after a cruise to have a look at her.

She was in dry dock when we got back to port, and the most smashed-up-looking object that any of us had ever seen come in from sea. The wonder was how she ever stayed up long enough to make port. That gaping after end open to sea and sky, and the bare propeller shaft sticking out from the insides of her—she sure did look like she needed nursing! They agreed that they were a lucky bunch to get her home.

One poor fellow was killed—a wonder there were not more—and all hands were sorry for him; but tragedy and comedy so often bunk together, and men who adventure are more apt to dwell on the humorous than the tragic side of things. There was that about the code-books. The instructions to all ships are to get rid of the code-books if there is ever any likelihood of the enemy capturing the ship. The code-books are bound in thick lead covers. They are kept in a steel box, and altogether they weigh—I do not know, I never lifted them—but some say they weigh 150, some say 200 pounds. After the 343 was torpedoed, an ensign grabbed up the code-book chest, tossed it onto his shoulder, and waltzed out of the ward-room passage and onto deck with it. You would think it was a feather pillow he was dancing off with. When the danger of capture was over our young ensign hooked his fingers into the chest handles to waltz back with it. But nothing doing. It took two of them to carry it back, and they did not trip lightly down any passageway with it either, proving once again that there are times when a man is stronger than at other times.

After the 343 made port the injured were handed over to the sick bay of the flag-ship. There were two of them who must have been pretty handy to the storm centre of the explosion. At least, it took two young surgeons on the flag-ship all of one day to pick the gun-cotton out of their backs.

There was another man. The doctors, when they came to look

him over, found the print of a perfect circle on the fleshiest part of his anatomy. It was so deeply pressed in that the blue and yellow flesh bulged out all around from it. The doctors said it must have been made by a wash-basin being blown against him as he ran up the ladder to the deck. But the man himself knew better than that. "Excuse me, doctor," he said, "but it was nothing so light and soft as a wash-basin hit me. It was something more solid and bigger than that. It was the water-cooler, and I didn't run up any ladder—I was blown up."

The destroyer people have great faith in the durability of their little ships. They are slim-built, and not much thicker in the plates than seven pages of the Sunday paper—they know that, but maybe that is their safety. There is no getting a fair wallop at them. They evade the issue. One man compared them to a hot-water bottle. Try to swat a loaded hot-water bottle. And what happens? "When you poke it in one place don't it bulge out in another to make up for it? Sure it does. And how do you account for that other one we were talking about? A couple o' years ago—the one that had her stern cut off so that the men in the after compartment leaned out where the bulkhead had been, but wasn't then, and chinned themselves up to the deck from the outside? And how do you account for her bouncing along at twenty knots or more in a gale of wind and a rough sea, and nothing happening them? Get shook up—yes. But they come home, don't they? They sure do. Maybe it's luck, but also maybe it's the way they're thrown together—loose and limber-like."

Whatever it is, they are dashing in and out over there on their job of convoying merchant ships and hunting U-boats. They expect to get their bumps, and they do; but so long as they get an even break they are not kicking. The chart-house gang on the 343 say that they are satisfied they get an even break all right. If she did not fill her little three-straight that time then nobody ever did get any cards in the draw.

They were sticking a new stern onto the 343 when I left the naval base. When they get it well glued on she is going out again. Maybe that same U-boat—you can't always tell, some people have luck—maybe that same U-boat will come drifting her way again. And if they see her first—pass the word for the gun crews!

CHAPTER 10

The Cargo Boats

I have spoken earlier of meeting cargo boats—tramp steamers, we call them at home—while crossing the Atlantic. In peace times a fellow would naturally expect to see them here, or almost anywhere else on the wide ocean; but to see them in these war days was to set a man wondering about them.

Wondering, because more than 90 per cent of U-boat sinkings are of ships of less than 12 knots' speed; which means that these rusty old junk heaps, wheezing along at maybe 9 or 10, but more likely at 7 or 8 knots, furnish most of the sinkings. They surely must be having great old times getting by the U-boats, and their captains and crews must surely have a view-point of their own!

At this naval base of which I have been writing, you could look almost any day and see 5, 10, or 20 of these cargo boats to moorings. And ashore was a pub—there were other pubs, plenty of them—but to this one particular pub came bunches of these cargo captains to forget things. (Without wishing to offend any prohibition advocate, I have to report that knocking around the world a man cannot help noticing that men who face peril regularly do sometimes take a drink to ease off things.)

A barmaid, answering to the name of Phyllis, presided over this pub, a blond, square-built, capable person, who had always about three or four of these captains standing on their heads. She was not without sentiment, but never letting sentiment interfere with business.

"Phyllis, my dear," a skipper would begin, and get about that far when she—her right hand reaching for the bottle of Scotch and her left for the soda—would be saying: "The same, captain?"—thereby choking off a great rush of words, and forwarding the business for which she drew one pound ten a week.

Before a creature of that kind these cargo captains were bound to preen themselves. They bought at frequent intervals, not at all like the ways of another group—not cargo captains—of whom one of our American warrant officers said: "You buy and buy and buy, and they drink and drink and drink. It comes time for them to buy, and when it does they submerge, and don't come up for air."

These cargo skippers were always coming up for air. They would hunt a man three stories up in his room, wake him out of his sleep, and haul him down-stairs to have just one more. Between drinks, after they got to know a man pretty well, they would talk of their sea experiences; and, after the fashion of all true adventurers, their talk was almost always of the humorous side of things.

There was a skipper there one morning who bid all hands, especially Phyllis, goodbye. He was off to Alexandria. He would not be back for three months—more likely five or six months. Phyllis pinned a flower in his coat and off he went. From the pub window they saw him board his ship, and an hour later saw her steam out of the harbour and to sea.

That was at ten in the morning. At five in the afternoon—the lights were just being turned on—those in the pub who happened to be looking out of the window thought they saw this captain's ghost coming up the waterside with his crew trailing behind him. The crew looked as if they had dressed in a hurry and were scampering along to keep warm. But our skipper was wearing all he wore when he left the pub.

He drew nearer. It was no ghost. It was himself, even to the rose in his coat. He hailed Phyllis. She was talking to another skipper. The other skipper turned to see who was butting in, and seeing who it was, said: "To Egypt and back in seven hours—the quickest voyage ever I 'eard of!" Which comment so depressed the voyager that he refused to say anything about what had happened, except that five miles outside of the harbour he had been torpedoed, and they had to take to the boats in a hurry.

The foregoing is by way of introducing the captain who commented on the quick voyage. A few mornings later I was up at the Admiralty House when he came into the waiting-room, let himself carefully down into a mahogany chair, dropped his new soft grey hat into his lap, and looked around.

"A solemn place, ain't it? Would they 'ang a chap, d'y' think, if he was to 'ave a bit of a smoke for 'imself while waitin'?"

I said that I thought the fashion nowadays was to take a man out and stand him up against the wall and shoot him.

He was tall, heavily built, fresh-coloured, with a way of seeming to reflect deeply before he replied to anything. By and by he said: "Oh, aye!" and lit his cigarette, but had not taken the second puff when the doorkeeper's feet sounded outside, at which sound he pinched the cigarette hurriedly by the neck, and looked around for somewhere to dump it. There was no ash-tray, and the table being bare mahogany, the floor all polished wood, the fireplace with no fire in it, so brassy and shiny that to put anything there would be treason—he dropped the cigarette into his hat.

The doorkeeper smelled something, but he wasn't one who looked on lowly things when he walked, and so did not see the little spiral of smoke curling up from the hat.

My seafarer was in a great stew. To sit there and watch him was to warm up to him. There he was, a man who regularly faced death by more ways than one at sea, but now in deep fear that this shore-going flunky would catch him smoking a surreptitious cigarette. He stared determinedly at every place except at his hat until the doorkeeper had passed on.

When he looked at his hat the cigarette had burned a hole in it. He viewed the hat sadly. "No gainsayin' it, war is 'ell, ain't it? I paid fourteen bob for that 'at three days back in Cardiff."

I went out to help him buy a new hat. Hat stores were scarce, but life does not end with hat stores; there were fleets of little places where a man could sit down and talk about more important things than hats.

In the hotel smoke-room after lunch there was no sugar for our coffee. His sea-training began to show at once. "The thing you 'ave to learn to do at sea is to go on your own. Nobody doing much for a chap that 'e don't do for hisself, is there?" From his coat pocket he drew an envelope which once held a letter from home—in place of the letter now was sugar. "Preparedness—'ere it is"—and sweetened our coffee from the envelope.

He spoke of his life at sea. "I can't say that I like it—I can't say I don't like it—but it was my life before the war and it 'as to be since. You've seen my ship, 'aven't you, lying to moorings? Nothing great to look at, is she? but the managing director of our company—he has the 'andling of maybe a 'undred more like her—'Let 'em 'ave their grand passenger ships,' 'e says, 'but give me my cargo boats that pays for theirselves every two voyages.' The right idea 'e 'ad, I'll say for 'im. And for my part of it there is no everlastin' polishin' o' brahss and painting o' white work and no buying o' gold-laced uniforms at your own cost. And there's the bonus for me. Oh, aye! A bit of bonus ain't a bit of 'arm, you know, especially when you've a wife that's no eyesore to look at, and little kiddies growin' up.

"Torpedoed? Oh, aye. It's not to be expected of a man to escape that these days. My chum Bob, remember 'im—that was seven hours to Alexandria and back—with a rose in his coat? His fourth time torpedoed, that was. I've been blowed up only three times myself. Nothing much of anything special, the last time and the time before that—a matter of getting into boats and by and by being picked up—no more than that—no. But the first time—maybe it was a novelty-like then. 'Owever, I'd carried a load of coal to Naples and getting twenty-two pounds a ton for coal that cost two pound ten in Cardiff maybe makes it a bit clearer what the managing director 'ad in mind when 'e said: 'let 'em have their grand passenger ships, but give me my little cargo boats.'

"From Naples I go on to Piraeus in Greece, and we take a load on there—admiralty stuff, and not to be spoken of—and we put out for 'ome. She was a good old single-crew, this one o' mine. Twenty-five year old—not the worst, though I'd seen better. Well warmed up she could squeeze out eight knots, or maybe eight and a 'alf. I 'ung close to the land along that Greek shore, for if anything should 'appen ther's no sense 'aving too long a row to the beach in boats.

"Very good. We're rollin' along one morning when the radio man came in with a message which read: *'Put into nearest port. U-boats.'*

"And without ado we puts into a little place down at the 'eel of Italy, and that night I 'ad a 'ot barth an' a lovely long sleep in my brahss bed which the missus 'ad given me for Christmas the last time 'ome. And a great pleasure it was, I say.

"Next mornin' we put to sea again, and next day after comes

another radio, and it says: *'Put into nearest port. U-boats.'* And we put into Malta, and that night again I 'ad another 'ot barth and a fine sleep in my brahss bed.

"We resume our voyage from Malta, and a two days later I gets another radio—more U-boats—and I puts into Algiers. Three times in one week that made with me 'aving me 'ot barth and a fine sleep in me brahss bed—grand good luck, I say now, and said it then to the mate, adding to it: 'There's a signal station west of Gibraltar—wouldn't it be delightful passing that signal station to get the word to put back to Gib and stop there for another night and I 'ave another 'ot barth and a lovely sleep in my four-poster bed.' But the mate 'e only says 'e didn't have no brahss bed aboard ship to sleep in, and he saved his 'ot barths, he did,'til he got 'ome to enjoy 'em proper.

"Summer-time it was, and I likes to take my little siesta after lunch—just like the Dons theirselves, y' know—and I'm 'aving me siesta next day after lunch when something woke me up. There's a shelf of books on the wall o' my room—chart-books and the like—and when all at once I see them pilin' down on top of me I say to myself: 'Somethin's 'appened.' And so it 'ad. The mate 'e sticks 'is 'ead in the door and says: 'We're torpedoed, sir.'

"'There goes my bonus,' I says, and goes on deck.

"We carried a 3-inch gun in a little 'ouse aft, and there was the mate firing at the U-boat, which was out of water and maybe two miles away. It was one of those out-of-date guns the navy would have no more to do with, and so they passes it on to us. New good guns would probably be wasted on us, and maybe that's true. None of us aboard ever fired a shot from the gory weapon till this day. The mate fired two shots at the U-boat, but 'e don't 'it anything. The U-boat fires two shots at us and she 'its something. One of 'em pahsses through the chart house, and the other tears a nice little 'ole in 'er for'ard.

"'That'll do for that gun practice,' I says.

"'Aren't you goin' to 'ave a go at 'em?' says the mate.

"'You can 'ave all the go at 'em you please,' I says, 'after we leave the ship. Besides you there's 19 men and 4 Eurasians in this crew, and some of 'em will maybe like to see 'ome again—I know I do!'

"We get into the boats, myself takin' along what was left of a second case of Scotch, and good old pre-war Scotch it was, not the gory infant's food they serve these days that a man 'as to take a tumblerful of to know 'e's 'aving a drink at all. I also took along three sofy cushions, hand-worked by the missus, with pink doves and cupids and the like—rare lookin' they was. 'A man might's well be comfortable,' I says.

"I 'ad a cook. 'If comfort's the word,' says the cook, 'I might's well take along the wife's canary,' and 'e takes it along in a cage in one 'and, and a bag of clothes in the other. 'E's in the boat when 'e thinks to go back for a package of seed 'e'd left for the canary on the shelf in the galley. 'Hurry up with your bird-seed,' I says, and as I do a shell comes along and explodes inside of 'er old frame somewheres, and the cook says maybe 'e'll be gettin' along without the seed—the canary not being what you'd call a 'eavy eater, anyway.

"The mate 'ad a cameraw, and when we're clear of the ship he would stand up and set the cameraw on the shoulders of a Eurasian fireman, and take shots of the ship between shells.

"In good time one last shell 'its 'er, and down she goes. The U-boat moves off, and we see no more of 'er.

"It's a fine day and a lovely pink sunset, and there's a beautiful mild sirocco blowing off the African shore to make the 'ot night pleasant as we approach it in the boats. A man could 'ardly arsk to be torpedoed under more pleasant conditions, I say, and we continue to row toward the shore in 'igh 'opes. It's maybe two in the mornin' when we see the side-lights of a ship. She's bound east—a steamer—and we know she's a Britisher, because we're the only chaps carried lights in war zones at that time. Carryin' lights at night o' course made us grand marks for the U-boats, but there was no 'elp for it. A board o' trade regulation, that was, and no gettin' away from what the board o' trade says. We had our choice of carryin' lights and losin' our ships, or not carryin' lights and losin' our jobs. So we lost our ships. After a year and a 'alf of war some bright chap in the board said that maybe it would be a good idea to change the regulation about carrying lights, and they did. And about time, we said.

"Some of the crew were for 'ailing the ship in the night. ''Ail 'ell!' I says. 'D'y' think I want to be took into that rotten 'ole of a Port Said, or maybe Alexandria, and that end of the Mediterranean fair lousy with U-boats. Besides, we'll get 'ome quicker this way,' I says, and allows her to pass on. In the mornin' we run onto the beach, and 'ardly there when a crowd of Ayrabs come gallopin' down on 'orseback to us. 'We'll be killed now,' says the mate, and talks under his breath of stubborn captains, who wouldn't 'ail a friendly ship's light in the dark, but the only killing the Ayrabs do is two young goats for breakfast. And they make coffee that was coffee, and we had a lovely meal on the sand. And by and by they steered us along the shore to where was a French destroyer, which takes us over to Gibraltar, and from Gib we passed on through Spain and France to Havre. Three weeks that took, and I never 'ad such a three weeks in all my life. 'Eroes, ragin' 'eroes—that's wot we were!

"At Havre the French authorities took the mate's pictures out of the cameraw, and they never did give 'em back. Except for that, it was a fine pleasure, that land cruise 'ome.

"Lucky? Oh, aye, you may well say it. Three times in one week I 'ad me 'ot barth and my lovely sleep in me brahss bed—it's not to be looked for with ordinary luck, you know."

* * * * *

One day the destroyer to which I was assigned put to sea. There were other destroyers, and we were to take a fleet of merchantmen from the naval base to such and such a latitude and longitude, and there turn them loose. My friend's ship was of the convoy.

We made such and such a latitude and longitude, and there we turned them loose, signalling the position to them and waiting for acknowledgment. They acknowledged the signal. We then hoisted the three pennants which everywhere at sea means: Pleasant voyage! They answered with the three pennants which everywhere spells: Thank you. And no sooner done than away they belted, each for himself, and let the U-boats get the hindmost.

The hindmost here was the rusty old cargo boat of my friend. I could see her for miles after the others were hull down; and long after I could see her I could picture him—walking his lonely bridge and his ship plugging away at her 7 or maybe 7½ knots across the lonely ocean.

Three times torpedoed and taking it all as part of his work! Some day they may get him and he not come back; and when they do the world will hear little about him. Hero? He a hero? Why a shore-going flunky had him bluffed for smoking a surreptitious cigarette in high quarters! 'Ero? Not 'im. Why 'e don't even wear a uniform.

So there they are, the wheezing old cargo boats and their officers and crew. British, French, Italian, American, but mostly British.

No heroes, but the Lord help their people if they hadn't stayed on the job.

Chapter 11
Flotilla Humour—At Sea

We were a group of American destroyers convoying twenty home-bound British steamers. There was one ship, a P. & O. liner, a great specimen of camouflaging.

She was the only ship in the convoy that was camouflaged, and she rode in stately style two lengths out in front of the others. All of which made her a prominent object. Our officers felt like telling her to dress back; but she had a British commodore aboard, and for an American two or three striper to try to advise a British commodore—well, it isn't done.

All day long she rode out in front of the column, and all day long our fellows kept saying things about her.

"Isn't she the chesty one!"

"Look at the big squab with all that war-paint on—how does she expect any U-boat to overlook her?"

"That big loafer, she'd better watch out or she'll be getting hers before the day's gone!"

U-boats were thick around there. One of them must have come up, looked the convoy over, and said, "Well, there's nothing to this but the big one!" and, Bing! let her have it, for it was not yet quite dark when those who were looking at her saw a column like steam go into the air, a black column like coal follow it, and after that a column of water boiling white.

One of our destroyers hopped to twenty-five knots, dumped over a 300-pound "ash-can," and got Mister U-boat. At least, the British admiralty later gave her 100 per cent on the circumstantial evidence. Two other destroyers—the 396 and the 384, we will call them—went at once to the job of taking off passengers from the sinking ship.

That was at five minutes to six, just before dark. It had interrupted dinner on our ship; but by and by we went back to the ward-room to finish eating. It is always good business to eat—no knowing when a man will be needing a good meal to be standing by him inside. And we were still eating when the messenger came in with a radio. He passed it to the skipper, who read it to himself, whistled, and then read aloud: *Torpedoed—Clan Lindsay*.

The *Clan Lindsay* was another of our convoy, and she had been within 1,000 yards of our ship when we last came about to zigzag back across the front of our column.

We looked at one another, and one said: "Well, you got to hand it to Fritz for being on the job every minute."

And another: "Yes, but it looks like a big night to-night. Two in an hour! And eighteen more ships and eight destroyers to pick from yet! If he starts off like that, what d'y' s'pose he'll be batting by morning?"

The ward-room on our ship opens onto the ship's galley; and from the ship's galley another door opens onto the deck. Through the open galley-door just then came a muffled explosion—a great Woof!

We all thought just one thing—they've got us too!—and we all sort of half curled up, and would not have been a bit surprised if the next instant we found ourselves sailing through the deck overhead. The feeling lasted for perhaps three seconds, and then our skipper, happening to look up, saw that the coloured mess-boy George was grinning widely.

"What the devil you laughing at?" barked out our skipper.

George took his eyes off the galley-door, but his grin remained. Said George: "Cap'n, I see de flame. The galley stove just done bust!"

The galley stove on our ship was an oil-burner. It had backfired, and so the loud Woof!

Later it came out that the *Clan Lindsay* wasn't torpedoed at all; but one of our destroyers dropped a depth charge so close to her to get a U-boat that she thought she was.

* * * * *

The camouflaged big liner sank, but not until the two of our destroyers standing by had taken off every one of the 503 passengers, one taking the people off the deck, the other picking up those in the small boats. One destroyer—the 396, say—took off 307 of these passengers. Her skipper passed the word by radio to the 384, which had gathered in 196 passengers, including the commodore. The 384 got the message, only she got it 7 instead of 307 people rescued.

"Seven survivors!" said the 384's skipper. "I wonder why she radioed that?" He meditated over the puzzle and by and by solved it to his satisfaction.

"Of course, what she wants is for us to take off the seven and add 'em to our own." He took measures to meet the emergency, and then followed this little incident:

Aboard the 396 they were busy trying to find space for their 307 passengers when a lookout heard a Putt! putt! putt! coming over the water. The officer of the deck listened. Everybody on the bridge listened. Putt! putt! putt! it came. The officer of the deck reported to the skipper. The skipper wondered who it could be, when just then a radio message arrived: "Am sending a boat—384."

"Sending a boat? What for?" He meditated over that puzzle and then he solved it—as he thought. "Sure. That British commodore she picked up is coming to see how the survivors aboard here are getting on. That's it"—he turned to the watch-officer—"you know how these Britishers are for regulations. Even in the midst of a mess like this we'll have to kowtow to his rank or he'll probably be reporting us. So rouse out six side-boys, line 'em up, rig up the port ladder, have the bugler stand by for *ta-ra-rums* and all that stuff."

They did that, shoving their crowded survivors out of the way to make room for the ceremony.

The Putt! putt! putt! comes nearer and nearer. Next, from out of the blackness of the ocean they make out a little motor-dory. Balanced out on the gunwale of the little dory, when it comes nearer, they see an American blue-jacket smoking a cigarette. No one else was in the dory.

The dory ran alongside. It was about a 14-foot dory—no smaller one in the flotilla. The skipper of the 396 looked down at him. "What you want?"

The blue-jacket removed the cigarette from his lips. "I'm from the 384, sir."

"Yes, yes, but what do you want?"

"I've come, sir"—he waved his cigarette-stub airily—"to take off the survivors. The captain thought I might be able to make one load of 'em."

* * * * *

When the big P. & O. liner reported herself torpedoed that evening, a destroyer—not one of ours—picked up the message 100 miles or so away; and at once radioed: *Coming to your assistance—give position, course, and speed.*

That was proper and well-intentioned, but as the 384 and the 396 were already standing by, a radio was sent back: *Everything all right—no help needed—thank you.*

That did not seem to satisfy the inquirer. *Would like to help—give position, speed, and course.*

Everybody being busy, nobody bothered to answer that. By and by came another radio: *This is the destroyer blank—give position, speed, and course.*

He was so evidently one of those Johnnies who are always volunteering to do things not needful to be done that nobody paid any further attention to him. But he kept right on sending radios. By and by, for perhaps the seventh time, came: *This is the destroyer blank—please give position, speed, and course of torpedoed ship.*

At which some one—nobody seemed to know who, but possibly some undistinguished enlisted radio man whose ears were becoming wearied—sparked out into the night: *Position of torpedoed ship? between two destroyers. her speed? about four feet an hour. her course? toward the bottom of the Atlantic.*

Nobody ever found who sent that message; nobody inquired too closely; but all hands thanked him. The flotilla heard no more from the bothersome destroyer.

* * * * *

The business of hunting U-boats is a grim one. The officers and men engaged in it do not like to dwell on the hard side of it. They do like to repeat stories of the humorous side of it.

One of our destroyer commanders over there has a personality that the others like to hang stories onto. He is a quick-thinking, quick-acting man named—well, say Lanahan. He was one day on the bridge of his ship when the lookout shouted: "Periscope!"

"Charge her!" yelled out Lanahan.

Away they went hooked-up for the periscope, which everybody could now see—about 200 yards ahead.

"He's a nervy one—see her stay up!" said the officer of the deck, who was standing beside the wheel, and had glasses on the periscope. And then, hurriedly: "I don't like the looks of her, captain—it looks like a phoney periscope to me—as if there was a mine under it!"

"To hell with her—ram her anyway!" snapped Lanahan.

The deck officer had not once taken the glasses off the periscope. Suddenly he let drop his glasses, grabbed the wheel and pulled it hard toward him.

Lanahan had stepped to the wing of the bridge and was leaning far out to get a glimpse of the U-boat. What he saw beneath him as his ship scraped by was not a U-boat, but a great white mine. He watched it slide safely past the bridge, past his quarter, past his stern. Then, turning around, he said gravely to his deck officer:

"You're right—it *was* a mine."

* * * * *

There was another young officer—Chisholm call him—who played poker occasionally. He commanded a *flivver*, which is the service name for the smaller class of destroyers, the 750-ton ones.

In our navy there are plenty of young officers who will tell you that they never built destroyers which keep the sea better than that same little flivver class. Young Captain Chisholm of the 323 was one.

One morning, having convoyed a fleet of merchant ships safely up the channel, the 323 was one of a group of destroyers making the best of their way to their base port. Officers and men who have been hunting U-boats for a week or so do not like to linger along the road home; so it was every young captain giving his ship all the steam she could stand and let her belt.

It was breaking white water all around when they started. It grew rougher. Chisholm in the 323 was going along at twenty knots when a poker-playing chum came along in his big 1,000-ton destroyer. Her nose hauled up on the quarter of the 323; up to her beam; up to her bridge. As he passed the 323—and he passed quite close to let all hands view the passing—the poker-playing friend leaned out and megaphoned across:

"What you making, Chiz?"

"Twenty knots!" hailed back Chisholm.

"I am seeing your twenty knots and raising you five!" returned the other, and passed on.

"The boiler-riveted nerve of him!" gasped Chiz. "But let him wait!"

The sea grew yet rougher. The 323 was bouncing pretty lively, but hanging onto her twenty knots. "And at twenty you let her hang if she rolls her crow's nest under!" said Chisholm to his watch-officer, "and I'll betcher we won't be acting rudder to this bunch going into port!"

It was at ten in the morning that the big one had passed them. It was four in the afternoon, and the 323 was still going along at twenty knots when from out of the drizzle ahead her bridge made out the stern and funnels of a destroyer. It was Chiz's poker-playing chum, and his ship was making heavy weather of it. The able little 323 came up to her stern; breasted her waist, her bridge, and as he passed her (and he came quite close to let all hands view the passing), young Captain Chisholm leaned out from his bridge and roared through a long megaphone: "I *call* yuh!"

He beat the big one fifty minutes into the naval base.

* * * * *

There are two channels leading into the naval base port—call them West and East. This same Chisholm was one day headed for port in the usual hurry and was already well into the west channel when a signal was whipped out from the signal hill. It was for his ship and it read: "West Channel mined last night by U-boats. Proceed to sea and come in by East Channel."

Chiz did not proceed to sea. All the harbour men who were watching saw him come straight on through the gap in the barrage, and safely on to his mooring. Also all the harbour knew that next morning he had to report to the admiralty and explain.

The story of his explanation was not told by himself. But an officer friend, a great admirer—call him Mac—had gone with him to the admiralty. Here the next day Mac told the story in the smoke-room of the King's Hotel:

"Well, Chiz went and—you know his courtly style—he has his cape over his shoulders—and he salaams and says, 'Good morning, sir.'

"The old man looks up and says like ice: 'You got my signal yesterday afternoon?'

"'I did, sir.'

"'Then why did you not turn back and come in by the other channel?'

"'Sir,' says Chiz, 'may I be allowed a few words?'

"'Very few. What have you to say?'

"'Sir,' says Chiz, 'I have been trained to believe that the one word a naval officer should not know is fear. In our navy, sir, we reverence the tradition of your own Admiral Nelson, who at the siege of Copenhagen put his glass to his blind eye and said: "I see no signal to withdraw!" and continued the fighting to a victory.'

"'Have you a blind eye, too?'

"'My sight is good, thanking you, sir, for inquiring, but in my own navy we also have the tradition of Admiral Farragut, who at Mobile Bay said: "Damn the torpedoes—go on!" and his fleet went on to victory. And there was Admiral Dewey, who said: "Damn the mines!" at Manilla, and went on to victory.'

"'What are you coming at?' roars the old man. 'Did you get my signal?'

"'I did, sir. And my first instinct—the instinct of all our naval officers—is to obey all orders of our superiors, sir. But I was well into that channel when I got the signal, sir. And as I have said, sir, my first instinct was to obey orders. But also I stop and reflect, for I have also been trained to believe that hasty judgments work many evils, sir, and I consider and find myself saying to my deck officer: "This ship, Mac, is 300 feet long, and under her stern there are two big propellers. If ever we turn this 300-foot ship in this channel with those two propellers churning and there's any loose German mines around, there won't be a blamed one of 'em she'll miss. But if I keep her straight on, there's a chance. So hell's afire!" I says to Mac—"there's only one thing for us to do now and that is to keep straight on!" And I kept straight on, sir—and, I beg leave to report it now, sir—we made our mooring safely.'

"And that's all there was to that," concluded Mac.

There was a long silence in the smoke-room when Mac had done, and then a voice asked: "If Chiz had gone to sea and come in by the other channel—it was almost dark at the time—he would have been too late to make the barrage, wouldn't he?"

"He sure would," said Mac.

"Which would mean that he would be kept turning his wheels over outside the net all night?"

"He sure would."

"As it was, he got in in plenty of time for that little game upstairs last night?"

"He was in a little game," admitted Mac.

Another silence, and then another voice: "Well, poker or no poker, Chiz's dope on that damn-the-torpedo stuff isn't the worst in the world!"

Chapter 12
Flotilla Humour—Ashore

The incident reported in the previous chapter was not young Chisholm's first interview with the British admiral.

Mac went on to tell how when, after his first cruise, Chiz came to the naval base to report. He had heard that the old fellow in charge believed that the Lord made the earth for admirals, especially British admirals, but beyond that he knew nothing of his peculiarities.

However, after his cruise, Chiz went whistling up the hill to report. By and by he was admitted to the presence of the admiral, who was seated at a flat desk in the middle of the room, gazing straight ahead.

The old chap looked pretty frosty. Chiz waited a moment, then ventured a cheery "Good morning, sir."

The face at the desk did not even turn to look at him, but the thin lips almost opened and a rasping voice said: "Got anything to say to me?"

Chiz was one of the sociable souls, and he would have liked to sit down and talk in an informal way of several little sea things that he thought were fairly interesting. But he had not been asked even to sit down, and the voice froze him. So, "Why, no sir, nothing special to report," was all he could find to say.

"H-m. Nothing to say? Then why waste my time or your own? Might as well get out, hadn't you?"

Chiz got out.

"An American lieutenant-commander in this place must rate about seven numbers below a yellow dog," said Chiz to Mac when he came out.

Chiz had four days in port (Mac is still telling the story) after that cruise, and two days after his visit to the hill there was a cricket-match between a team from our flotilla and a team from theirs. The idea was for all hands to forget rank for a while, get into the game, and so cement the entente between the two nations.

Chiz was picked for one of our team, and you all know what a husky he is, and what he used to do with a baseball-bat. There aren't many who ever hit 'em any further or oftener than Chiz on the old Annapolis ball-field. He was one of the first of our fellows to go to bat. He's standing there—in the box, or whatever they call it, waiting for one to his liking; and looking around the field wondering where he will place it when he gets one to his liking. And as he looks he spies his friend the admiral, playing what we'd call left field. And just beyond the admiral the ground sloped away for a hundred yards or so.

Chiz hefts his bat—and you know those cricket-bats, what they look like and how they feel after you've been used to meeting fast ones with a narrow baseball-bat. They are wide and heavy and springy. Chiz doesn't pay any attention to three or four balls that come along, except to fend them away from the wicket with his wide cricket-bat. He knew what he wanted, and by and by he got one—one about knee-high with a little incurve to it. Chiz sets himself and swings and whale-O it goes, over the old admiral's head and down the slope beyond.

Chiz makes all the runs the law allows—six, I think it is—and he's sitting resting on the wide part of his cricket-bat before the admiral even shows the top of his head over the hill with the ball. When he does and heaves it about half-way to the pitcher, or bowler, or whatever they call him, he's out of breath.

Chiz sets himself for another one knee-high with an in-shoot, and when he gets one he whales it again, and away trots the admiral on another hunt down the hill. And Chiz makes six more runs before they even see the top of the admiral's head over the brow of the hill.

The third time, and the fourth time, Chiz sets for a knee-high one with an in-shoot to it, and the third time and the fourth time he belts it over the old fellow's head and down the long slope. But on the fourth time the old fellow doesn't throw the ball in.

He walks in with it and he calls in the high official umpires, or whoever they are in charge, and they have a conference, and the next thing they call the game off. By this time, doubtless (so the word was passed), the American officers have caught the idea of the game, and next time there would be a real game and so on.

But there was no next game. However, next day Chiz puts out to sea, and when he's into port again he calls up on the hill as per instructions. And by and by he is passed again into the presence, who is sitting just as before at the flat desk in the middle of the room, and gazing straight before him.

This time Chiz doesn't speak, not even to say; "Good morning, sir." And the graven image at the desk doesn't speak either, and there's a silence for maybe a minute, and then the old fellow barks out: "What are you standing there for? You wish to see me?" And Chiz barks out in his turn: "No, sir, I don't wish to see you."

"You do not wish to see me? Then what are you doing here?"

And Chiz cracks out: "I'm here because your orders compel me to be here, sir."

Zowie!—that straightened the old boy up. He took a look at Chiz, and he says, after a while and almost pleasantly: "Have a chair."

And Chiz has a chair, and they have a talk, and after that Chiz finds him a lot easier to get along with. Chiz says now that the old fellow isn't such a terrible chap—not after you get onto his curves.

* * * * *

When we first came over (Mac is still speaking), most of the topsiders over here were strong for the entente stuff, and a good thing, too—why not?

Our fellows were mostly strong for it, too—two or three so strong that it was hard to tell whether they were Americans or something else—even their accents.

And, as I say, most of the officers of our own over here were for it—most of them. But you can't rid everybody overnight of long-inherited notions. There was one chap we used to meet, and he sure was the most patronizing thing!

Now, we know we haven't the biggest navy in the world, but as far as it goes we think it is pretty good. As good as anybody's, man for man, and ship for ship—but let that pass.

This chap, who never could see anything in our navy, came in here one day. He wasn't bad. He was just one of those naturally foolish ones who thought he was a little brighter than his company. The topsiders would be working night and day to create good feeling, and he was the kind would come along and break up the show—not exactly meaning to.

This was in the hotel bar here, where a bunch of us were easing off after a hard cruise, when he comes along. He doesn't like the names of our destroyers. In his navy there was significance in the names they gave to a class of ships.

"Take *Viper, Adder, Moccasin,* and so on—they suggest things y' know. Dangerous to meddle with and all that sort of thing, y' know. But your people name your ships after men evidently—*David Jones, Conyngham, McDonough.* I say, who are they—Presidents or senators or that sort, or what?"

Lanahan was there—the hell-with-her-ram-her-anyway Lanahan—and we all just naturally turned him over to Lanahan, who had west-of-Ireland forebears, and never did believe in letting any Englishman put anything across—nothing like that anyway.

"You never read much, I take it, of our history?" says Lanahan.

"Your history? My dear chap, I had hard work keeping up with my own."

"No doubt. But you've heard of the American Revolution?"

"I dessay I have—Oh, yes, I have!"

"Well, you spoke of Jones. If you mean John Paul, then there was a naval fight one time in the North Sea—the *Serapis* and the *Bonhomme Richard.*"

"I say, old chap, I didn't mention John Paul Jones. *David Jones* is the name of your destroyer out in the harbour now."

"David Jones? Let me see. Why, sure, David Jones was a New England parson who boarded around among the God-fearing neighbours for his keep on week-days and preached the wrath of God and hell-fire for his cash wage—five pound a year—on Sundays. He was a devout man. If thy finger offend thee, cut it off. But a sort of muscular Christian, too. If thy enemy cross thee, go out and whale the livers and lights out of him—same as we're trying to do to the U-boats now.

"Well David lived in the shadow of the church till he was thirty-seven years of age. Then the Revolution broke, and David, in whose veins flowed the blood of old Covenanters, took a running long jump into it. He started in as deck-hand or, perhaps, it was cook's helper, but there was salt in his veins too, and rapidly he learned his trade. And soon rose in his new profession until he was master of his own ship, and, as master, raising the devil among the coasters which used to cruise out of Maritime Province ports in those days. The captures he made of vessels loaded with hay and potatoes, and so on, materially reduced the high cost of living for New England folks in those days.

"Conyngham? He was a young American lad who did not come of any particularly good old stock, meaning that he did not come from Massachusetts or Virginia probably. He went to sea as a midshipman on an American sloop-of-war. And he turned out to be some little middy. Ensign, lieutenant, commander—man, he just ran up the ladder of naval rank. And got a ship of his own—a fine, young, able sloop-of-war, and with this sloop-of-war he would run out from the French channel ports and harry the English coast and English shipping. Never heard of him? No? Well, well!—and he so famous in his day that King George put up a reward of 1,000 pounds for his capture dead or alive. But they never captured him.

"And Barry? He was the Wexford boy who captured 200 English prizes more or less in the West Indies. Paul Jones trained under Barry before he had a ship of his own. And McDonough? He—but am I boring you?"

"No, no—it is very interesting."

"I am glad. Well, McDonough was the commodore who fought the battle of Lake Champlain against your people. He opened that battle with prayers for the living and closed it with prayers for the dead. You want to watch out for those fellows who pray when they go to war. Their technique is sometimes pretty good. Their spirit is always good. While Mac was looking over the booty after that fight, a funny thing happened. He—"

"I say, old chap, it's all very interesting, exceedingly interesting, but what d'y' say to another little nip before I go? I've got to run along to see the chief now. What will you have to drink?"

"Sure. A nip of Irish, if you please. And here"—Lanahan held up his glass—"here's to the memory of dead heroes—may they always be preferred to crawling reptiles when it comes to naming our fighting ships!"

After the other fellow had gone Lanahan turned to us. "Say, fellows, I know I got Paul Jones and Barry and McDonough right, but how near was I on Davey Jones and Conyngham? Something tells me I got their histories mixed."

* * * * *

This admiral, of whom our fellows used to spin the yarns, was a unique character. He lacked imagination, and he had the manner of a rat-terrier toward people not of his own kind; but he was one good executive.

Devotion to duty—conscience—those were his beacon lights. He had been known, when the minister of the local church wasn't up to standard, to walk into the pulpit, and deliver the sermon himself. Before he came to take command of this coast district the U-boats had been raising Cain there. There was a fleet of steam-trawlers handled by their old fishing captains and crews, whose special duty it was to sweep up the waters just outside the harbour for mines. It was at that time a dangerous business, but it was also monotonous. It was a duty most easy to evade.

Who was to say they had not swept up? No cove at a naval base five hundred miles away, that was sure! Even if mines were found there after they reported it swept clear, what would that prove? The Huns were laying mines all the time, weren't they? So—war days are hard enough anyway—why not ease up now and again?

They eased up. Many a snug little place there was along the coast where a crew could go ashore and have a pleasant time for a day or two. There were reports to fill out, but what were reports? Ship a clerk in the crew and who would know? Surely not some aide at the naval base who spent his busiest hours taking the admiral's niece to tea fights!

The British public will probably stand more from their lawfully ordained rulers than any other public on earth. They stood for a good many ships being mined on that coast before they began to ask the why of it.

The powers returned with facts and figures, percentage tables, and so on, of ships departing and ships arriving; proving clearly that the number of ships lost was no more than was to be expected. Whereupon the British public took to writing letters to the press. British politicians take letters to the press seriously; a new man, the admiral we have been talking of, was sent to take charge of the district.

He got down to business. He fitted out a 30-knot despatch-boat and away he went! All along that coast he pounced in on little harbours where mine-sweepers should be found working outside, but where he found them working mostly inside at little sociable gatherings where there was a dance or the like going on in front and a little something nourishing to drink in back. Our stern and efficient admiral lit into them like a gull into a school of herring. Out by their gills he hauled them, and pretty soon the B. P. began to read less of percentages and more of results.

One of the first results was that some trawler skippers lost their jobs, and new skippers took their places. This was at the time that rewards of five pounds or so were offered the skippers bringing a mine into port.

That five pounds looked pretty good to one of the new skippers; and when one night at a pub a discharged skipper confided to him where there was a nest of German mines, out he goes into the grey dawn to be there first. He's there first, and sure enough it's a grand little spot for mines. He hooks into one, lashes it under his quarter and goes scooting back to harbour, which happens to be the naval base.

Proudly and noisily he steamed along, shouting to everybody he met of his good luck, and asking the course to the admiral's ship. Everybody he met gave him the course and also the full width of the channel as he passed. He ran alongside the flag-ship, hailing loudly for the admiral as he steamed up.

The admiral was not on board, but his aide was, and the aide came on to have a look over the side. He saw the mine bouncing up and down between the mine-sweeper's quarter and his own ship's side. Shove off—"get away from us!" yelled the aide. "Suppose you press one of those little feelers and blow us all to pieces—get away, I tell you!"

The mine-sweeper skipper looked up—"Feelers, sir?"—and

then looked down at the mine. "Feelers, sir? Oh-h, you mean them little 'orns stickin' out on 'er? Bly-mee, sir, I thought I'd knocked 'em all hoff afore I lashed her alongside. But 'ave no fear, sir, there's only two of 'em left, and I'll bloomin' well soon"—he reaches for an oar and went bouncing aft—"bloomin' well soon knock them hoff, too, sir!"

Chapter 13

The Unquenchable Destroyer Boys

One day last summer a group of our destroyers were sent across the Atlantic. It was a night-and-day strain for all hands—watching out for raiders, watching out for U-boats, watching out for everything, and grabbing snatches of sleep when they could.

Arriving at their naval base, every skipper of the little fleet felt pretty well used up. But every worth-while skipper thinks first of his men. One we have in mind passed the word to his crew that whoever cared to take a run ashore to stretch his legs and forget sea things for a while, why—to go to it. And stay till morning quarters if they wished.

As fast as they could clean up and shift into shore clothes they were going over the side. Our young captain felt then that perhaps there was a little something coming to himself; so he turned in, and he was logging great things in the sleeping line when the anchor watch, who was also a signal quartermaster, woke him up with:

"Signal from the admiralty, sir."

"Read it."

The S. Q. M. read it—an order to proceed at once to an oil dock and take oil.

It was nine o'clock at night when our skipper had come to moorings. It was now one in the morning, and he knew he could have slept for another week; however, orders were to oil up.

He turned out and mustered what remained aboard of his crew. There were about a dozen. He sent three to the fire-room, three to the engine-room, one here, another there, himself took the wheel, and with his signal quartermaster acting as a sort of officer of the deck, set out to find the oil dock.

He had never seen that harbour before that night, but he sheered close in to every ship's anchor light he saw and hailed for the course to the oil dock. Most of them did not know, but one now and then passed him a word or two, and so he bumped along and by and by made the oil dock.

Officers who have business with it will tell you that the naval organization of the British is pretty complete. Our young skipper found everything ready for him now. Men ashore made fast his lines, connected up his pipes, filled his tanks—all in good order. Sister destroyers were oiling up with him, and with tanks filled they all bumped their way back to moorings, again without sinking anything along the way.

It was then daylight, and right after breakfast they all had to report to the admiralty, so no use trying to sleep any more. Arrived at the admiralty, the officer in command complimented them on their safe run across, and then went on to say that of course they had had a trying passage, and naturally their ships, especially engines and boilers, would have to be overhauled—all very natural and proper—and of course the needful time for overhauling, and for officers and crew—two, three, four days, whatever it was—would be granted; but (they knew the need) the question was: How long before they would be ready to go to sea?

The young destroyer commanders had discussed that and other possibilities in the reception-room outside, so when the senior of the group looked from one to the other of his colleagues they had only to nod, for him to turn to the admiral and say:

"We are ready now, sir."

Which remark should become one of the historic remarks of this war.

At this time—at the gates to the North Sea, the English Channel, the Irish coast—the U-boats were collecting frightful toll. In the Mediterranean they were running wild. Five ships from one convoy in one day—three of them big P. & O. liners—was one of their records in the Eastern Mediterranean.

To the natural question, Why haven't you checked them? almost any young British naval officer felt like saying: "Check 'em? Try it yourself and check 'em! You go out there and keep your ship zigzagging full speed night and day for three years and see how you like it! Go out there in rough weather and fog with not a minute's let-up, and see if you get to where the fall of a bucket of a dark night will make you jump three feet in the air or not! Our ships were not built, and our chaps were not trained, to beat their rotten game."

So things were when our fellows took hold, and hearing no word from them for a long time and then but a meagre one, it may be that many a citizen on this side was saying to himself:

"Well, they're gone, that little flotilla, swallowed up in the mists of the Atlantic, and that is all we know about them. And now I wonder what they're doing over there? Are they doing great work or are they tied up to a dock at the naval base, and their officers and crews roistering ashore?"

I can say from several weeks' observation later that they were not doing too much roistering ashore. Before leaving this side I found no evidence that anybody in Washington wished to suppress the record of what that little fleet was doing. Secretary Daniels and Chairman Creel of the Committee on Public Information believed with me that our little fellows over there were doing things worth recording. This fact is set down here because many people last summer believed there was too much suppression of the news of our fighting forces; and suspicion of suppression breeds distrust. Our fellows perhaps were not doing well. If they were doing well, wouldn't we be told more?

But they have ideas of their own on these matters over on the other side, and it is the other side which has most to say of what shall or shall not be given out for publication. In a previous chapter I have reported the answer of the British admiral in charge to my request to be allowed to cruise on an American destroyer. The reply was a flat and immediate: "No." They did not allow British writers on British ships; why should they allow an American writer on an American ship?

It had to be explained that despite what they allowed or did not allow, English papers did publish praiseful items about the deeds of the British navy; and even if they did not publish such items, conditions governing publicity in the United States and the British Isles were not equal. The British navy was a tremendous one and it was operating just off their own shores; officers and men were regularly going ashore by the thousands and to their friends and families, if to nobody else, they talked of what was going on; and it does not take long for thousands of blue-jackets to spread the gossip in a country where no spot in it is more than forty miles from tide-water, whereas our nearest Atlantic ports were three thousand miles from our base of operations in Europe, and it was another three thousand miles to our west coast.

It also had to be pumped into the admiralty over there that possibly the American and British publics did not hold to quite the same ideas about their respective navies. It was possible that the 110,000,000 people of the United States looked on our navy as not altogether the property of the officers and men in it; possibly our 110,000,000 people over here looked on the navy as their navy, that they had a right to know something of what it was doing; and so (this item had to be pointed out to one of our own topside officers, too) as that same public were paying the bills of the navy, no harm perhaps to let them in on a few things or, this being the twentieth century, they might take it into their heads some day to have no navy at all.

It took the foregoing talk and something more before I could get the permission of the British Admiralty to cruise on one of our own destroyers over there. This isn't so much a criticism of the British Admiralty as to show that their point of view differs from ours; and to show that it was not Washington which was holding up news of our navy over there.

As to what they have been doing! They have been doing great work. I cruised over there on one of our destroyers. She was five years old, yet one day during an 85-mile run to answer an S O S call she exceeded her builder's trial by half a knot. Incidentally, she saved a merchantman which had been shelled for four hours by a U-boat and her $3,000,000 cargo; also she ran the U-boat under—one of the new big U-boats with two 5.9 deck guns. On the same day two other destroyers of our group took from a sinking liner 503 passengers without the loss of a life. One of these destroyers lashed herself to the sinking ship the more quickly to get them off; and as the liner went down our little ship had to use her emergency steam to get away in time. A fourth destroyer of ours got the U-boat which sank the liner. That was the record of one little group of destroyers in one day; and it is detailed here because the writer happened to be present when these things happened.

When our fellows first went over they had to learn a few things from the British. We had first to get rid of some childish ideas about depth charges. We brought over a toy size of 50 to 60 pounds. They showed us a man's size one—300 pounds of TNT, a contraption looking so much like a galvanized iron ash-barrel with flattened sides that they call them "ash-cans."

These ash-cans do not have actually to hit the U-boat; to explode one anywhere near is enough. When our fellows let go one of them, the ship has to be going 25 knots to be safe. One of our destroyers was making 11 knots one night—the best she could do under the weather conditions—and an ash-can was washed overboard by a heavy sea. Our destroyer's stern came so near to being blown off that her crew thought sure she was gone; she had to feel the rest of the way most carefully to port.

This U-boat hunting has been found so wearing on men's nerves that the British Admiralty has a law that our destroyers must remain in port after every cruise for periods that average about two-thirds of their time at sea. Once our destroyers are back to port and tied up to moorings, a U-boat might come up and sink a ship at the harbour entrance and our fellows not allowed to up-steam and at 'em. It was only after a hard experience against U-boats that they evolved this law to save men from breaking down.

It is a dangerous, hard service on one of the roughest coasts in the world—a coast where for seven months or so in the year wind and sea and strong cross tides seem to be their daily diet; a service where for days on a stretch it is nothing at all for destroyer crews not to be able to take a meal sitting down, not even in chairs lashed to stanchions and one arm free hooked around a stanchion; a service where officers live jammed up in the eyes of the ship and never think at sea of taking off their clothes, and where they sleep (when they do sleep) mostly by snatches on chart-house or ward-room transoms.

And for watches: eight hours in every twenty-four, night and day watching of their convoy, of their colleagues, of periscopes. (The prospect of collision with their close-packed convoy and themselves is a bad chance in itself.) On a destroyer convoying ships the officer of the deck has to stand with one eye to the compass ordering, say, two hundred changes of course in every hour.

And one watch-officer of every destroyer has the extra job of acting as chief engineer of the ship; and when a watch-officer had to go aboard a torpedoed ship, or to go in the crow's nest in a critical time, to spend hours, it may be, the time so spent is in addition to his regular eight hours.

If he is the executive officer he must also act as navigator; and as it is important to know just where the ship is any moment of the day or night, the navigator does not figure on sleep in any long stretches. About twenty waking hours out of twenty-four is his portion. As for the skipper: Every single waking hour of his is a heavy strain. I went to sea with the commander of the alert, intense type. Most of them are of that type, but this one particularly so, with eyes, ears, nerves, and brain working always at full power. Three hours in twenty-four was a pretty good lay-off for him.

Lively? Our destroyers are about 11½ times as long as they are wide; which does not mean that they cannot keep the sea. They can keep the sea. Put one of them stern-on to a 90-mile breeze and all the sea to go with it, give her 5 or 6 knots an hour head of steam, and she will stay there till the ocean is blown dry. But they are engined out of all proportion to their tonnage, with their great weight of machinery deep down; which means that they roll. Oh, but they do roll! *Whoopo*—down and back like that! Most any of them will make a complete roll inside of six seconds. Ours was a 5¼-second one. When she got to rolling right, she would snap a careless sailor overboard as quickly as you could snap a bug off the end of a whalebone cane. There is one over there which rolled 73 degrees—and came back.

Take one of them when she is hiking along at 20 knots, rolling from 45 to 50 degrees, and just about filling the whale-boat swinging to the skid deck davits as she rolls! See one dive and take a sea over her fo'c's'le head and smash in her chart-house bulkhead maybe! Their outer skin is only three sixteenths of an inch thick. See that thin skin give to the sea like a lace fan to a breeze! Watch the deck crawl till sometimes the deck-plates buckle up into V-shaped ridges! See them with the seas sloshing up their low freeboard and over their narrow decks, so that men have to make use of a sort of trolley line to get about. A man is aft and has to go forward, say. He hooks onto a rope loop, the same hanging from a fore-and-aft taut steel line about seven feet above deck, and when her stern rises he lifts his feet and shoots and fetches up Bam!—up against the fo'c's'le break. He is forward and wants to go aft—he hooks onto the loop, waits for her bow to rise, lets himself go and there he is—back to her skid deck.

That sounds like rough work. Sometimes it gets rougher than that, and then you hear of the wireless operator who was held in his radio shack for forty hours. He got pretty hungry, but he preferred the hunger to coming out and being washed overboard.

But let a machinist's mate tell you in his own way of the night he was standing a fire-room watch—this with all due respect to the chart-house bulkhead, the trolley line, the buckling decks, and the radio operator who was confined—this night he was on watch in the fire-room. Was it rough? He thought so. When he looked down at his feet, there were the fire-room deck-plates folding in and out like a concertina.

Destroyer crews do not loaf overmuch around deck. They can't. They live below decks mostly, strapped in when it is rough to a stretch of canvas laced to four pieces of iron pipe, set on an angle down against the ship's sides, and called a bunk. Even strapped in so they are sometimes, when she has a good streak on, hove out into the passageways. It was a young doctor of the flotilla who said that, except for their broken arms and legs, his ship's crew were disgustingly healthy.

Our officers over there volunteer for this service, and for every one who went, there were a dozen who wanted to go. And there is a lot of difference between men who go to a duty because they are ordered to go, and men who go because they want to go. These officers and men—there is no beating them, except by blowing them off the face of the waters. And even then they are not always beaten. One of our destroyers was cut down one night by collision. (With so many ships being crowded into a small steaming area, collisions are sure to happen.) All hands had to take to the rafts in a hurry. It was about two in the morning, one of those summer nights in the North when the light comes early. They watched her going under. Her deck settled level with the sea, and as it did so a young irrepressible one sang out: "What do you say, fellows, to having a race around the old girl before she flops under?" Away they started, four or five gangs of them, paddling their life rafts with their hands around the sinking ship at two in the morning.

That is youth; and there is no beating youth. We have had stories of our soldiers singing a song that has become very popular since we entered the war. We have been told of them singing it under the most varying conditions: as they camped on the granite blocks of the Hoboken water-front; as they climbed over the gangways of ships bound across; debarking from ships in European ports; singing it from behind the drawn shades of coaches rolling across France. There were even those who sang it while waiting to step into the life-boats on a torpedoed troop-ship; but for light-hearted courage has any one beaten that destroyer lad who was torpedoed one night last winter?

When the torpedo struck his ship the two depth charges astern were exploded also. Two 300-pound charges of TNT they were. The little ship seemed to be lifted out of the water. There was just time to throw over a few life rafts and take a high dive after the rafts. There was no time to get an S O S message away before the ship went down; so there they were—a November night in northern waters, more than half their crew known to be dead, their ship sunk, no other ship near and no hope of one coming near. It was about as tough a case as men could be expected to face and hope to live. But there was a boy there—he was jouncing up and down in the water to keep warm, and jouncing up and down he was singing (from out of the dark they heard him), singing cheerfully:

"O boy, O boy, where do we go from here!"

It is the thing spoken of in the early part of this book. Material is a great thing; but personnel has it beaten a dozen ways. Paul Jones with his capable sea-goers in his little sloop-of-war could raise the devil with the enemy. Paul Jones with a line of battleships and forty crews of men without spirit would not have caused them ten minutes' loss of sleep. That singing lad in northern waters was worth a dozen guns.

Our destroyers went over there at a time when the U-boats were sinking more tonnage in one month than Great Britain was building in four; and because of U-boat activities the loss of ships in the usual marine ways was far beyond normal. To the weary British our fellows brought a fresh vigour, a new aggressiveness.

Only half a dozen were in that first group, but other groups followed, and groups are still following. They have not driven the U-boats from under the seas, but they have made it possible for merchant ships to live in that part of the ocean they are covering.

Somebody has broken into print somewhere to say that Germany has trouble getting U-boat crews; that men have to be driven into U-boats to man them. What a queer idea of human courage people who say such things have! There are always volunteers, probably always will be—plenty of volunteers for any dangerous service. If the U-boat crews were the kind that have to be driven to sea, there would be no great harm in them. But they are not that kind. They have courage, and they have skill, and because they have courage and skill they are dangerous.

After a year of the U-boat drive England saw a danger of being some day starved out; and with England starved out, our army might as well have stayed on this side last summer; but though the drive is still on, England is not yet starved out, for much of which comfort they can thank the officers and men of our little destroyer flotilla.

At a time when England was worn and weary with the U-boat game, our fellows went over to hearten them up; and they are still heartening them up; and, besides heartening them up, they are getting the U-boats regularly. How many they are getting I could not say, even if I knew; but one of our vice-admirals has publicly stated that they once got five in one day. And with malice toward none, let us hope for more days like it.

Chapter 14

The Marines Have Landed

It was a little girl at home, not old enough to read long words, but able to read a picture, as she put it; and there was a print of a company of marines leaving one of our navy-yards, and she said: "The marine soldiers going away—more trouble somewheres, isn't there, papa?"

Which caused her papa to recall that from where he was born and lived the first years of his life he had only to look out of his top window and across the harbour to see a big navy-yard; and while he was still too young to read a paper, he had seen marines boarding ships and marching off to trains; and just as sure as he did the older people would read from that night's or next morning's paper of trouble somewhere abroad.

And always they went without any fuss. Most of us would have more to say about going to the office of a snowy morning than do the marines on leaving for some far-away country, from where, as they know by past records of the corps, quite a few of them are never coming back. They were the original efficiency boys. They slung their rifles, hooked on their packs and went; and that ended that part of it.

But after they were gone people living near naval quarters waited for the next word; and that next word so often came in the form of one laconic sentence, the same cabled back by the topside naval officer or some American consul, that we used to wonder if they had a rubber stamp for it—that laconic, reassuring sentence! When our country erects a memorial structure to the United States Marine Corps, she should chisel over the main front: *The Marines Have Landed and Have the Situation Well in Hand.*

Landed in some tropic port with some hard-pronouncing name, they have, shoving off from the ship's side with their rifles and their packs, to get a toe-hold somewhere against two, five, ten times their number blazing away at them from behind sand-hills, or roof-tops, or a fine growth of jungle, it may be.

The others are not always as well equipped as our fellows and they may have no advance supply-base; but they know how to campaign. South of us are multitudes who will take a bag of corn, a water-bottle, and a pair of straw sandals and go shuffling over the hill trails for forty or fifty miles a day. And don't think they won't fight. They will. In countries where boys of twelve and thirteen pack a gun and go off with their fathers in the army, they probably do not worry overmuch about dying early.

From their retreats they like to sally forth at intervals and have a wallop at our fellows. There was a corporal in Haiti, on outpost, with half a dozen loyal natives acting as policemen with him. The native guards slept in barracks by themselves; our marine in a little low shack set up on posts a hundred yards away, with a native who acted as cook and general helper. The next outpost was six miles away.

A band of outlaws rushed the native police in their barracks at this post one night, and such as they did not shoot up they ran into the brush. Our corporal was awakened from sound slumber by the firing and shouting at the barracks. A few volleys through the sides of his own shack waked him up good. He pulled on his trousers, taking time to fasten them only by one button at his waist. There was no time for socks; he pulled on his shoes, but had no time to lace them. A marine is trained to be neat in his attire, and so our corporal apologetically explained later that he had got no farther than that in his dressing when he heard them trying to burst in his front door.

The corporal sent his native cook to the rear door, while he fixed his bayonet to his rifle and stood guard over the front door. They had it all but stove in when he began cutting loose like three men with his rifle through the door. He killed a man there.

They then began to smash in the window nearest the door. He pried open the window with his bayonet, and got there before them. There was a big black fellow at the broken window. Our marine shot him dead, which gave him time to turn to the side window, which they had now broken in with the butts of their rifles. He got one there. There was another close up whom he hit but did not kill; and he dropped another one on the edge of the shadows outside. The cook, catching the spirit of the thing, killed one at the rear door on his own account.

The bandits had enough, and left. Next evening, when his officer came along with a squad, he found our corporal with his wounded under guard, his four dead ones in a neat row, and himself and his cook frying chicken in the twilight, cheerfully able to report that he had the situation well in hand.

They are a sharpshooting rifle outfit. Down in Vera Cruz during the late trouble a platoon of marines were at the foot of a street leading up from the water-front. They had cleaned up things all about them and thought they were in for a rest; and they wanted their rest—a hot tropic day with the heat rolling off the asphalt where they lay.

There came a ping! of a rifle bullet among them; and half a minute or so later another ping! They watched, and up the street they saw the head, arm, and shoulder of a man with a rifle come poking around the corner of a building, and ping! another one, and this time one of their men hit. A bad hombre, that one.

"Get him!" said their officer, and named two of them to get him.

The two men lay down on the asphalt; and when their friend next poked his head and shoulders around the corner, they fired. They saw the adobe plaster spatter from a corner of the building just under the man's chin; but that wasn't getting him. They jacked their sights up 50 yards, making it 800 yards; and when next the native showed around the corner they both got him—one plumb between the eyes.

It was good shooting; but there was no special comment after it. The talk would have come if they hadn't got him.

But it is not always a matter of fighting or shooting efficiency. There was that bad hombre, Juan Calcano of Santo Domingo— Juan the Terrible, the natives called him. Juan and his gang had a headquarters in the mountains. From there they came riding down into the valleys—shooting, robbing, standing quiet natives on their heads generally. Juan had quite a little territory under tribute. He came down into La Ramona, where was a custom-house and guard. He shot up the guards, took all the gold in the custom-house, and rode away, saying: "Come after me who dares!"

The marines did not worry about the daring part; but he was too strongly entrenched for a direct attack. Your professional soldier, above all men, prefers not to throw away good men's lives. They considered matters; and one day they set out, three marine officers and thirty men, for Juan's country. One of those tropical hurricanes came along the same day they started, blew down trees, filled rivers to over their banks, and made them wade waist-deep in the mud of the roads. It was tough going, but it had its good side—there were not many people abroad.

They arrived near the village where Juan was known to be. An American marine would not have stood much chance to get back if Juan had known one was around; but one of the officers rigged up as a mule trader and went looking for Juan. He found him, taking it easy until the roads after the storm should become passable, and allow himself and his men to sashay into the valley again.

All kinds of people—white, and black, and brown—came Juan's way to do business—to buy mules and horses, for instance. In the course of his travels in the valley Juan had helped himself to some very fine mules and horses. Along comes this man this day—American, English, French, Spanish, who knows? Or cares? He talked money—cash—for a good pair of mules. No old spavined creatures, but young, strong, sound ones.

Yes, Juan had just such a pair of mules. Oh, a superb young pair! He would see. Truly yes. Would the stranger *señor* come into his house so that Juan might speak more confidentially of them? The stranger would. And did. But before Juan could unload all he had to say about his mules the mule buyer drew a large service automatic and slipped Juan out to where thirty-two marines, officers and men, were in hiding. And they put Juan in jail, and all it cost was one mule—not Juan's—drowned while crossing a stream during the hurricane.

The marines have a great fighting record; but the marines do more than fight. After all, men cannot be handling rifle and bayonet every waking minute—they would become abnormal creatures if they did, of use only in war time; and it would be a terrible world if war were our end and aim. The marines get aviation, search-light, wireless, telegraphic, heliograph, and other signal drill. They plant mines, put up telegraph and telephone lines in the field, tear down or build up bridges, sling from a ship and set up or land guns as big as 5-inch for their advance base work.

It is a belief with marines that the corps can do anything. Right in New York City is a marine printing plant with a battery of linotypes and a row of presses. They set their own type, write their own stuff (even to the poetry), draw their own sketches, do their own photography, their own colour work—everything. Every man in that plant is a marine, enlisted or commissioned. Every one has seen service somewhere outside his country.

One was in a tropic country one time after an all-night march to a river where the ferry was a water-soaked bamboo raft. They had to wait until some native might happen along with a bull—or it might be a cow—to tow the raft across. After crossing the river twice in that day, the young marine commander halted on the bank and said: "That's sure not crossing in a hurry if we had to. Might's well go to it and build a bridge right now."

They cut down trees, got a portable pile-driver from their transport, rigged it up and set to work. They hoisted the hammer—a good heavy one—and let it drop. Bam! she struck, and into the mud for about two feet went the pile. Fine! They hoisted the hammer again—four men hauling on pulley blocks did the hoisting—and let her go again. This time instead of a fine *bam!* the hammer went a fine *splasho!* into the river. The great heat and dampness of the place had warped the runways; almost every other time they let that hammer drop, it jumped the runways and into the river.

But that was all right. They could fish her out and hoist her up by man power again. It was when they left the solid bank and had to put out into the river that their troubles began. A pile-driver ought to have a pretty solid foundation. Ought to have! They took two dugout canoes, lashed them together, put a bamboo deck across, set their pile-driver on the deck and turned to again. It made a kind of a wobbly base; besides hauling the hammer out every time it jumped into the river, they had to see that it didn't come bouncing down atop of their own heads or through the canoe deck. However, they were getting action. They finished driving the piles and setting up the stringers.

For their bridge floor they laid down wood shingles, and over that a mat made out of woven bamboo strips. For a top deck? Well, it was a coral island and the roads of that country were of pounded coral; they put a top dressing of pounded coral across the bridge.

And then the young marine commander looked her over and figured on the dimensions of his struts and stringers, and said: "Some class! She'll stand a two-ton load." And then along came a steam-roller from off the transport, and the roller weighed five tons and it was important that it be passed across. "Go ahead," said the marine commander—"only I hope you can swim!" And they all camped on the bank to watch. The steam-roller man was an optimist and a literary person: "You may have builded better than you know, captain!" The bridge settled down another foot, but the roller got across, and back and over many more times; which set the younger marines to standing on the bank and saying: "That's us—bridge builders!"

The fight in the shack, the capture of Calcano, the sharpshooting at Vera Cruz, the building of that coral-floored bridge, are not set down here as wonderful stunts. They are set down because the writer happened to bump into them during a casual hour's inspection of their records. Scores of more heroic or ingenious samples could be served up by anybody who cared to dig deep into the records. These are detailed here, because they could be briefly told and at the same time show the marine's characteristic qualities: courage, ingenuity, technique, and industry.

Here we might mention that it is not in itself an act of war to land marines on foreign soil. It was sending ashore the blue-jackets at Vera Cruz that made it an act of war. To protect American lives and property in Nicaragua a battalion of marines landed there a few years ago. They had some sharp fighting, but it was not an act of war. Do you begin to see him as a diplomatic asset? And perhaps why all this landing action comes his way? Most of us have probably forgotten the details of that Nicaraguan landing; but—unless they have been jacked out lately—a company of those marines are still there, looking out for American interests. Only a company, but still hanging on.

Courage, ingenuity, industry—they need them all. Most of us will probably have to stop to remember that the marines who landed in Haiti and Santo Domingo are still there. And running things in their usual efficient fashion. There was the usual fighting to get a toe-hold, the usual fighting to retain place, the usual establishing of outposts, with the usual killed and wounded already probably forgotten by most of us. Perhaps they are too far away to make absorbing newspaper items; perhaps it is the Big War overshadowing all else.

In Haiti and Santo Domingo it was the old story of political factions, each faction having its own little gang of fighting men till our fellows came in and ran most of them into the hills. When the marines took charge they found that pretty much everything on the island had gone to wrack. As, for instance, under the old French regime there had been some splendid roads in Haiti, but now they were hardly more than sewers in the towns and a drainage for the hill slopes of the country.

The marines repaired the roads; not always using the picks and shovels themselves, but seeing to it that somebody did, paying a living wage for such work to the natives. Sometimes bandits—who are quite often gentle creatures when out of training—captured bandits were allowed to quit jail to do useful work in this line. The marines installed sanitary methods, saw that courts of justice were resumed, marine officers themselves serving as justices until they found natives who could do that service. Likewise they collected and disbursed taxes.

Above all, they did away with the old reign of terror, when no man's life was safe if he happened to be on the wrong side. When the bandits were running around unchecked, it was not safe for a whole family to go to market together. Generally the women went to sell their little produce, while the men stayed behind to guard the little property at home. Now—the natives speak of the wonder of it—the roads on market-days are crowded with both men and women.

At first they had distrust of the marine; not altogether because he was a foreigner (the tropical people probably are less distrustful of us than we of them)—he was an armed soldier. But they learned to know him, and now the native salutes and smiles without effort at the marine in passing. When one particular marine officer left there to come home recently, crowds of native men, women, and children came down, some to weep, but all to wish him Godspeed in going.

The marine is sometimes termed soldier and sailor too, which is not correct. He is not a sailor and does not claim to be. When not in barracks ashore he lives aboard some war-ship afloat; and on shipboard he does certain guard work and handles the secondary batteries. But he does not have to sailorize; the blue-jacket takes care of that part, and takes care of it well. The notion that a marine must qualify as a sailor aboard ship has probably cost the corps many a prospective recruit.

To call him a seagoing soldier is more nearly correct. When it is not an act of war to land marines on foreign soil, it is good business to keep them where landings can be quickly made with them. So his being kept aboard ship, perhaps. Blue-jackets have taken part in landing-parties, too, but it is not to black the blue-jacket's eye to say that it is not his regular job. The blue-jacket's work is aboard ship—on the bridge, in magazines, in turrets, below decks. Advance shore work is the marine's specialty, and he goes to it pretty much as a man with a dinner-pail goes to work in the subway.

He is the first to land, the last to leave, and to name the places where he has seen service—well, one of them wrote a song once.

"From the hills of Montezuma to the shores of Tripoli," it began. But he has seen more than Mexico or the Mediterranean since. He could now say:

"From the hills of Montezuma to the gates of old Peking He has heard the shrapnel bursting, he has heard the Mauser's *ping!* He has known Alaskan waters and the coral roads of Guam, He has——"

But it's like calling a roll—Egypt, Algeria, Tripoli, Abyssinia, Mexico, China, Japan, Korea, Cuba, Porto Rico, Panama, Nicaragua, Haiti, Santo Domingo, Alaska, the Philippines, Formosa, Sumatra, Hawaii, Samoa, Guam—like calling the roll of tropic countries and a few less warm to say where he has been.

He has been most everywhere, done most everything. Did you ever see any mounted marines? There is a guard of mounted marines right now with the legation in Peking; and once a platoon of marines, on duty in Africa, not being able to get big enough horses, rode camels through the wilds of Abyssinia to the palace of old Menelik.

In speaking here of the marines, no man or officer has been named. That is done of a purpose. In talking of the corps, from the topsiders down—generals, colonels, majors, captains lieutenants, and enlisted men—one fact stuck out: They all played up the corps. All individuals—officers and men—were made subordinate to the corps. So here, taking the tip, no names are named. A soldier speaks of his regiment, a blue-jacket of his ship. The Marine Corps is made up of companies, regiments, battalions, divisions; but it is the corps of which the marine always speaks.

If you ask the members of any other outfit to name the model military unit, they may name their own branch of the service first; but if they do, it is almost a sure bet that they will name the United States Marine Corps next. When they do not name themselves first, they name the marines first. And this does not apply to outfits in this country alone.

By the look of things now, there probably will be plenty of war before we are done. If any young fellow is wishful to be in the middle of it, we would say: Consider the marines. You may not see them mentioned every morning in the press reports, but be sure of this—they are there and on the job.

Chapter 15
The Navy as a Career

A young fellow reading all this stuff about the doings of our destroyers might be inclined to look on the navy as pure adventure, which would not be to get it quite right. The adventure is there, but there is something more. The navy will take a young man, feed and clothe him, give him a good all-round training, and while he is yet in middle age retire him with at least $60 a month for the rest of his life. No matter how low his rating has been, that $60 a month is certain after his thirty years of service; while, if he has shown moderate intelligence and ambition, he can count on close to $100 a month, and this without his having ever been a commissioned officer. The years after his retirement he may spend as he pleases—go into business, get another job, and make another wage on top of his pension. He can go to jail if he prefers: whatever he does, always there is that sheet-anchor of a pension to windward.

Apart from the fighting end of it, most of us possibly do not know just what navy life means to-day. We all know that man-of-war's men no longer lie out on rolling yard arms to reef salt-crusted sails in gales of wind; but in what else lies the difference? Some of us, possibly, do not know that.

The navy still wants men with the seagoing instinct—men who can sailorize, who can hand, splice, and steer; but more than ever the navy is looking for men who can do other things. The navy wants ship-fitters, blacksmiths, plumbers, electricians, wireless operators, carpenters, boiler-makers, painters, printers, store-keepers, bakers, cooks, stewards, drug clerks; even as it wants gunners, boatmen, quartermasters, sail-makers, firemen, oilers, and it will take clarinet, trombone, and cornet players and the like for the ship's band.

If a man has no trade the navy will teach him one. There are navy schools for electricians, shipwrights, ship-fitters, carpenters, painters, coppersmiths, ship's cooks, bakers, stewards, and musicians. There are schools where yeomen (ship's clerks) are taught all about departmental papers; there is a Hospital Corps school; an aeronautic school; a school for deep-sea diving. (There are no schools for blacksmiths or boiler-makers; these must have mastered their trades before enlistment.)

When a young fellow enlists he is sent to one of several naval training-stations. Here they are quartered in barracks—well-aired, well-lighted, well-heated buildings. At one place, where the climate is mild, the boys sleep in barracks in bungalows with upper sides of canvas, which are rolled down to let in sun and air in fine weather and laced up against bad weather.

At all training-stations there are mess-halls, reading-rooms, libraries; also gymnasiums, athletic fields, and ball parks. At all stations there are setting-up drills, gymnastic, swimming and signal exercises, ship and boat training. The men go on hikes, fight sham battles, dig trenches. Line-officers give them advice which will be of use to them on shipboard later; service doctors and chaplains hand them hygienic and moral truths that will be of use to them anywhere at any time.

A recruit goes from the training-school to a cruising ship, where he may find himself—according to his work—doing watch duty four hours on to eight hours off; or working at hours like a man ashore—turning to at eight or nine o'clock and knocking off at four or five or six o'clock in the afternoon.

War-ships formerly meant close living quarters; and ships formerly went off on cruises on which the men sometimes did not set foot on shore for six months or a year, and quite often they had to go for months without taste of fresh meat or vegetables. Those days are gone. Ships still make long cruises from home, but they do not keep the sea as they used to. Service regulations require that men now be given a run ashore once in three months; and "beef boats" travel with all fleets.

The everlasting holystoning of wooden decks and the dim lanterns hung at intervals from low-hanging beams—they are gone. The only dim lanterns now are the "battle-lanterns" in use at night war practice; and they are swung to steel bulkheads by electric wires. Quarter-decks, forecastle heads, and bridges are still planked on the big ships, and such do still have to be holystoned on special days; but the great stretches between decks are now laid in linoleum on the hard steel itself; electric lights are all over the ship, and, as for the low beams, the new big ships are so high-girdered that hammock-hooks on the berth-deck have to be made extra long so the men won't have to get stepladders to turn in. A battleship nowadays is about 600 feet long, 100 feet wide, has seven or eight decks, with turrets, bridges, military masts, and smoke-pipes topside. Between decks are magazines, storerooms, engine-rooms, boiler-rooms, dynamo-rooms, mess-rooms, ice-rooms, repair-shops, staterooms, office-rooms, sick-bays, galleys, laundries, pantries—but only ship-constructors can tell you offhand how many hundreds of compartments are below decks of a present-day big war-ship.

She is a great workshop, an office-structure, a big power-plant, a floating hotel—and a few other things. But above all she is meant to be a home for ten or twelve hundred officers and men.

A man may not be given duty on a battleship or battle cruiser; he may be sent to a scout cruiser or a beef boat or a gunboat, which, being smaller, will bounce and roll around more in heavy weather and not offer so much room to move around in; but he will get used to the bouncing around, and always he will find some variety and some comfort in his daily life.

That item of comfort might as well be counted in as important. It is something to know that, no matter what else happens, there are hot meals waiting a man three times a day, and a dry change of clothing, and a dry hammock to turn into nights. Even on deck duty in bad weather a man can get into slicker, rubber boots, and rain-hat, and at the worst be almost comfortable.

Navy life is not meant to be a perpetual entertainment—not though they do hold regular smokers on the quarter-decks of the big ships. To lie for months off a tropic port waiting for something to happen—that is not exhilarating; and coaling ship, even with the band playing—that is no joy. But the watching of tropic ports passes; and the ship has to steam many a mile before she must be coaled again. So, taking it in the long perspective, it is a moderately varied life, an outdoor life, and under hygienic conditions of the best. Right now, war with us, there is going to be some danger; but we are assuming that any man who thinks of joining the navy is prepared for a little danger.

A man may enlist in the navy up to thirty-five years of age, provided he is at least 5 feet 4 inches tall, weighs 128 pounds, has a 33-inch chest, possesses normal vision, a moderate number of sound teeth, is free from disease or deformity, and is an American citizen. Sometimes men shy on some measurement are passed if above average otherwise. A boy seventeen (the youngest enlistment age) must be 5 feet 2 inches and weigh 110 pounds. When a boy or a man enlists he goes at once on the payroll. With his pay goes a clothing allowance sufficient to cover all service demands; with his pay also goes nourishing and abundant food.

Enlistments are of four years for men. A boy's enlistment runs to his majority. A man may work up to be a C. P. O. (chief petty officer) in his first enlistment. The navy is full of men who have done that. During this war many a recruit should make his C. P. O. quickly, for there is nothing in the Regulations to prevent a recruit from making his C. P. O. overnight. The habit of most officers is to rate up good men in their divisions as fast as vacancies will permit.

A C. P. O.'s base pay may run up to $77 a month. With re-enlistment that base pay is increased. A man re-enlisting without delay gets a bounty of four months' pay. (Figure that extra re-enlistment money—four months' pay every four years, the same with interest at the navy savings-account rate of 4 per cent—and see what it amounts to after thirty years' service.) That extra re-enlistment money is not figured into the pension probabilities, as stated in the beginning of this article. Consider that and then consider how many men have to work until they are too old to work any further and who, after all their years of labour, go on the scrap-heap without a dollar against the poverty of their old age.

Besides the base pay of a man's rating there is extra money for men doing special work. (Neither has this been reckoned in the pension possibilities.) Certain gun-pointers, gun-captains, coxswains, stewards, and cooks get extra money up to $10 a month. Men in submarines get $1 extra for every day their boat submerges up to $15 a month. Men acting as mail-clerks draw up to $30 a month extra;

ship's tailors up to $20 a month extra. Men in the Flying Corps get 50 per cent more than the base pay their rating calls for. Every man in the service draws a small extra sum for good conduct.

A chief petty officer is not the highest rating of the enlisted service. There is a most efficient body of men called warrant-officers, who wear a sword, are called "Mr.," and draw up to $2,400 a year. There are warrant boatswains, gunners, machinists, carpenters, pharmacists, and pay-clerks. But they must remain in service, even as most commissioned officers, till they are sixty-four, before they draw their pension of three-quarters pay. Also, like commissioned officers, they get no clothing allowance and have to pay for their food.

The matter of becoming a commissioned officer may interest the recruit. One hundred appointments may be made to Annapolis every year from among the younger enlisted men of the navy. Young fellows who wish to try for this are given special opportunities for study. The proviso that an applicant must be under twenty years of age and have been at least one year in service to make Annapolis is going to bar the way to some. For such there is another way—warrant. A warrant boatswain, gunner, or machinist of four years' standing and still under thirty-five years of age may take an examination for ensign. Twelve warrant-officers may be made ensigns annually. If they pass, they thereafter go on up exactly as any Annapolis graduate. A warrant pay-clerk may go up to be junior paymaster, where he will rank with an ensign.

The foregoing is for the business or ambitious side. Somebody may ask: Will the young fellow who looks on the navy as a business proposition make a good fighting man?

Well, in the judgment of men who study the game, almost any young fellow you meet along the street has it in him to make a good fighting man. The fighting habit is more a habit of mind than of body. Habituating the mind to the fighting game is what makes our sailors, soldiers, and marines do the right thing almost automatically in crises; and this almost automatically correct action makes for the greater safety of shipmates or comrades in time of peril.

In this book only the work of our destroyers in this war has been spoken of. That is because only our destroyers have come in contact with enemy ships; but all along the line the personnel is of equal calibre.

Our navy is crowded with men who will face any danger. Some years ago one of our battleships was on the battle-range, with bags of powder stowed in her turrets to save time in loading and firing the guns. A spark got to the bags of powder. There was an explosion and a fire. Directly underneath was the handling-room. Burning pieces of cloth fell from the turret down into the handling-room. The crew of that handling-room could have jumped into the passageway, made their way up a ladder, and so on to the free and safe air of the open deck. What they did was to stand by to stamp out what fire they could.

Leading from the handling-room were the magazines. The doors of the magazines were open. Men jumped into the magazines and buttoned the keys of the bulkhead doors so that there would be no crevice for sparks. In doing that they locked themselves in; and once in they had to stay in. Above them, they knew, was a turret full of men and officers dead and dying; they knew that fire was raging around them, too, and that the next thing would be for the people outside to flood the magazines. The magazines were flooded; when things were under control and the doors opened, the water in the magazines was up to the men's necks.

While that was going on below decks, in the turret were other men and officers, including the chaplain, not knowing what was going on below, and expecting every moment to be blown up into the sky; but there they were, easing the last moments of the men who were not already dead. Thirty all told were killed in the turret. All concerned behaved well, but no better than they were expected to behave.

A few years ago there was a destroyer off Hatteras. It was before daybreak of a winter's morning in heavy weather. A boiler explosion blew out her side from well below the water-line clear up through to her main deck. Men were killed by the explosion; others were badly scalded. A steam burn is an agonizing thing, yet some of these scalded men went back into that hell of a boiler-room and hauled out shipmates who, to their notion, were more badly burned than themselves. One such rescuer died of his burns. The hole in the deck and top side of that destroyer was twelve feet across, yet her commander and crew got her to Norfolk under her own steam. Commander and crew behaved well, but no better than they were expected to behave.

There is a chief boatswain in the navy who had the duty of taking a ship's steamer with a crew to look after the ship's target at battle practice. A target is a frame of canvas set up on a raft of logs. The duty of the steamer was to stand off to one side and make a record of the hits.

This boatswain likes to joke, to try out new men. On the run from the ship he called the roll and said: "Now, boys, in this work one of you will have to stay on the raft to count the hits. Of course it is dangerous work. I won't say that it isn't. The man going may not come back. The chances are"—he eyed them one after another—"that whoever goes will never come off the raft alive. Now, I can name the one who will have to do that work. But I don't want to have to name him. I'll let you draw lots."

He took a sheet of paper and cut it into strips. His crew—all apprentice boys, all fresh from the training-school—drew the slips. The lad who drew the short slip was no better or braver to look at than most of the others. He looked at his slip of paper and then in a sort of wonder at the sea and sky.

He came back to his short slip. His lips trembled. He prayed to himself. Then he went down into his blouse pocket and fished out a stub of a pencil. He was whiter than ever, and shaking. "Can I have a sheet of paper, sir?"

"What do you want a sheet of paper for?"

"I'd like, sir, to write a note to my mother before I go."

To pick out a few isolated instances from service records and shout: "There is the proof of general efficiency, of courage, of—" whatnot—that would be idle. These were not taken from the service records. Officers and men in the turret explosion, in the destroyer accident, in the raft incident, are mentioned here because the writer, at different times, has cruised with them.

They all behaved well; but no better than they were expected to.

When I asked the boatswain in the raft case if he expected the boy to quit, he said: "Quit! They never quit."

This talk of heroism and pensions in the same breath may not seem to jibe; somebody is going to wonder if the man who thinks of the money side of the navy in the beginning isn't going to think too much of it in the end. But there is a point of view which should be reckoned with, and a type of man, of a good fighting man, who should be listened to in this matter. Why should not a man who risks his life in his daily calling have the normal comforts and his family the ordinary necessities of life?

I know a fireman, an efficient, brave man—a man with a record. One night—we were in a drug store in a crowded city—he was answering the argument of a man working in a big factory.

Said the fireman: "You're making your five or six—yes, and eight—dollars a day, in lively times like now. All right. But the lively times will pass, and there'll come weeks when you won't make any four or five or six dollars a day, and there'll come weeks when you'll be on half-time. Average it up and you won't get any more than I will in the long run. And when I'm through, when I'm fifty-five, I get a pension, and with a few good years left to me. And where are you then? Out on the street or some home for the aged—if they will take you.

"Save money as I go along? I don't figure on it—not with a family and trying to give them the kind of food they need and the little things that live boys and girls—especially girls—care as much for as the grub they eat and the clothes they wear. But if I do spend all my pay, my family are getting the good of it, I don't go into the discard at the end. And when I'm up on a shaky roof in a bad fire, maybe I'll be more ready to take a chance, knowing that if I go through and cripple myself, there's something coming to the wife and family after it."

The fireman's argument holds for the navy, except that in the navy they get through younger and with a bigger pension.

Is there any romance in the navy nowadays? Who can answer for all? Probably as much now as ever there was. Why should substituting smoke-pipes for spars, and propellers for sails, kill the thing that thrills us? I've seen men washing down decks of a tropic morning, and, ninety miles inland, old Orizaba showing his white head above the clouds; and some of those men thought it was slow work and others thought it was great.

On a scout cruiser to African ports, or a thousand miles up a Chinese river on a gunboat, among the South Sea Islands on a light cruiser, some men return with dumb lips and others can keep you awake till morning with the tales of what they've seen.

A nineteen-year-old big-gun pointer sits atop of his bicycle saddle, and the enemy fleet is swinging into range. Will it be like shooting clay pipes in a gallery or will a warmer wave go rolling through his veins as he presses the button?

Romance! Is it something always dead and gone, or something a man carries around with him?

Whatever it is, the navy is there to try it out, and no danger of starving while we try it.

Chapter 16

The Sea Babies

Submarines have been cutting a large figure in this war. There is probably a general curiosity to know how they are operated. I know I was curious to know, and, *Collier's* having secured me permission from the Electric Boat Company, I went over to Cape Cod to take in a trial trip or two of some boats they were building for the British Government.

There was one all ready for sea.

Long and narrow, and modelled like a stretched-out egg she was, with one end of the egg running to a point by way of a stern, and the other flattened to an up-and-down wedge-like bow. A heavy black line marked her run.

Below her run she was tinted to the pale green of inshore waters, and to a greyish blue above. Everything above her deck, which was only a raised fore-and-aft platform for the crew to walk on, with countless little round scupper-holes in its sides—above the deck her conning-tower, and above that again her periscope casing—all were blue-grey.

The feeling of the morning was of heavy wind and rain or snow to come; and a hard, cold breath of the sea and a taste of the rain were already on us as we crossed the plank from the mother ship to the deck of the "sub" and, one after the other, fitted ourselves into the main hatchway and wiggled down into her.

Our submarine, from the inside, was an amazing collection of engines, tanks, gauges, tubes, pipes, valves, wheels, torpedoes, tube heads, electric registers, electric lights, and whatnot. A flat steel floor ran from the forward end to the engine-room aft. Between the floor and the arched deck overhead were three heavy steel bulkheads with heavy steel doors. A narrow iron skeleton ladder led up to her conning-tower; small steel rungs bolted to the casing showed the way to a square after-deck hatch.

When all the others of us were below, the captain came squeezing down from the conning-tower hatch and took his position at the periscope.

To the captain's left stood a man whose job it was to hold the sub to the depth of water desired. This was the diving-rudder man, a most expert one, we were told, who had been known to hold a submerged sub at full speed to within six inches of one depth for two miles at a stretch. A thin brass scale and a curved tube of coloured water with an air bubble in it helped out the diving-rudder man's calculations. The least deviation of the sub's course from the horizontal and these two instruments, lit up by electric lamps, showed it at once. There was a big dial, with a long green hand, which also marked the depth of the sub; but that was an insensitive and rather slow-acting gauge—all right for the crew to look at from half the length of the sub, but not fine or quick enough for the diving-rudder man.

He was the busy man while we were under water. The others could now and again grab a moment of relaxation from their tenseness, but while the sub was moving the diving-rudder man never took his eyes off the little brass scale with the electric light playing on it. Stop and consider that our sub had only to get a downward inclination of ever so little while running hooked-up under water, and in no time she would be below her lowest safety depth of 200 feet, where the pressure is 7 tons to every square foot of her hull. And should she collapse there would be no preliminary small leak by way of warning. She would go as an egg-shell goes when you crush it in your palm. *Plack!*—like that—and it would be all over. Above this same middle compartment, the smallest and most crowded of all, up through the grilled spaces of a steel grating, we could see the wide feet and boot-legs of the man who held the ship to her compass course; and for a wheel, we knew, he was holding a little metal lever about as long and thick as his middle finger, with a little black ball about as big as the ball of his thumb on the end of it.

To the right of the foot of the conning-tower ladder stood the

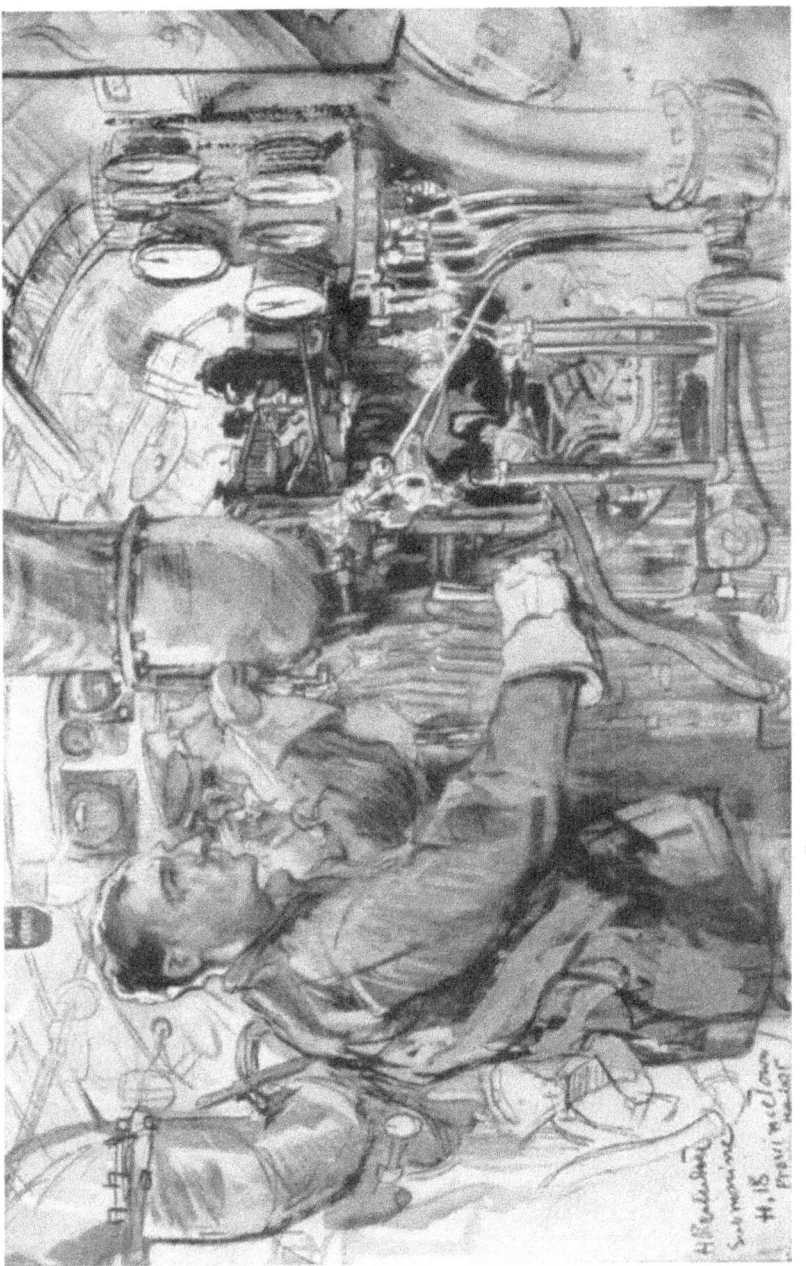

In the engine-room of a submarine.

ballast-tank man; and when the captain from the foot of his periscope gave the word—after first looking forward, aft, and to each side of him to see that all hands were at their proper stations—it was the ballast-tank man who went violently at once into action. He grabbed a big valve and gave it a twist; grabbed another and gave it a twist; and another, and one more; and, standing near by, we could hear—or thought we could—the in-rush of great waters.

A man got to wondering then what would happen if this chap got his valves mixed. But a look around showed every lever and every valve, everything marked with its own name and number. Nothing was left unmarked—in deep-cut black lettering on brass plates generally, but here and there coloured-light signs, too. After another look at the multiplicity of them, almost any man would agree that it is a good scheme.

But to get back: the tank man has done his part and our sub is sinking. There is no unusual feeling to inform a man she is sinking. Only for the starting of the engines, the diving-rudder man getting busy, and the wide-faced gauge's long green finger beginning to walk around, a man who didn't know could easily believe that the sub was still tied up alongside her supply-ship. But the long green finger is walking, and marking 5 feet, 10 feet, 11, 12, as it walks. At 16 feet the finger oscillates and stops, and to that depth our diving-rudder man holds her while she speeds on for a mile or so.

That first little dash is by way of warming her up. The officer for whose government this submarine was built is aboard. He now asks for a torpedo demonstration. So two 1,500-pound dummy torpedoes are got ready, the breeches to two of the four forward tubes opened, the torpedoes slipped in, the breeches closed. The bow caps are then opened.

The captain, during all this time, has never left the periscope, which—to have it explained and over with—is no more than a long telescope set on end, with a reflecting mirror top and bottom. From the lower end of the periscope project two brass arms, by means of which the skipper now swings the periscope all the way around. In this way he is able to look at any quarter of the sea he pleases.

Running at the depth we were then, the periscope showing about six feet out of water, the captain at the periscope was, of course, the only man who could see anything outside of her.

The captain gave the needful preliminary orders; and at the proper time, sighting through the periscope as he did so, he pressed the button of a little arrangement which he held, half concealed, in the palm of his hand. There was a soft explosion, a sort of woof!—and a torpedo was on the way to a hypothetical enemy, with only the captain able to see that it reached its mark.

As the torpedo left the sub the rudder man gave her a "down" rudder, which was to offset the tendency of the sub to shoot her nose to the surface; when the torpedo had gone the tank man turned on the air-pressure, which blew out what water had entered the torpedo chamber. By and by the other torpedo was fired.

One reason for this trial run was to prove that she could run so many miles an hour under water by the power of her storage-batteries alone. And soon she went at that. And no mild racket inside her then; for a sub's engine power and space are out of all proportion to her tonnage. Not to decrease the noise, the man to whom the trial meant most was standing by with a stop-watch, and every half-minute or so he would yell at the top of his lungs, "Go!" or "Hold!" to the engineer, who was imprisoned in a narrow alley-way with engines to right and to left and below him. The engineer would look at a register and yell back at the manager, who would then set some figures in a book and rush over to the man who was reckoning up the decreasing or increasing amperes or kilowatts or whatever they were of her storage-batteries, and set down more figures; and if the boss had to yell his head off to make himself heard, be sure that the others had to yell even louder. Only on trial trips, probably, where tests have to be proved, does all this yelling happen; but the total effect was to make a shore-goer feel, not as if he were in a ship under water, but rather in a subway section under construction, or some overdriven corner of some sort of night-working machine-shop, or some other homelike place ashore. The bright electric lights helped out the machine-shop illusion.

For a time during the run the diving-rudder man had his troubles keeping her on a level, whereupon the skipper—an easy-going man ordinarily—jerked his head away from his periscope and had a peek for the reason. Through the forward bulkhead door he spied the torpedo man, who, feeling pleased, perhaps, at the successful execution of his part of the programme, was fox-trotting fore and aft for himself in his section of the ship. "Would you mind picking out one spot and staying on it?" asked the skipper, at which the torpedo man took his camp-stool, picked out his one spot, and planted himself on it, and piously read the stock-market quotations of a week-old newspaper for the rest of the run.

While this hour run—full speed, submerged—was in progress, a tickling in our throats set most of us to coughing. A naval constructor of note, who was also a shark on chemistry, explained how this coughing was not caused by the chill in the air, but by the particles of sulphuric acid thrown off by the action of the storage-batteries. These little particles, it seems, went travelling about in the air seeking a home—some place, any place where they could tuck in out of the way; but all the air homes being already occupied by other tenants—the usual ingredients or components of the air—they could find no place to butt in; and so they went around and about till innocent people like ourselves made a home for them by breathing them in out of the way. After which explanation—yelled above all the other noises—these sulphuric hoboes caused less suspicion and discomfort. It was good to hear that what we were swallowing was not the chlorine of a hundred stories of fiction.

The sub had now to prove her diving qualities. So tanks were blown out and up she went to the surface again; and there, while she was resting like a bird on the water, ballast-tanks were suddenly filled and down she went. Down, down, down she went—the long green finger on the broad-faced gauge walking around at a fine clip. Dropping so—on an even keel, by the way—she gave out no sense of action such as a man gets on an aeroplane. Flying around in the air, you see what's doing every second. If anything happens, you know you will see it coming, and—perhaps—going: your eyes, ears, brains, and nerves prove things to you.

But action in a submarine lies largely in a man's imagination, unless he be the periscope man; and even there, when she is completely submerged, he sees no more than the others. However, a man did not need to have too much imagination to think of a few things as he looked at the long green finger walking around: 30 feet, 40 feet, 50 feet—This particular observer had no idea she could drop so fast; and as she dropped, he could not help wondering how deep the ocean was around there—this in case anything happened. Sixty feet, 70 feet—she was gathering great speed by then, but at 82 feet she stopped—a pleasant thing to see. And then, maybe to show it was no accident, she did it all over again. Did we feel any difficulty in breathing during all this? We did not, nor during the three to four hours we were under that morning. And let a man listen to these submarine enthusiasts telling how they can live three or four weeks on their compressed air, if they have to, without coming to the surface! Only give them food enough, of course. And coffee—they have an electric range to make the coffee. As it happened, they made coffee for us—not that day, but next morning going home. It was good coffee. The 82-foot-drop stunts were done with each of the crew at his station, ready at any instant to check her.

To meet the further requirements our sub had to rise to the top, fill her tanks, let herself go, and then, by an automatic safety device, fetch up all by herself. So the tank man applied the air-pressure, blew his tanks free of all water, closed his outer valves and brought her up. She was now stretched out on the surface—not quite motionless, for the first of the breeze predicted the night before was on and we could feel that she was rolling a little. A peek through the periscope while she was up disclosed further evidence of the breeze—tossing white crests, two coasters hustling for harbour under short sail, an inbound fisherman with reefed mainsail making great leaps for home. Looking through the periscope so, it was easy enough to understand the feeling of power which might well come to the master of a submarine in war time. The sub can be lying there—in dark or bright water will make no difference; on such a day no eye is going to discern the white bone of the moving periscope; and he can be standing there, with a quick peek now and then to see what is going on above him; and by and by she can come swinging along majestically in her arrogance and power—the greatest battleship afloat, with guns to level a great city, or the biggest and speediest ship ever built—and he can be there and when he gets good and ready—Woof! she's gone. War-ship or liner, she's gone and all aboard gone with her; and the submarine skipper can go along about his business of getting the next one.

However, the automatic device was set for action at the required depth and the word given.

In this same middle compartment—the operating compartment of the ship—was a man with the spiritual face of one who keeps lonely, intense vigils. He sat on a camp-stool, and his business seemed to be not ever to let his rapt gaze wander from several rows of gauges which were screwed to the bulkhead before him. Since I first stepped down into the sub I had spotted him, and had been wondering if his ascetic look was born with him or was a development of his job—whatever his job might be. Now I learned what his job was. He was the man who stood by the automatic safety devices. If anything happened to the regular gadgets and it was life or death to get her at once to the surface, he was the man who pressed a button, or moved a switch, or in some highly mechanical way applied the mysterious power which would get her safe to the surface.

The skipper gave the word, the main ballast lad opened his outer valves, and down she started. We knew this, as always, by the moving green finger on the wide-faced gauge. Downward she kept on going, and to a man not too long shipmates with the creature she certainly did seem to be going down in a hurry. She was nearing the appointed depth; she made the appointed depth, and—went on by. "What's this!" said one observer to himself, and directed an interested eye toward the saint-like lad on the camp-stool.

But it was only for a few feet. The indicator slacked up, fluttered, stopped dead. And then—without the husky tank boy to lift a finger—we heard the *rumph-h* and rumbling of the valve-seats as the sea-water was driven out of her ballast-tanks; and then up she started. Soon there she was—did it all by herself—atop of the water. And the face of the young fellow of the automatic devices was like the face of the devout missionary who has just put something over on the heathen.

Later, when you express the feeling of almost holy comfort which these little automatic safety devices give you, the manager—the same with the stopwatch and the notebook—says, "Puh! Look here," and sits down and details—drawing good working plans of them on a pad while he talks—three different ways by which a submarine crew can beat the game should any evil happen to the ordinary and regular means of getting to the surface.

She has a turn at porpoising then; that is from a moderate depth the diving-rudder man shoots her near enough to the surface for the captain to have a look through the periscope—a long-enough look to plot the enemy on a chart, but not long enough to give that enemy much of a chance to pick him up; and then under again. And then up for another peek; and quickly under again, the captain at the periscope taking each time a fresh bearing of the enemy, who is supposed to be at some distance and steaming at good speed. After two or three such quick sights, changing course after each sight, it will be time to discharge a torpedo or two at her. And—the layman may note it—with expert men at the periscope and diving-rudder, a porpoising sub can sight, discharge her torpedo, and dive—all within five seconds.

Steaming back to harbour after our trial run that day, we caught the first rip of the gale which the gummed-over moon and the low barometer had forecast the night before. It was too rough to tie her up to the supply-ship, so the sub was anchored—they carry anchors too—a short distance away, with three men left on her for an anchor watch, the idea being to take them off later for a hot meal. But after the rest of us were safe and warm and well fed aboard the mother ship, the increasing winds came bowling over the increasing seas, and the crew of the sub had to wait.

At intervals we could hear them emitting beseeching, doleful, disgusted moans and shrieks and howls from her air-whistle. But it was too rough for any little *choo-choo* boat to be battling around. It was 9.30 that night before they could safely be taken off. They were a moderately good-natured lot; but that was the blear-eyed trouble with making sub trial trips with bad weather coming on—a man never knew about his regular meals.

The supply-ship was quite a little institution herself. Approaching her from shore the night before, her lights beneath the dull moon and thin, drifting clouds had loomed up like a dancing-hall across the lonesome harbour waters. When we got aboard, we found her the relic of what had once been a fine block of a three-masted coaster; but moored forward and aft she was now, as if for all time, and no longer showing stout spars and weather-beaten canvas—nothing but two floors of white-painted boarding above her old bulwarks.

She was a boarding-place, a sort of club, for the crew and attendants, as well as a supply station for the submarines which in these New England waters were being tried out for one of the warring Powers. Voices and cigar-smoke as we stepped aboard, and more or less quiet breathing, with partly closed and open living and sleeping rooms, denoted that men were discussing, arguing, sleeping, and otherwise passing a normal evening. Looking farther, we saw that down in the insides of her—where formerly she stowed noble freights of coal or lumber or, sometimes, hay and ice—were now a boiler and engine room, and a good, big repair shop.

This night, while the gale came howling and the sea rolling and the solid rain sweeping against the sober old sides of our supply-ship—on this night, the finest kind to be sitting in a warm cabin, we sat and, while the smoke rolled high, aired our views of the real things in the world; and the most real thing in the world just then being a submarine, we got this:

"Danger? Of course, there's some danger. So is there danger in bank-fishing, in log-jamming down in Maine, in mining deep down, and in aeroplaning.

"You want to get a sub right. A sub is a ship modelled different from most ships, of course, and built stronger to stand pressure, but only a ship, after all, with special tanks in her. She's on top of the water and wants to go down. Good. She fills her tanks and down she goes. She's down and wants to come up. All right. She empties her tanks and up she comes. She's got to. She couldn't stay down with her tanks empty if she wanted to—not unless she blew a hole in her side, or left her hatches open.

"Of course if her tanks don't work right! But we showed you three different ways to-day how she can beat that game. And anyway, no matter what happens, unless you're cruising deep, it's only a few feet to the top. Not like a crazy aeroplane a thousand feet up in the air! Something happens in an aeroplane, and where are you? With a busted stay or bamboo strut and you a mile in the air, where are you? Volplane? Maybe. But if you didn't—down you'd come a-tumbling like a hoop out of the clouds. That's 90 per cent—yes, maybe 99 per cent—of the submarine game: See that everything is right mechanically with your sub, then get a competent crew and—well, you're ready."

That is for the submariner's point of view. As for the danger from a shore-goer's point of view: Ashore we make the mistake, perhaps, of thinking of a submarine as a heavy, logy body fighting always for her life beneath an unfriendly ocean; whereas she is a light-moving easily controlled creature cruising in a rather friendly element.

The ocean is always trying to lift her atop and not hold her under water. A submarine could be sent under with a positive buoyancy so small—that is, with so little more than enough in her tanks to sink her—that an ordinary man standing on the sea bottom could catch her as she came floating down and bounce her up and off merely by the strength of his arms. Consider a submarine under water as we would a toy balloon in the air, say. Weight that toy balloon so that it just falls to earth. Kick that toy balloon and what does it do? Doesn't it bounce along, and after a few feet fall easily down again, and up and on and down again?

Picture a strong wind driving that toy balloon along the street, and the balloon, as it bumps along, meeting an obstacle: Will the balloon smash itself against the obstacle, or what will it do? What that balloon does is pretty much what a submarine would do if, while running along full speed under water, she suddenly ran into shoal water. She would go bumping along on the bottom; and, meeting an obstacle, if not too high, she would be more likely to bounce over it than to smash herself against it.

But sometimes they do run into things and fetch up?

That is right, they do. Let our naval men tell of the old C plunger—the first class of sub in our navy—which hit an excursion steamer down the James River way one time. She was a wooden steamer about 150 feet long, and the C's bow went clear through the steamer's sides. The steamer's engineer was sitting by his levers, reading the sporting page of his favourite daily, when he heard a crash and found himself on the engine-room floor. Looking around, he saw a wedge of steel sticking through the side of his ship. He did not know what it was, but he could see right away it didn't have a friendly look; so he hopscotched across the engine-room floor and up a handy ladder to the deck, taking his assistant along in his wake. After rescuing the passengers it took three tugboats to pry sub and steamer apart.

Our C boat must have hit her a pretty good wallop, for as they fell apart the steamer sank. They ran the little old C up to the navy-yard to see how much she was damaged. Surely after that smash she must be shaken up—her bow torpedo-tubes at least must be out of alignment! But not a thing wrong anywhere; they didn't even have to put her in dry dock. Out and about her business she went next morning.

Later another of the same class came nosing up out of the depths, and bumped head on and into a breakwater down that same country—a solid stone wall of a breakwater. What did she do? She bounced off, and, after a look around, also went on about her business.

* * * * *

In the morning our sub up-anchored for her run across the open bay. On the conning-tower was rigged a little bridge of slim brass stanchions and thin wire-rope rail, with the canvas as high as a man's chin for protection; and away she went in a wind that was still blowing hard enough to drive home-bound Gloucester fishermen down to storm trysails and sea enough to jump an out-bound destroyer of a thousand tons under easy steam to her lower plates whenever she lifted forward.

There was not a soul standing around on the main deck of the destroyer as we passed her, nor on her high forward turtle-deck, which was being washed clean; and surely not much comfort being bounced around on transoms in that destroyer below, nor too much dryness on her flying bridge. And yet here was our little sub—full speed and all—heading straight into high-curling seas and making fine weather of it.

Plunging her bow under, and through she'd go; and when she did the seas would go swashing up atop of her make-believe deck and come rolling down her round-top plates and squishing through the hundreds of round holes in her deck sides. But steady? Up on her little bridge we did not half the time have to hold on to her little steel-rope rail lines to keep our balance. She kept on going, hooked-up all the way, seas and wind and all to hinder her, and finished her five-hour run without so much as wetting our coat fronts up on the conning-tower bridge. A great little sea boat—a submarine.

Now for the personnel of the crew. The crew of the sub described were not sailors. The captain was an old sea-goer—yes; and it would be a safe guess that the diving-rudder man had a seagoing experience; and one other perhaps; but the fellows who stood by the other things below came straight from the boat works. They had helped, most of them, to build her: which was one good reason for having them along on her trial trip.

And there are thousands of young fellows working around garages and in machine-shops and electric-light plants ashore who are the very men needed for submarines. There will always have to be a sailor or two in a submarine; or there should be, for a real sailor is always a handy man to have around—he knows things that nobody else knows.

And so, if hanging around there are any young fellows with a taste for adventure and a trend for naval warfare, these submarines look to be the thing. They are only little fellows now, and, as they stand to-day, limited as to range and power of offence, but stay by and grow up with them, and by and by be with them when they will be as big as the battleships and of a radius of action that will stretch from here to—well, as far as they like; drawing their energy from the sun above them, or the sea-tides about them, and not having to see enemy ships to be able to fight them—equipped with devices not now invented but which will serve to feel those other ships and, feeling them, to plot their direction and distance!

Imagine a fleet of those lads battling under water some day—allowing no surface craft to live—feeling each other out and plotting direction and distance as they feel, and then letting go broadsides of torpedoes ten or a hundred times as powerful as anything we now have; and at the same time the air full of war-planes battling above them.

Infants, sea babies, is what they are to-day. But wait till they grow up!

The Diary of a
U-Boat Commander

by Karl von Schenk

With an introduction and
explanatory notes by

Etienne

WE RAMMED A DESTROYER, PASSING THROUGH HER LIKE A KNIFE THROUGH CHEESE

...THEY ARE SO BLACK AND SWIFT I DON'T GO NEAR THEM

Introduction

"I would ask you a favour," said the German captain, as we sat in the cabin of a U-boat which had just been added to the long line of bedraggled captives which stretched themselves for a mile or more in Harwich Harbour, in November, 1918.

I made no reply; I had just granted him a favour by allowing him to leave the upper deck of the submarine, in order that he might await the motor launch in some sort of privacy; why should he ask for more?

Undeterred by my silence, he continued: "I have a great friend, Lieutenant-zu-See Von Schenk, who brought *U.122* over last week; he has lost a diary, quite private, he left it in error; can he have it?"

I deliberated, felt a certain pity, then remembered the *Belgian Prince* and other things, and so, looking the German in the face, I said:

"I can do nothing."

"Please."

I shook my head, then, to my astonishment, the German placed his head in his hands and wept, his massive frame (for he was a very big man) shook in irregular spasms; it was a most extraordinary spectacle.

It seemed to me absurd that a man who had suffered, without visible emotion, the monstrous humiliation of handing over his command intact, should break down over a trivial incident concerning a diary, and not even his own diary, and yet there was this man crying openly before me.

It rather impressed me, and I felt a curious shyness at being present, as if I had stumbled accidentally into some private recess of his mind. I closed the cabin door, for I heard the voices of my crew approaching.

He wept for some time, perhaps ten minutes, and I wished very much to know of what he was thinking, but I couldn't imagine how it would be possible to find out.

I think that my behaviour in connection with his friend's diary added the last necessary drop of water to the floods of emotion which he had striven, and striven successfully, to hold in check during the agony of handing over the boat, and now the dam had crumbled and broken away.

It struck me that, down in the brilliantly-lit, stuffy little cabin, the result of the war was epitomized. On the table were some instruments I had forbidden him to remove, but which my first lieutenant had discovered in the engineer officer's bag.

On the settee lay a cheap, imitation leather suit-case, containing his spare clothes and a few books. At the table sat Germany in defeat, weeping, but not the tears of repentance, rather the tears of bitter regret for humiliations undergone and ambitions unrealized.

We did not speak again, for I heard the launch come alongside, and, as she bumped against the U-boat, the noise echoed through the hull into the cabin, and aroused him from his sorrows. He wiped his eyes, and, with an attempt at his former hardiness, he followed me on deck and boarded the motor launch.

Next day I visited *U.122*, and these papers are presented to the public, with such additional remarks as seemed desirable; for some curious reason the author seems to have omitted nearly all dates. This may have been due to the fear that the book, if captured, would be of great value to the British Intelligence Department if the entries were dated. The papers are in the form of two volumes in black leather binding, with a long letter inside the cover of the second volume.

Internal evidence has permitted me to add the dates as regards the years. My thanks are due to K. for assistance in translation.

Etienne

The Diary of a U-Boat Commander

One volume of my war-journal completed, and I must confess it is dull reading.

I could not help smiling as I read my enthusiastic remarks at the outbreak of war, when we visualized battles by the week. What a contrast between our expectations and the actual facts.

Months of monotony, and I haven't even seen an Englishman yet.

Our battle cruisers have had a little amusement with the coast raids at Scarborough and elsewhere, but we battle-fleet fellows have seen nothing, and done nothing. So I have decided to volunteer for the U-boat service, and my name went in last week, though I am told it may be months before I am taken, as there are about 250 lieutenants already on the waiting list.

But sooner or later I suppose something will come of it.

I shall have no cause to complain of inactivity in that Service, if I get there.

* * * * *

I am off tonight for a six-days trip, two days of which are to be spent in the train, to the Verdun sector.

It has been a great piece of luck. The trip had been arranged by the Military and Naval Inter-communication Department; and two officers from this squadron were to go.

There were 130 candidates, so we drew lots; as usual I was lucky and drew one of the two chances.

It should be intensely interesting.

* * * * *

At ——

I arrived here last night after a slow and tiresome journey, which was somewhat alleviated by an excellent bottle of French wine which I purchased whilst in the Champagne district.

Long before we reached the vicinity of Verdun it was obvious to the most casual observer that we were heading for a centre of unusual activity.

Hospital trains travelling north-east and east were numerous, and twice our train, which was one of the ordinary military trains, was shunted on to a siding to allow troop trains to rumble past.

As we approached Verdun the noise of artillery, which I had heard distantly once or twice during the day, as the casual railway train approached the front, became more intense and grew from a low murmur into a steady noise of a kind of growling description, punctuated at irregular intervals by very deep booms as some especially heavy piece was discharged, or an ammunition dump went up.

The country here is very different from the mud flats of Flanders, as it is hilly and well wooded. The Meuse, in the course of centuries, has cut its way through the rampart of hills which surround Verdun, and we are attacking the place from three directions. On the north we are slowly forcing the French back on either river bank—a very costly proceeding, as each wing must advance an equal amount, or the one that advances is enfiladed from across the river.

We are also slowly creeping forward from the east and north-east in the direction of Douaumont.

I am attached to a 105-cm. battery, a young Major von Markel in command, a most charming fellow. I spent all today in the advanced observing position with a young subaltern called Grabel, also a nice young fellow. I was in position at 6 a.m., and, as apparently is common here, mist hides everything from view until the sun attains a certain strength. Our battery was supporting the attack on the north side of the river, though the battery itself was on the south side, and firing over a hill called L'Homme Mort.

Von Markel told me that the fighting here has not been previously equalled in the war, such is the intensity of the combat and the price each side is paying.

I could see for myself that this was so, and the whole atmosphere of the place is pregnant with the supreme importance of this struggle, which may well be the dying convulsions of decadent France.

His Imperial Majesty himself has arrived on the scene to witness the final triumph of our arms, and all agree that the end is imminent.

Once we get Verdun, it is the general opinion that this portion of the French front will break completely, carrying with it the adjacent sectors, and the French Armies in the Vosges and Argonne will be committed to a general retreat on converging lines.

But, favourable as this would be to us, it is generally considered here that the fall of Verdun will break the moral resistance of the French nation.

The feeling is, that infinitely more is involved than the capture of a French town, or even the destruction of a French Army; it is a question of stamina; it is the climax of the world war, the focal point of the colossal struggle between the Latin and the Teuton, and on the battlefields of Verdun the gods will decide the destinies of nations.

When I got to the forward observing position, which was situated among the ruins of a house, a most amazing noise made conversation difficult.

The orchestra was in full blast and something approaching 12,000 pieces of all sizes were in action on our side alone, this being the greatest artillery concentration yet effected during the war.

We were situated on one side of a valley which ran up at right angles to the river, whose actual course was hidden by mist, which also obscured the bottom of our valley. The front line was down in this little valley, and as I arrived we lifted our barrage on to the far hill-side to cover an attack which we were delivering at dawn.

Nothing could be seen of the conflict down below, but after half an hour we received orders to bring back our barrage again, and Grabel informed me that the attack had evidently failed. This afternoon I heard that it was indeed so, and that one division (the 58th), which had tried to work along the river bank and outflank the hill, had been caught by a concentration of six batteries of French 75's, which were situated across the river. The unfortunate 58th, forced back from the river-side, had heroically fought their way up the side of the hill, only to encounter our barrage, which, owing to the mist, we thought was well above and ahead of where they would be.

Under this fresh blow the 58th had retired to their trenches at the bottom of the small valley. As the day warmed up the mist disappeared, and, like a theatre curtain, the lifting of this veil revealed the whole scene in its terrible and yet mechanical splendour.

I say mechanical, for it all seemed unreal to me. I knew I should not see cavalry charges, guns in the open, and all the old-world panoply of war, but I was not prepared for this barren and shell-torn circle of hills, continually being freshly, and, to an uninformed observer, aimlessly lashed by shell fire.

Not a man in sight, though below us the ground was thickly strewn with corpses. Overhead a few aeroplanes circled round amidst balls of white shell bursts.

During the day the slow-circling aeroplanes (which were artillery observing machines) were galvanized into frightful activity by the sudden appearance of a fighting machine on one side or the other; this happened several times; it reminded me of a pike amongst young trout.

After lunch I saw a Spad shot down in flames, it was like Lucifer falling down from high heavens. The whole scene was enframed by a sluggish line of observation balloons.

Sometimes groups of these would hastily sink to earth, to rise again when the menace of the aeroplane had passed. These balloons seemed more like phlegmatic spectators at some athletic contest than actual participants in the events.

I wish my pen could convey to paper the varied impressions created within my mind in the course of the past day; but it cannot. I have the consolation that, though I think that I have considerable ability as a writer, yet abler pens than mine have abandoned in despair the task of describing a modern battle.

I can but reiterate that the dominant impression that remains is of the mechanical nature of this business of modern war, and yet such an impression is a false one, for as in the past so today, and so in the future, it is the human element which is, has been, and will be the foundation of all things.

Once only in the course of the day did I see men in any numbers, and that was when at 3 p.m. the French were detected massing for a counter-attack on the south side of the river. It was doomed to be still-born. As they left their trenches, distant pigmy figures in horizon blue, apparently plodding slowly across the ground, they were lashed by an intensive barrage and the little figures were obliterated in a series of spouting shell bursts.

Five minutes later the barrage ceased, the smoke drifted away and not a man was to be seen. Grabel told me that it had probably cost them 750 casualties. What an amazing and efficient destruction of living organism!

* * * * *

Another most interesting day, though of a different nature.

To-day was spent witnessing the arrangements for dealing with the wounded. I spent the morning at an advanced dressing station on the south bank of the river. It was in a cellar, beneath the ruins of a house, about 400 yards from the front line and under heavy shell-fire, as close at hand was the remains of what had been a wood, which was being used as a concentration point for reserves.

The cover afforded by this so-called wood was extremely slight, and the troops were concentrating for the innumerable attacks and counter-attacks which were taking place under shell fire. This caused the surgeon in charge of the cellar to describe the wood as our main supply station!

I entered the cellar at 8 a.m., taking advantage of a partial lull in the shelling, but a machine-gun bullet viciously flipped into a wooden beam at the entrance as I ducked to go in. I was not sorry to get underground. A sloping path brought me into the cellar, on one side of which sappers were digging away the earth to increase the accommodation.

The illumination consisted of candles set in bottles and some electric hand lamps. The centre of the cellar was occupied by two portable operating tables, rarely untenanted during the three hours I spent in this hell.

The atmosphere—for there was no ventilation—stank of sweat, blood, and chloroform.

By a powerful effort I countered my natural tendency to vomit, and looked around me. The sides of the cellar were lined with figures on stretchers. Some lay still and silent, others writhed and groaned. At intervals, one of the attendants would call the doctor's attention to one of the still forms. A hasty examination ensued, and the stretcher and its contents were removed. A few minutes later the stretcher—empty—returned. The surgeon explained to me that there was no room for corpses in the cellar; business, he genially remarked, was too brisk at the present crucial stage of the great battle.

The first feelings of revulsion having been mastered, I determined to make the most of my opportunities, as I have always felt that the naval officer is at a great disadvantage in war as compared with his military brother, in that he but rarely has a chance of accustoming himself to the unpleasant spectacle of torn flesh and bones.

This morning there was no lack of material, and many of the intestinal wounds were peculiarly revolting, so that at lunch-time, when another convenient lull in the torrent of shell fire enabled me to leave the cellar, I felt thoroughly hardened; in fact I had assisted in a humble degree at one or two operations.

I had lunch at the 11th Army Medical Headquarters Mess, and it was a sumptuous meal to which I did full justice.

After lunch, whilst waiting to be motored to a field hospital, I happened to see a battalion of Silesian troops about to go up to the front line.

It was rather curious feeling that one was looking at men, each in himself a unit of civilization, and yet many of whom were about to die in the interests thereof.

Their faces were an interesting study.

Some looked careless and debonair, and seemed to swing past with a touch of recklessness in their stride, others were grave and serious, and seemed almost to plod forward to the dictates of an inevitable fatalism.

The field hospital, where we met some very charming nurses, on one of whom I think I created a distinct impression, was not particularly interesting. It was clean, well-organized and radiated the efficiency inseparable from the German Army.

*****

Back at Wilhelmshaven—curse it!

Yesterday morning, when about to start on a tour of the ammunition supply arrangements, I received an urgent wire recalling me at once!

There was nothing for it but to obey.

I was lucky enough to get a passage as far as Mons in an albatross scout which was taking dispatches to that place.

From there I managed to bluff a motor car out of the town commandant—a most obliging fellow. This took me to Aachen where I got an express.

The reason for my recall was that Witneisser went sick and Arnheim being away, this has left only two in the operations ciphering department.

My arrival has made us three. It is pretty strenuous work and, being of a clerical nature, suits me little. The only consolation is that many of the messages are most interesting. I was looking through the back files the other day and amongst other interesting information I came across the wireless report from the boat that had sunk the *Lusitania*.

It has always been a mystery to me why we sank her, as I do not believe those things pay.

* * * * *

Arnheim has come back, so I have got out of the ciphering department, to my great delight.

I have received official information that my application for U-boats has been received. Meanwhile all there is to do is to sit at this —— hole and wait.

2ND JUNE, 1916

I have fought in the greatest sea battle of the ages; it has been a wonderful and terrible experience.

All the details of the battle will be history, but I feel that I must place on record my personal experiences.

We have not escaped without marks, and the good old *König* brought 67 dead and 125 wounded into port as the price of the victory off Skajerack, but of the English there are thousands who slept their last sleep in the wrecked hulls of the battle cruisers which will rust for eternal ages upon the Jutland banks.

Sad as our losses are—and the gallant *Lutzow* has sunk in sight of home—I am filled with pride.

We have met that great armada the British Fleet, we have struck them with a hammer blow and we have returned. I was asleep in my cabin when the news came that Hipper was coming south with the British battle cruisers on his beam. In five minutes we were at our action stations. We made contact with Hipper at 5.30 p.m.,[1] and Beatty turned north with his cruisers and fast battleships and we pursued.

Two of the great ships had been sunk by our battle cruisers, and we had hopes of destroying the remainder, when at 6.55 the mist on the northern horizon was pierced by the formidable line of the British Battle Fleet.

Jellicoe had arrived!

Three battle cruisers became involved between the lines, and in an instant one was blown up, and another crawled west in a sinking condition. Sudden and terrible are events in a modern sea-battle.

Confronted with the concentrated force of Britain's Battle Fleet we turned to east, and for twenty minutes our High Seas Fleet sustained the unequal contest.

It was during this period that we were hit seventeen times by heavy shell, though, in my position in the after torpedo control tower, I only realized one hit had taken place, which was when a shell plunged into the after turret and, blowing the roof off, killed every member of the turret's crew.

From my position, when the smoke and dust had blown away, I looked down into a mass of twisted machinery, amongst which I seemed to detect the charred remains of bodies.

At about 7.40 we turned, under cover of our smoke screen, and steered south-west.

Our position was not satisfactory, as the last information of the enemy reported them as turning to the southward; consequently they were between us and Heligoland.

At 11 p.m. we received a signal for divisions of battle fleets to steer independently for the Horn Reef swept channel.

Ten minutes later we underwent the first of five destroyer attacks.

The British destroyers, searching wide in the night, had located us, and with desperate gallantry pressed home the attack again and again. So close did they come that about 1.30 a.m. we rammed one, passing through her like a knife through a cheese.

It was a wonderful spectacle to see those sinister craft, rushing madly to their destruction down the bright beam of our powerful

---

1: This is 4.30 G.M.T.

searchlights. It was an avenue of death for them, but to the credit of their Service it must stand that throughout the long nightmare they did not hesitate.

The surrounding darkness seemed to vomit forth flotilla after flotilla of these cavalry of the sea.

And they struck us once, a torpedo right forward, which will keep us in dock for a month, but did no vital injury.

When morning dawned, misty and soft, as is its way in June in the Bight, we were to the eastward of the British, and so we came honourably home to Wilhelmshaven, feeling that the young Navy had laid worthy foundations for its tradition to grow upon.

We are to report at Kiel, and shall be six weeks upon the job.

Frankfurt

Back on seventeen days' leave, and everyone here very anxious to hear details of the battle of Skajerack.

It is very pleasant to have something to talk to the women about. Usually the gallant field greys hold the drawing-room floor, with their startling tales from the Western Front, of how they nearly took Verdun, and would have if the British hadn't insisted on being slaughtered on the Somme.

It is quite impossible in many ways to tell that there is a war on as far as social life in this place is concerned.

There is a shortage of good coffee and that is about all.

* * * * *

Arrived back on board last night.

They have made a fine job of us, and we go through the canal to the Schillig Roads early next week.

We are to do three weeks' gunnery practices from there, to train the new drafts.

1916 (about August)

At last! Thank Heavens, my application has been granted. Schmitt (the Secretary) told me this morning that a letter has come from the Admiralty to say that I am to present myself for medical examination at the board at Wilhelmshaven tomorrow.

What joy! to strike a blow at last, finished for ever the cursed monotony of inactivity of this High Seas Fleet life. But the U-boat war! Ah! that goes well. We shall bring those stubborn, blood-sucking islanders to their knees by striking at them through their bellies.

When I think of London and no food, and Glasgow and no food, then who can say what will happen? Revolt! rebellion in England, and our brave field greys on the west will smash them to atoms in the spring of 1917, and I, Karl Schenk, will have helped directly in this! Great thought—but calm! I am not there yet, there is still this confounded medical board. I almost wish I had not drunk so much last night, not that it makes any difference, but still one must run no risks, for I hear that the medical is terribly strict for the U-boat service. Only the cream is skimmed! Well, tomorrow we shall see.

* * * * *

Passed! and with flying colours; it seemed absurdly easy and only took ten minutes, but then my physique is magnificent, thanks to the physical training I have always done. I am now due to get three weeks' leave, and then to Zeebrugge.

I have wired to the little mother at Frankfurt.

* * * * *

At Zeebrugge, or rather Bruges

I spent three weeks at home, all the family are pleased except mother; she has a woman's dread of danger; it is a pleasing characteristic in peace time, but a cloy on pleasure in days of war. To her, with the narrowness of a female's intellect, I really believe I am of more importance than the Fatherland—how absurd. Whilst at Frankfurt I saw a good deal of Rosa; she seems better looking each time I meet her; doubtless she is still developing to full womanhood. Moritz was home from Flanders. He had ten days' leave from Ypres, and, though I have a dislike for him, he certainly was interesting, though why the English cling to those wretched ruins is more than I can understand.

I felt instinctively that in a sense Moritz and I were rivals where Rosa was concerned, though I have never considered her in that light—as yet. One day, perhaps? These women are much the same everywhere, and I could see that having entered the U-boat service made a difference with Rosa, though her logic should have told her that I was no different. But is that right? After all, it is something to have joined this service; the Guards themselves have no better cachet, and it is certainly cheaper.

Here we live in billets and in a commandeered hotel. The life ashore is pleasant enough; the damned Belgians are sometimes sulky, but they know who is master. Bissing (a splendid chap) sees to that.

As a matter of fact we have benefited them by our occupation, the shops do a roaring trade at preposterous prices, and shamefully enough the German shopkeepers are most guilty. These pot-bellied merchants don't seem to realize that they exist owing to our exertions.

I was much struck with the beautiful orderliness of the small gardens which we have laid out since 1914, and, in fact, wherever one looks there is evidence of the genius of the German race for thorough organization. Yet these Belgians don't seem to appreciate it. I can't understand it.

I find here that social life is very much gayer than at that mad town of Wilhelmshaven. At the High Seas Fleet bases there was the strictness and austerity that some people seem to consider necessary to show that we are at war, though Heaven knows there was precious little war in the High Seas Fleet; perhaps that was why the "blood and iron" regime was in full order ashore. Here, in Bruges, at any rate as far as the submarine officers are concerned, the matter is far different. When the boats are in, one seems to do as one likes, with a perfunctory visit to the ship in the course of the day.

Witnitz (the Commodore) favours complete relaxation when in from a trip. In the evenings there are parties, for which there are always ladies, and I find it is necessary to have a "smoking."[1] I went to the best tailor to buy one, and found that I must have one made at the damnable price of 140 marks; the fitter, an oily Jew, had the incredible impertinence to assure me it would be cut on London lines!

I nearly felled him to the ground; can one never get away from England and things English? I'll see his account waits a bit before I settle it.

There are several fellows I know here. Karl Müller, who was 3rd watch-keeper in the *Yorck*, and Adolf Hilfsbaumer, who was captain

---

1: A dinner jacket.

of *G.176*, are the two I know best. They are both doing a few trips as second in commands of the later U.C. boats, which are mine-laying off the English coasts. This is a most dangerous operation, and nearly all the U.C. boats are commanded by reserve officers, of whom there are a good many in the Mess.

Excellent fellows, no doubt, but somewhat uncouth and lacking the finer points of breeding; as far as I can see in the short time I have been here they keep themselves to themselves a good deal. I certainly don't wish to mix with them. Unfortunately, it appears that I am almost bound to be appointed as second in command of one of the U.C. boats, for at least one trip before I go to the periscope school and train for a command of my own. The idea of being bottled up in an elongated cigar and under the command of one of those nautical plough-boys is repellent. However, the Von Schenks have never been too proud to obey in order to learn how to command.

* * * * *

I have been appointed second in command to *U.C.47*. Her captain is one Max Alten by name. Beyond the fact that I saw him drunk one night in the Mess I know nothing of him.

I reported to him and he seems rather in awe of me. His fears are groundless.

I shall make it as easy as possible for him, for it must be as awkward for him as it is unpleasant for me.

To celebrate my proper entry into the U-boat service, I gave a dinner party last night in a private room at "Le Coq d'Or." I asked Karl and Adolf, and told them to bring three girls. My opposite number was a lovely girl called Zoe something or other. I wore my "smoking" for the first time; it is certainly a becoming costume.

We drank a good deal of champagne and had a very pleasant little debauch; the girls got very merry, and I kissed Zoe once. She was not very angry. I think she is thoroughly charming, and I have accepted an invitation to take tea at her flat. She is either the wife or the *chère amie* of a colonel in the Brandenburgers, I could not make out which. Luckily the gallant "Cockchafer" is at the moment on the La Bassée sector, where I was interested to observe that heavy fighting has broken out today. I must console the fair Zoe!

Both Karl and Adolf got rather drunk, Adolf hopelessly so, but I, as usual, was hardly affected. I have a head of iron, provided the liquor is good, and *I* saw to that point.

* * * * *

We were sailing, or rather going down the canal to Zeebrugge on Friday, but the starting resistance of the port main motor burnt out and we were delayed till Sunday, as they will fit a new one.

I must confess the organization for repair work here is admirable, as very little is done by the crews in the U-boats, all work being carried out by the permanent staff, who are quartered at Bruges docks. Taking advantage of the delay I called on Zoe Stein, as I find she is named.

It appears she is *not* married to Colonel Stein. She told me he was fat and ugly, and laughed a good deal about him. She showed me his photograph, and certainly he is no beauty. However, he must be a man of means, as he has given her a charming flat, beautifully decorated with water-colours which the Colonel salved from the French château in the early days—these army fellows had all the chances.

I bade an affectionate farewell to Zoe, and I trust Stein will be still busily engaged at La Bassée when I return in a fortnight's time! I am greatly obliged to Karl for the introduction, and told him so; he himself is running after a little grass widow whose husband has been missing for some months. I think Karl finds it an expensive game; luckily Zoe seems well supplied with money—the essential ingredient in a joyous life. On Friday night we had an air-raid—a frequent event here, but my first experience in this line. Unpleasant, but a fine spectacle, considerable damage done near the docks and an unexploded bomb fell in a street near our headquarters.

Two machines (British) brought down in flames. I saw the green balls[1] for the first time. A most fascinating sight to see them floating up in waving chains into the vault of heaven; they reminded me of making daisy chains as a child.

1: Known as "Flying-onions."

We are alongside the mole in one of the new submarine shelters that has been built.

The boat is under a concrete roof over three feet thick, which would defy the heaviest bomb.

We have much improved the port since our arrival. The port, so-called, is purely artificial, and actually consists of a long mole with a gentle curve in it, which reaches out to seaward and protects the mouth of the canal. The tides are very strong up and down the coast, and constant dredging is carried out to keep 20 feet of water over the sill at the lock gates.

On arrival last night we went straight into No. 11 shelter, as an air-raid was expected, but nothing happened, so I went up to the "Flandre," which seems to be the best hotel here, full of submarine people, and I heard many interesting stories. There seems no doubt this U-boat war is dangerous work; I find the U.C. boats are beginning to be called the Suicide Club, after the famous English story of that name, which, curiously enough, I saw on the kinematograph at Frankfurt last leave. We Germans are extraordinarily broad-minded; I doubt if the works of German authors are seen on the screens in England or France.

The news from the West is good, the English are hurling themselves to destruction against our steel front. We are now to load up with mines. I must stop writing to superintend this work.

At sea. Near the South Dogger Light

We loaded up the ten mines we carry in an hour and five minutes. They were lifted from a railway truck by a big crane and delicately lowered into the mine tubes, of which we have five in the bows.

The tubes extend from the upper deck of the ship to her keel, and slope aft to facilitate release. Having completed with fuel at Bruges, we took in a store of provisions and Alten went up to the Commodore's office to get our sailing orders.

We sailed at 6 p.m. and at last I felt I was off. To-day, the 22nd, we are just north of the South Dogger, steering north-westerly at 9½ knots.

The sea is quite calm and everything is very pleasant. Our mission is to lay a small minefield off Newcastle in the East Coast war channel. I have, of course, never been to sea for any length of time in a U-boat, and it is all very novel.

I find the roar of the Diesel engine very relentless, and last night slept badly in a wretched bunk, which was a poor substitute for my lovely quarters in the barracks at Wilhelmshaven. One thing I appreciate, and that is the food; it is really excellent: fresh milk, fresh butter, white bread and many other luxuries.

I have spent most of the day picking up things about the boat. Her general arrangement is as follows:

Starting in the bows, mine tubes occupy the centre of the boat, leaving two narrow passages, one each side. In the port passage is the wireless cabinet and signal flag lockers, with store rooms underneath. In the starboard passage are one or two small pumps and the kitchen.

The next compartment contains four bunks, two each side, these are occupied by Alten, myself, the engineer, and the Navigating Warrant Officer. Proceeding further aft one enters the control room, in which one periscope is situated, and the necessary valves and pumps for diving the boat. The next compartment is the crew space; ten of the company exist here.

Overhead on each side is the gear for releasing the torpedoes from the external torpedo tubes, of which we carry one each side. I think we borrowed this idea from the Russians. Then comes the engine-room, an inferno of rattling noises, but excellent engines, I believe. At the after end of the engine-room are the two main switchboards, of whose manner of working I am at present in some ignorance.

The two main sets of electric motors are underneath the boards, in the stern, where we have a third torpedo tube.

* * * * *

I had hardly written the above words when a message came that the captain would like me to come to the bridge.

I went up in a leisurely fashion, through the conning tower, which is over the control room, and reported myself. He indicated a low-lying patch of smoke on the horizon far away on the starboard bow. I was obliged to confess that it conveyed nothing to me, when he aroused my intense interest by stating that it was, without doubt, being emitted from a British submarine, who are known to frequent these waters. He was proceeding away from us, and was, even then, six or seven miles away, so an attack was out of the question. The engineer, who had joined us, drew my attention to the thin wisp of almost invisible blue-grey smoke from our own stern. The contrast was certainly striking!

Over dinner I gave it as my opinion that the British boats were pretty useless. Alten would not agree, and stated that, though in certain technical aspects they were in a position of inferiority, yet in personnel and skill in attacking they were fully our equals. He seemed to hold them in considerable respect, and he remarked that, when making a passage, he was more anxious on their account than in any other way. He informed me that, on the last passage he made, he was attacked by a British boat which he never saw, the only indication he received being a torpedo which jumped out of the water almost over his tail. Luckily it was very rough at the time, which made the torpedo run erratically, otherwise they would undoubtedly have been hit.

What appeared to astonish him was the fact that the British boat had been able to make an attack in such weather. We are now charging on one engine, 500 amperes on each half-battery.

* * * * *

We are due back at Zeebrugge at 10 p.m. tonight. We should have been in at dawn today, but we received a wireless from the senior officer, Zeebrugge, to say that mine-laying was suspected, and we were to wait till the "Q.R." channel, from the Blankenberg buoy, had been swept. We lay in the bottom for eight hours, a few miles from the western end of the channel. Our trip was quite successful, but not without certain excitements.

On the night of the 23rd we passed fairly close to a fishing fleet on the Dogger Bank, and saw the lights of several steamers in the distance. As our first business was to lay our mines in the appointed place, we did not worry them.

We burnt usual navigation lights, or rather side lights which appear to be usual, except that, by a little fitting which Alten has made himself, the arcs of bearing on which the lights show can be changed at will. His idea is that, should we appear to be approaching a steamer which he wishes to avoid, in many cases, by shining a little more or less red and green light, we can make her think that we are a steamer on such a course that it is her duty by the rules of the road to keep clear of us.

He tells me it has worked on several occasions, and he has also found it useful to have two small auxiliary side lights fitted which are the wrong colours for the sides they are on. It is, of course, only neutral shipping which carry lights nowadays, though Alten says that many British ships are still incredibly careless in the matter of lights.

However, to resume my account of what happened. We reached our position at dawn or slightly after, the weather was beautifully calm and the sea like glass. As we were only three miles from the English coast, and close to the mouth of the Tyne, we were extraordinarily lucky to have nothing in sight, if one excepts a long smudge of smoke which trailed across the horizon to the southward.

The land itself was obscured by early morning banks of mist, yet everything was so still that we actually faintly heard the whistle of a train. I could hardly restrain from suggesting to Alten that we should elevate the 10-cm. gun to fifteen degrees and fire a few rounds on to "proud Albion's virgin shores," but I did not do so as I felt fairly certain that he would not approve, and I do not wish to lay myself open to rebuffs from him after his behaviour concerning the smoking incident. I boil with rage at the thought, but again I digress.

The fact that the land was obscured was favourable from the point of view that we were not worried by coast watchers, but unfavourable from the standpoint that we were unable to take bearings of anything and so ascertain our exact position.

The importance of this point in submarine mine-laying is obvious, for, owing to our small cargo of eggs, it is quite possible that we may be sent here again, to lay an adjacent field, in which case it is highly desirable to know the exact position of one's previous effort.

We were somewhat assisted in our efforts to locate ourselves by the fact that a seven-fathom patch existed exactly where we had to lay. We picked up the edge of this bank with our sounding machine, and steering north half a mile, laid our mines in latitude—No! on second thoughts I will omit the precise position, for, though I shall take every precaution, there is no saying that through some misfortune this Journal might not get into the wrong hands.

STEERING NORTH-WESTERLY...;
TO LAY A SMALL MINEFIELD OFF NEWCASTLE

HE HAD SUDDENLY SEEN THE BOW WAVES OF A DESTROYER
APPROACHING AT FULL SPEED TO RAM.

I am very glad I decided to keep these notes, as I shall take much pleasure in reading them when Victory crowns our efforts and the joys of a peaceful life return.

I found it a delightful sensation being so close to the enemy coast, in his territorial waters, in fact. For the first time since the Skajerack battle I experienced the personal joys of war, the sensation of intimate and successful contact with the enemy, and the most hated enemy at that.

We had hardly finished laying our eggs when a droning noise was heard. With marvellous celerity we dived, that damned fellow Alten, who, under these circumstances leaves the bridge last, treading on my fingers as he followed me down the conning tower ladder.

The engineer endeavoured to sympathize with me, and made some idiotic remark about my being quicker when I had had more practice. I bit his head off. I can't stand this hail-fellow-well-met attitude in these U.C. boats, from any lout dressed in an officer's uniform. They wouldn't be holding commissions if it wasn't for the war, and they should remember that fact. I suppose they think I'm stand-offish. Well, if they had my family tree behind them they would understand.

We dived to sixty feet, and then came up to twenty. Alten looked through the periscope, and then invited me to look. Curiosity impelled me to accept this favour and, putting the focussing lever to "skyscrape" I swept round the sky.

At last I saw him; he was a small gas-bag of diminutive size, beneath which was suspended a little car, the most ridiculous little travesty of an airship I have ever seen. He was nosing along at about 800 feet and making about 40 knots.

Suddenly he must have seen the wake of our periscope, for he turned towards us. Simultaneously Alten, from the conning tower (I was using the other periscope in the control room), ordered the boat to sixty feet, and put the helm hard over.

We had turned sixteen points,[1] and in about two minutes heard a series of reports right astern of us. It was evident that our ruse had succeeded and that he had overshot the mark.

Inside the boat one felt a slight jar as each bomb went off.

1: 180°

We gradually came round to our proper course, and cruised all day submerged at dead slow speed. Every time we lifted our periscope he was still hanging about sufficiently close to make it foolish for us to come to the surface.

Towards noon a group of trawlers, doubtless summoned by wireless, appeared, and proceeded to wander about. These seemed to concern Alten far more than the airship, and he informed me that from their, to me, aimless movements he deduced they were hunting for us by hydroplanes. Occasionally we lay on the bottom in nineteen fathoms.

By 4 p.m. the atmosphere was becoming rather unpleasant and hot, and gradually we took off more clothes. Curiously enough, I longed for a smoke, but wild horses would not have made me ask Alten for permission.

At 8 p.m. it was sufficiently dark to enable us to rise, which gave me great pleasure, though the first rush of fresh air down the hatch made me vomit after hours of breathing the vitiated muck. On coming to the surface we saw nothing in sight, but a breeze had sprung up which caused spray to break over the bridge as we chugged along at 9 knots.

Everyone was in high spirits, as always on the return journey, when the mind turns to the Fatherland and all it holds.

My mind turns to Zoe. I confess it to myself frankly. I hardly realized to what extent this woman had begun to influence me until we received the wireless signal ordering us to delay entering for twelve hours. The receipt of this news, trivial though the delay has been, threw a mantle of gloom over the crew. I participated in the depression and, upon thought, rather wondered that this should be so. Self-analysis on the lines laid down by Schessmanweil[1] revealed to me that the basis of my annoyance is the fact that my next meeting with Zoe is deferred! I feel instinctively that I shall have trouble here, and that I had better haul off a lee shore whilst there is manoeuvring room, and yet—and yet I secretly rejoice that every revolution of the propeller, every clank and rattle of the Diesels brings us closer together.

Alten has just come down from the bridge, and we chatted for

1: Apparently some German author, of obscure origin, as I cannot find him in any book of reference.

some moments; it is evident that he wishes to apologize for his rudeness over the smoking incident.

I was in error, I admit it frankly; at the same time I did not know that the battery was on charge, and to dash a match from my hand! I could have shot him where he stood. However, I am not vindictive, and as far as I am concerned the incident is ended.

One thing I find trying in this small boat, and that is that I can find no space in which to do half my Müller exercises, the leg-and-arm-swinging ones. I must see whether I can't invent a set of U-boat exercises!

Good! in two hours we reach the Mole-end light buoy.

* * * * *

Submarine Mess, Bruges

It is midnight, and as I write in my room at the top of the house the low rumble of the guns from the south-west vibrates faintly through the open window, for it is extraordinarily warm for the time of year, and I have flung back the curtains and risked the light shining.

We spent the night at Zeebrugge and came up to the docks here next day. We shall probably be in for a week, and I am on four days' "extended absence from the boat," which practically means that I can go where I like in the neighbourhood provided I am handy to a telephone.

After a short inward struggle I rang Zoe up on the telephone; fortunately I did not call first.

A man's voice answered, and for a moment I was dumbfounded. I guessed at once it was the Colonel, and I had counted so confidently on his being still away at the front.

For an instant I felt speechless, an impulse came to me to ring off without further ado, but I restrained myself, and then a fine idea came into my head.

"Who is that?" I said.

"Colonel Stein!" replied the voice, and my fears were confirmed, but my plan of campaign held good.

"I am speaking," I continued, "on behalf of Lieutenant Von Schenk——"

"Ah, yes!" growled the voice, and for an instant a panic seized me, but I resumed:

"He met Madame Stein at dinner some days ago, and she kindly asked him to call; he has asked me to ring up and inquire when it would be convenient, as he would like to meet you, sir, as well. He has been unable to ring up himself, as he was sent away from Bruges on duty early this morning."

I smiled to myself at this little lie and listened.

"Your friend had better call tomorrow then, for I leave tomorrow evening for the Somme front; will you tell him?"

I replied that I would, and left the telephone well satisfied, but cursing the fates that made it advisable to keep clear of No. 10, Kafelle Strasse for thirty-six hours. Needless to say next day I rang up again in order to tell the Colonel that Lieutenant Schenk had apparently been detained, as he was not yet back in Bruges, and how I felt sure that he would be sorry at missing the Colonel, etc., etc., but all this camouflage was unnecessary, as she herself came to the 'phone. I could have kissed the instrument when I told her of my stratagem and heard her silvery laughter in my ear.

"It is arranged that tomorrow, starting at 10.30, we motor for the day to the Forest of Meten, taking our lunch and tea with us—pray Heaven the weather holds."

To-night in the Mess it is generally considered that *U.B. 40* has been lost; she is ten days overdue and was operating off Havre, she has made no signal for a fortnight. Such is the price of victory and the cost of war—death, perhaps, in some terrible form, but bah! away with such thoughts, tomorrow there is love and life and Zoe!

* * * * *

Once more it is night, still the guns rumble on the same old dismal tones, and as it is raining now it must be getting bad up at the front. Except for the rain it might have been last night, but much has happened to me in the meanwhile.

To-day in the forest by Ruysslede I found that I loved Zoe, loved her as I have never yet loved woman, loved her with my soul and all that is me. The day was gloriously fine when we started, and an hour's run took us to the forest. We left the car at an inn and wandered down one of the glades.

I carried the basket and we strolled on and on until we found a suitable place deep in the heart of the forest.

I have the sailor's love for woods, for their depths, their shadows, their mysteries, which are so vivid a contrast to the monotony of the sea, with the everlasting circle of the horizon and the half-bowl of the heavens above.

In the forest today, though the leaves had turned to gold and red and brown, the beeches were still well covered, and overhead we were tented with a russet canopy.

I say, at last we found a spot, or rather Zoe, who, with girlish pleasure in the adventure, had run ahead, called to me, and as I write I seem to hear the echoes of "Karl! Karl!" which rang through the wood. When I came up to her she proudly pointed to the place she had found.

It was ideal. An outcrop of rock formed a miniature Matterhorn in the forest, and beneath its shelter with the old trees as silent witnesses we sat and joked and laughed, and made twenty attempts to light a fire.

After lunch, a little incident happened which had an enormous effect on me; Zoe asked me whether I would mind if she smoked.

How many women in these days would think of doing that? And yet, had she but known it, I am still sufficiently old-fashioned to appreciate the implied respect for any possible prejudices which was contained in her request.

After lunch, I asked her a question to which I dreaded the answer.

I asked her whether, now that the old Colonel had gone to the Somme, whether that meant that she would be leaving Bruges.

She laughed and teasingly said: *"Quien sabe, señor,"* but seeing my real anxiety on this point, she assured me that she was not leaving for the present. The Colonel, she said, had a strange belief that once a man had served on the Flanders Front, and especially on the Ypres salient, he always came back to die there.

It appears that the Colonel has done fourteen months' service on the salient alone, and is firmly convinced he will end his career on that great burial ground. As we were talking about the Colonel I longed to ask her how she had met him, and perhaps find out why she lives with him, for I cannot believe she loves him, but I did not dare.

Strangely enough I found that a curious shyness had taken hold of me with regard to Zoe.

I said to myself, "Fool! you are alone with her, you long to kiss her; you have kissed her, first at the dinner-party, secondly when you said goodbye at her flat," and yet today it was different.

Then I was kissing a pretty woman, I was on the eve of a dangerous life, and I was simply extracting the animal pleasures whilst I lived.

To-day it was a case of Zoe, the personality I loved; I still longed to kiss her, but I wanted to have the unquestioned right to kiss her, as much as I wanted the kisses.

I wanted to have her for my own, away from the contaminating ownership of the old Colonel, and I determined to get her.

I think she noticed the changed attitude on my part, and perhaps she felt herself that a subtle change in our relationship had taken place, and whilst I meditated on these things she fell into a doze at my side.

I was sitting slightly above her, smoking to keep the midges away, and as I looked down on her childish figure a great tenderness for her filled my mind. She is very beautiful and to me desirable above all women; I can see her as she lay there trustfully at my feet. I will describe her, and then, when I get her photograph, I will read this when I am far away on a trip.

She is of average height, for I am just over six feet and she reaches to just above my shoulder. Her hair is gloriously thick and of a deep black colour, and lies low on her forehead. Her complexion is of the purest whiteness beyond compare, which but accentuates the red warmth of the lips which encircle her little mouth. Her figure is slight and her ankles are my delight, but her crowning glories, which I have purposely left till last, are her eyes.

I feel I could lose my soul; I have lost it, if I have one, in the violet depths of those eyes, which were veiled as she slept by the long black eyelashes which curled up delicately as they rested on her cheeks. I have re-read this description, and it is oh, so unsatisfying; would I had the pen of a Goethe or a Shakespeare, yet for want of more skill the description shall stand.

How I long for her to be mine, and yet, unfortunate that I am, I cannot for certain declare that she loves me.

A thousand doubts arise. I torment myself with recollections of her behaviour at the dinner-party, when within two hours of our first meeting she gave me her lips.

Yet did I not first roughly kiss her as we danced?

I find consolation in the fact that, though she has said nothing, yet her conduct today was different. She was so quiet after tea as we wandered back through the forests with the setting sun striking golden beams aslant the tree trunks.

Before we left I sang to her Tchaikovsky's beautiful song, "To the Forest," and I think she was pleased, for I may say with justice that my voice is of high quality for an amateur, and the song goes well without an accompaniment, whilst the atmosphere and surroundings were ideal.

There was only one jarring note in a perfect day; when we returned to the car the chauffeur permitted himself a sardonic grin. Zoe unfortunately saw it and blushed scarlet.

I could have struck him on his impudent mouth, but for her sake I judged it advisable to notice nothing.

I feel I could go on writing about her all night, but it is nearly 2 a.m. I must get some sleep.

The guns rumble steadily in the south-west, and the sky is lit by their flashes; may the fighting on the Somme be bloody these coming days.

Probably about ten days later

We leave tonight, having had a longer spell than usual. I am in a distracted state of mind. Since our glorious day in the forest I have seen her nearly every afternoon, though twice that swine Alten has kept me in the boat in connection with some replacements of the battery.

I have found out that, like me, she is intensely musical. She plays beautifully on the piano, and we had long hours together playing Chopin and Beethoven; we also played some of Mussorgsky's duets, but I love her best when she plays Chopin, the composer pre-eminent of love and passion.

She has masses of music, as the Colonel gives her what she likes. We also played a lot of Debussy. At first I demurred at playing a living French composer's works, but she pouted and looked so adorable that all my scruples vanished in an instant, so we closed all the doors and she played it for hours very softly whilst I forgot the war and all its horrors and remembered only that I was with the well-beloved girl.

The Colonel writes from Thiepval, where the British are pouring out their blood like water. He writes very interesting letters, and has had many narrow escapes, but unfortunately he seems to bear a charmed life. His letters are full of details, and I wonder he gets them past the Field Censorship, but I suppose he censors his own.

She laughs at them and calls them her Colonel's dispatches; she says he is so accustomed to writing official reports that the poor old man can't write an ordinary letter.

I told her that I thought the way he mentioned regiments and dispositions rather indiscreet, and she agrees, but she says he has asked her to keep them, with a view to forming a collection of letters written from the front whilst the incidents he describes are vivid in his mind. I suppose the old ass knows his own business, and one day the collection may be completed by a telegram "Regretting to announce, etc. etc." The sooner the better.

So the days passed pleasantly enough, and never by a gesture or word of mouth did she show that I was more to her than any other pleasant young man.

I kissed her when I arrived, I kissed her when I left, each day was the same. She would put her arms round my neck and look long and deeply into my eyes, then she would gently kiss my lips. Not an atom of emotion! not a spark from the fires which I feel must be raging beneath that diabolically[1] extraordinary[1] amazingly calm exterior.

On ordinary subjects she would chatter vivaciously enough and she can talk in a fascinating manner on every subject I care to bring up, but as soon as I drew the conversation round to a personal line she gradually became more silent and a far-away and distant look came into those wonderful eyes.

I have found out nothing about her beyond the fact that she has travelled all over Europe. I don't even know how old she is, but I should guess twenty-six.

I tried to find out a few details by means of discreet remarks at the Club and elsewhere.

She simply arrived here about a year ago—as a singer, and met the Colonel—beyond that, all is mystery. Everything about her attracts me powerfully, and this mystery adds subtleties to her charms.

1: These words are crossed out.

This afternoon I went to say goodbye; I told her we were leaving "shortly," and she gently reproved me for disobeying the order which forbids discussion of movements, but I could see she was not greatly displeased. After tea she played to me, music of the modern Russian school—Arensky, Sibelius and Pilsuki; a storm was brewing and we both felt sad.

She played for an hour or so, and then came and sat by me on a low divan by the fire. We were silent for a long while in the gathering gloom, whilst a thousand thoughts chased each other swiftly through my brain, as I endeavoured to summon up courage to say what I had determined I must say before I left her, perhaps for ever.

At last, when only her profile was visible against the glow of the logs, I spoke.

I told her quietly, calmly and almost dispassionately that I had grown to love her and that to me she was life itself. I told her that I had tried not to speak until I could endure no longer.

She sat very still as I spoke, and when I had finished there was a long silence and I gently stretched out my hand and stroked her lovely black hair. At last she rose and with averted face walked across the room, and stood looking at the storm through the big bow windows. I watched her, but did not dare follow.

At length she returned to me, and I saw what I had instinctively known the whole time—that she had been crying. I could not think why.

She put her arms round my neck, kissed me on the forehead and murmured, "Poor Karl."

I felt crushed; I dared not move for fear of breaking the magic of the moment, yet I longed to know more; I felt overwhelmed by some colossal mystery that seemed to be enveloping me in its folds. Why did she pity me? Why did she weep? Why didn't she answer my avowal? Why didn't she tell me something? Such were some of the problems that perplexed me.

It was thus when the clock chimed seven. I told her that my leave was up at seven o'clock, and that at 7.15 I had to be back on board the boat. She remembered this, and in an instant the past quarter of an hour might never have existed. She was all agitation and nervousness lest I should be late on board—though at the moment I would have cheerfully missed the boat to hear her say she loved me.

I tried to protest, but in vain. With feminine quickness she utilized the incident to avoid a situation she evidently found full of difficulty, and at 7.10, with the memory of a light kiss on my lips and her God-speed in my ears I was in a taxi driving to the docks in a blinding rain-storm—and we sail tonight.

For five, six, seven, perhaps ten days at the least, and at the most for ever, I am doomed to be away from her and without news of her. And I don't even know whether she loves me!

I think I can say she cares for me up to a certain point, but I want more.

Oh Zoe! of the violet eyes,
And hair of blackest night
Thy lips are brightest crimson,
Thy skin is dazzling white.

Oh! lay your head upon my breast,
And lift your lips to mine;
Then murmur in soft breathings,
Drink deep from what is thine.

Then let the war rage onward,
Let kingdoms rise and fall;
To each shall be the other,
Their life, their hope, their all.[1]

AT SEA

We are bound for the same old spot as last time.

Alten must have been drinking like a fish lately; his breath smells like a distillery; he is apparently partial to schnapps, which he gets easily in Bruges.

I can't help admiring the man, as he is a rigid teetotaller at sea, though he must find the strain well nigh intolerable, judging from the condition he was in when he came on board last night. He was really totally unfit to take charge of the boat, and I virtually took her down the canal, though with sottish obstinacy he insisted on remaining on the bridge.

1: I am indebted to Commander C. C. for the above rough translation of Karl's effusion.

This morning, though his complexion was a hideous yellow colour, he seems quite all right. I shall play a little trick on him at dinner tonight.

I have begun to get to know some of the crew by now; they are a fine lot of youngsters with a seasoning of half a dozen older men. The coxswain, Schmitt by name, is a splendid old petty officer who has been in the U-boat service since 1911.

His favourite enjoyment is to spin yarns to the younger members of the crew, who know of his weakness and play up to it.

He has a favourite expression which runs thus:

"His Majesty the Kaiser said Germany's future lies on the sea; I say Germany's future lies under the sea."

He is inordinately fond of this statement, and the youngsters continually say: "What made you take to U-boat work, Schmitt?" and the invariable reply is as above. When he has been asked the question about half a dozen times in the course of a day, he is liable to become suspicious, and if his questioner is within range Schmitt stares at him for a few seconds in an absent-minded way, then an arm like that of a gorilla shoots out, and the quizzer (*Untersucher*) receives a resounding box on the ears to the huge delight of his companions. The old man then permits his iron-lipped mouth to relax into a caustic smile, after which he is left in peace for some time.

At the wheel he is an artist, for he seems to divine what the next order is going to be, or if he is steering her on a course he predicts the direction of the next wave even as a skilful chess player works out the moves ahead.

* * * * *

I am rather weary and ought to go to bed, but before I lose the savour I must record the splendid fun I had with Alten at dinner.

We were dining alone, as the navigator was on the bridge, and the engineer was busy with a slight leak in the cooking water service. I have said that, though a heavy drinker by nature, Alten is a strict abstainer at sea. Accordingly I produced a small flask of rum, half-way through dinner, and helped myself to a liberal tot, placing the liquor between us on the table. As the sight met his eyes and the aroma greeted his nostrils, a gleam of joy flashed across his face, to be succeeded by a frown.

With an amiable smile I proffered the flask to him, remarking at the same time: "You don't drink at sea, do you?"

In a thick voice he muttered, "No! Yes—no! thank you."

With an air of having noticed nothing, I resumed my meal, but out of the corner of my eye I watched his left hand on the table near the flask. It was most interesting, all the veins stood out like ropes, and his knuckles almost burst through the skin.

This went on for about thirty seconds, when he choked out something about needing a breath of fresh air. As he got up his face was brick red, and I almost thought he'd have a fit.

Whether by accident or design he pulled the cloth as he got out from between the settee and the table and upset the flask.

He was apparently incapable of apologizing, for he rushed up on deck.

A few minutes later the navigating officer came down and asked what was up?

I said: "What do you mean?"

He said: "Well, the Captain came up just now, swearing like a trooper, and told me to get to the devil out of it; it didn't seem advisable to question him, so I got out of it and came down."

I expressed my opinion that the Captain must be feeling seasick and was ashamed to say so. I also suggested to the navigator that he should take the Captain a little brandy in case he was not feeling well, but the navigator declared he was going to stay down in the warmth till he was sent for. Alten is a great coarse brute. Fancy allowing a material substance such as alcohol to grip one's mentality.

Thank Heaven I have nerves of iron; nothing would affect me!

And now to bed, though I must just read my account of our day in the forest. Darling girl, may I dream of thee.

*****

We laid our mines without trouble at 5 a.m. this morning, though at midnight we had a most unpleasant experience.

I was asleep, as it was my morning watch, when I was awakened by the harsh rattle of the diving alarms.

The Diesel subsided with a few spasmodic coughs into silence, and as I jumped out of my bunk and groped for my short sea boots, the navigator and helmsman came tumbling down the conning tower, with the navigator shouting, "Take her down," as hard as you like.

The men at the planes had them "hard-to-dive" in an instant.

The vents had been opened as the hooters sounded, and Alten, who had jumped into the control room, immediately rang down, "All out on the electric motors."

In thirty seconds from the original alarm we were at an angle of twenty degrees down by the bow, and I had sat down heavily on the battery boards, completely surprised by the sudden tilt of the deck.

It occurred to me that the air was escaping through the vents with a strangely loud noise, but before I could consider the matter further or even inquire the reason for this sudden dive, the noise increased to a terrifying extent, and whilst I prepared myself for the worst it culminated into a roar as of fifty express trains going through a tunnel, mingled with the noise of a high-powered aeroplane engine.

The roar drummed and beat and shook the boat, then died away as suddenly as it came; a moment later there was a severe jar. We had struck the bottom, still maintaining our angle.

I painfully got to my feet and then discovered from the navigator that he had suddenly seen two white patches of foam 800 yards on the starboard bow, which resolved themselves into the bow waves of a destroyer approaching at full speed to ram.

We had dived just in time, and her knife-edged bow, driven by 30,000 horse power, had slid through the water a very few feet above our conning tower.

Luckily he had not dropped any depth charges. We were not, however, completely free of our troubles, though we had cheated the destroyer.

Examination of the chart, showed the bottom to be mud, and on attempting to move the foremost hydroplanes, the plane motor fuses blew out. This showed that the boat was buried in the mud right up to her foremost planes, which were immovable.

The hydrophone watch-keeper reported that he could still hear fast-running propellers, though probably some distance away, and as this showed that our old enemy was still nosing about we were very anxious not to break surface. We just blew "A."[1] At least we started to blow "A," but Alten wisely decided that, as it was a calm night with a half-moon, the bubbles on the surface might be rather conspicuous, so we stopped the blow and put the pump on. We also flooded "W".[2] This had no effect on her at all.

We then pumped out "Q" and "P," leaving "W" full, and adjusted our trim to give her only three tons negative buoyancy, just enough to keep us on the bottom if she came out of the mud.

In this position we went full speed astern on the motors, 1,500 amps on each, and all the crew in the after-compartment. No result. We then pumped the outer diving tanks on the port side to give her a list to starboard. Still she remained fixed. So at 2 a.m. we decided to risk it and we put a slow blow on all tanks.

When she had about fifty tons positive buoyancy she suddenly bucketed up, and, as the motors were running full speed astern at the time, we came up and broke surface stern first. In a few seconds we were trimmed down again, and as a precautionary measure we proceeded for a couple of miles at twenty metres, when, coming up to periscope depth, we surfaced, and finding all clear we proceeded. We were put down by a trawler at dawn, though she never saw us. After half an hour's hanging about she moved off, which was lucky, as she was right on our billet.

We are now proceeding to a spot somewhat to the eastward of Cape St. Abbs,[3] as we have instructions to do a two-days patrol here and sink shipping.

We ought to start business tomorrow morning.

* * * * *

We should be in tonight, then for my little Zoe!

But I must record what we have done. Already I am getting much pleasure from reading my diary. Strange how it amuses one to see little bits of oneself on paper, and the less garnished and franker the truths the more entertaining it is.

The hours here are so long and boring at times that I feel I want to talk intimately with someone. Failing Zoe I turn to my notebooks.

1: Probably their foremost internal tank.
2: Presumably their after internal tank.
3: St. Abbs Head.

THE TORPEDO HAD JUMPED CLEAN OUT OF THE WATER A HUNDRED YARDS SHORT OF THE STEAMER AND HAD THEN DIVED UNDER HER.

A MOMENT LATER THERE WAS A SEVERE JAR; WE HAD STRUCK THE BOTTOM.

The first steamer we sighted raised high hopes, at least her smoke did, for we saw enough smoke on the horizon to make us think we were to see the Grand Fleet, and we promptly dived. We cruised towards her for about half an hour, and then hung about where we were, as we found that her course would take the ship close to us.

As the situation developed, Alten, who was up in the conning tower at the "A" periscope, gave us a certain amount of information, and we gathered that all this smoke was pouring out of the pipe-stem tunnel of a wretched little English tramp.

I found it most irritating, standing in the control room (my action station) and not knowing what was going on.

There is only one good job in a submarine and that is the Captain's. He knows and decides everything. The rest of us are in his hands and take things on trust. I object on principle to my life being held in Alten's hands. It is all very well for the crew, for, to start with, they have no imagination, and to most of them their mental horizon stops at the walls of the boat. Secondly, they have the consolation of mechanical activities; they make and break switches and open and close valves—they work with their hands. An officer has imagination, and only works with his head.

As we attacked the steamer, all one heard was murmurs from Alten, such as: "Raise!" "Lower!" "Take her down to ten metres!" "Half speed!" "Slow!" "Bring her up to five metres!" "Raise!" "Lower!"

I endeavoured to simulate an air of unconcern which I was far from feeling.

Not that I was a prey to physical fear; I flatter myself it is so far unknown to me, and there was no great danger, but simply that I longed to know what was happening. At length I heard the welcome order:

"Starboard tube. Stand by!"

Which was followed almost immediately by the order: "Fire!"

There was a kind of coughing grunt, and the starboard torpedo proceeded on its errand of destruction.

Every ear was strained for the sound of the explosion, but all we were vouchsafed was a torrent of blasphemy from Alten.

The torpedo had jumped clean out of the water a hundred yards short of the steamer, and had then evidently dived under the ship; so I gathered later when Alten had calmed down somewhat.

We were about to surface and give her the gun, when luckily Alten took a good sweep round with the skyscraper and discovered one of those wretched little airships about a mile away, coming towards the steamer, which was wailing piteously, on her siren.

As the chart showed forty metres we decided to bottom and have lunch.

Over lunch we discussed the misadventure. Alten was loud in his curses of Tanzerman (the torpedo lieutenant at Bruges), from whom he had got the torpedo in guaranteed good condition only forty-eight hours before we sailed. He launched forth into a tirade against the torpedo staff at Bruges, and, warming to his subject, he roundly abused the whole of the depot personnel, whom he stigmatized as a set of hard-drinking, shore-loafing ruffians, who were incapable of realizing that they existed for the benefit of the boats' personnel and "material."

I naturally disagreed, and did so the more readily that I conscientiously disagree with him. I find that there is a tendency on the part of some of these submarine officers, who have been U-boating a long time, to get into narrow grooves. Most reserve officers are not like this, as they have only been in during the war. Alten is an exception; he left the Hamburg-Amerika on two years' half pay in 1912, and was, of course, kept on in 1914. After all, the depot staff are Germans, and as such labour for the Fatherland, and though their work in office and workshop is not so dangerous as ours, on the other hand they have not got the stimulation before their eyes, of glory to be gained. Personally I am of the opinion that the torpedo broke surface because, being fired from the outside tubes, it probably started too shallow, dived deep, recovered shallow and dived deep, broke surface and dived very deep. A sticky motor or sluggish weight would give this effect.

And are these external tubes water-tight? Theoretically, yes, but what of practice? We have been down to forty metres several times during this trip, and not once have we had a chance on the surface of getting at the two external tubes; add to which our depth gear, with the pivots of the weight exposed to water if the tube does flood and then you have rust, corrosion and heaven knows what complications.

I saw a British Mark 11.50 torpedo at the torpedo shop at

Bruges the other day, and I was much struck with their deep depth gear, which is of the unrestrained Uhlan type, *i.e.*, weight and valve interdependent. But then the main feature is that the whole gear is contained in a separate water-tight chamber.

Our system is certainly a great saving in space, and is much neater in design, whilst I prefer the Uhlan principle of valve conjuncting with weight, but it would be interesting to know whether the British have much trouble with the depth-keeping of their torpedo.

I have written quite a disquisition on depth gears; I must get on with my record of events.

After lunch we had a good look round, but the small airship was still hanging about, flying slowly in large circles.

We were rather surprised to meet one of these despicable little sausages or "Zeppelin's Spawn," as the navigator calls them, so far from land, and at dark we surfaced and proceeded on one engine on an easterly course, charging the battery right up with the other engine.

Dawn revealed a blank horizon, not a vestige of mast, funnel or smoke in sight.

We ambled along in fine though cold weather, and I took advantage of the peacefulness of everything to do a really good series of Müller on the upper deck, stripped to the waist, and allowed the keen air to play its invigorating currents on my torso.

Alten silently watched me from the conning tower, with a sneering expression on his face. The navigator, who is quite a decent youngster, though of no family, was, I could plainly see, struck by my development, and asked to be initiated into the series of exercises. I agreed willingly enough to show them to him. I will confess I wish Zoe could have seen me as I perspired with healthy exercise.

At about 11 a.m. a couple of masts, then two more, then another, appeared above the horizon. The visibility was extreme, so we at once dived and proceeded at full speed, ten metres.

We had been going thus for perhaps half an hour when Alten remarked that he would have another look at the convoy. We eased speed, came up to six metres, and Alten proceeded up into the conning tower to use "A" periscope.

He had hardly applied his eye to the lens when he sharply ordered the boat to ten metres, accompanying this order with another to the motor room demanding utmost speed (*Ausserste Kraft*). I went up to the conning tower and found him white with excitement.

"Look!" he exclaimed, pointing to the periscope, entirely forgetful of the fact that we were at ten metres. I looked, and of course saw nothing; furious at the trick I considered he had played on me I turned on him, to be disarmed by his apology.

"Sorry! I forgot! The whole British battle cruiser force is there."

It was now my turn to be excited, and I rushed down to the motor room determined to give her every amp she would take. The port foremost motor was sparking like the devil, rings of cursed sparks shooting round the commutator, but this was no time for ceremony. I relentlessly ordered the field current to be still further reduced.

We were actually running with an F.C. of 3.75 amps,[1] for a period, when the sparking assumed the appearance of a ring of fire and, fearing a commutator strip would melt, I ordered an F.C. of five amps.

We thus passed a quarter of an hour full of strain, the tension of which was reflected in the attitude of all the men. Alten had announced his intention of using the stern torpedo tube after his failure in the morning, and the crew of this tube were crouched at their stations like a gun's crew in the last few seconds preparatory to opening fire. The switchboard attendants gripped the regulating rheostats as if by their personal efforts they could urge the boat on faster. Old Schmitt, at the helm, never lifted his eyes from the compass repeater.

At length: "Slow both!" "Bring her to six metres!" came from the conning tower, to which place I proceeded to hear the news.

Slowly the periscope was raised and I held my breath; a groan came from Alten and he turned away. For a fraction of a second I was almost pleased at his obvious pain, then, sick with disappointment, I took his place.

Yes! it was all over. There they were, and with hungry eyes and depressed heart I saw five great battle cruisers, of which I recognized the *Tiger* with her three great funnels, the *Princess Royal*, *Lion* and two others, zigzagging along at 25 knots, at a distance of 12,000 metres, across our bow.

1: The lower the field current the faster the motor goes. 3.75 is almost incredibly low for a motor of this type—at least according to British practice.

They were surrounded by a numerous screen of destroyers and light cruisers, the former at that range through the periscope appearing as black smudges.

It is not often one is permitted such a spectacle in modern war, and I could not tear myself away from the sight of those great brutes, whom I had fought when in the *Derflingger* at Dogger Bank and again when in the *König* at Jutland. So near and yet so far, and as they rapidly drew away so did all the visions of an Iron Cross. As soon as they were out of sight, we surfaced in order to report what we had seen to Zeebrugge and Heligoland.

Everything seemed against us. I had gone on the bridge with the navigator; Alten, with a face as black as hell, had gone to the wardroom. About ten minutes elapsed when I heard a fearful altercation going on below. I stepped down to find the young wireless operator trembling in front of Alten, who was overwhelming him with a flood of abuse. As I reached the wardroom, Alten shook his fist in the man's face and bellowed:

"Make the d—— thing work, I tell you."

"Impossible, Captain, the main condenser——" the man began.

Purple with rage, Alten seized a heavy pair of parallel rulers, and before I could check him hurled them full in the operator's face. Bleeding copiously, the youth fell to the deck in a stunned condition.

It was then, for the first time, that I noticed a half-empty bottle of spirits on the table, which colossal quantity he must have consumed in about a quarter of an hour.

Turning to me, this semi-madman pointed to the wireless operator with his foot and growled:

"Have him removed."

This I did, and then, lowering the periscope, I ordered the boat to fifteen metres. We proceeded at this depth until 8 p.m., when I was informed that the Captain was in his bunk and wished to see me.

I discovered him with his face to the ship's side, and upon my reporting myself he ordered me, firstly to throw that blasted bottle overboard (an unnecessary proceeding, as it was empty), and secondly to surface and shape course for Zeebrugge.

At midnight he relieved me, apparently perfectly normal.

The wireless operator has been laid up all day and has a nasty cut on the head. The navigator, a great scandal-monger, has heard from the engineer that Alten was speaking to him alone this morning, and the engineer believes that Alten has given him five hundred marks to say he fell down a hatch.

Hooray! Blankenberg buoy has just been reported in sight! Soon I shall see my Zoe!

*****

With what high hopes did I write the last few lines a few hours ago, and how they were dashed to the ground, for on going into the Mess at Bruges I found amongst my letters a note from her, which was terrible in its brevity. She simply said:

Dear Karl,
I am going away for some days, and as I shall be travelling it is no good giving you an address. To our next meeting!
Zoe

How horribly vague; not an indication of her destination, her object, or the probable length of her absence. Of course I rushed round to the flat, but found the place shut up. The porter told me she had gone away with her maid. He couldn't say when she'd be back—if at all! I gave him ten marks, and he said she might be away a fortnight. If I'd given him twenty he'd have said a week; he obviously didn't know.

I feel I could do anything tonight; any mad, evil thing would appeal to me.

There is a most fearful uproar coming from the guest-room, where a large and rowdy party are entertaining the chorus of a travelling *revue* company. I saw them when they arrived, horribly common-looking women, with legs like mine tubes.

*****

Another day and still no news; I don't know how I shall stick it. She might have had the softness of heart to write to me. She knows my address.

This evening a letter from the little mother, who asks whether I can find time to go to Frankfurt when I have leave; at the end of the letter she mentions that Rosa has joined the Women's Voluntary Auxiliary Corps of Army Nurses. I suppose she thought she'd like her photograph taken in some fancy uniform as "Rosa Freinland, one of our Frankfurt beauties, now on war work!" Holding the patient's hand is about the only work she intends doing.

Women as a class are the same the world over. We are well supplied with English papers in the Mess here; they come regularly from Amsterdam, and in their pages I see, just as in ours, pictures of the Countess this and the Lord that, photographed in becoming attitudes doing war work. It seems agricultural pursuits are the fashion in England at present—wait till our U-boat war gets its knife well into their fat guts, it will be more than fashionable to work in the fields then.

The British Empire is undeniably a great creation, or rather not so much a creation as a thing arrived at accidentally, but it lacks solidarity. It sprawls, a confused mass of races and creeds, around the world. Its very immensity lays it open to attack, it has a dozen Achilles heels from Ireland to Egypt and South Africa to India.

I met a man only yesterday who was recently at the propaganda department of the Foreign Office, and without going into details he gave me a very good idea of the good work that is going on in Britain's canker spots.

Ireland is considered particularly promising to those in the know.

Now for an agitated night! To think that a girl should disturb me so!

* * * * *

Two days have passed, or, rather, dragged their interminable lengths away, for there is still not a vestige of news. I have been twice to the flat with no result, except to receive a piece of impertinence from the porter the last time I was there.

No news.

* * * * *

Still no news, and we sail in forty-eight hours.

At sea, off the Isle of Wight

It is some days since I turned for solace and enjoyment, amidst the discomforts of this life, to my pen and notebook.

What strange tricks fate plays with us, and how lucky it is that one cannot foresee the future.

Here I am in *U.39*—but I must start at the beginning. My last entry was the depressing one of still no news. Well, I have had news, but it was like a drop of water in the mouth of a parched-up man. Another agonizing twenty-four hours passed, and I was sitting in my room about ten o'clock, trying to resign myself to the idea that the next night I should be starting out for my third trip without news of her, when the telephone bell rang. I lifted the receiver and to my amazed joy heard a voice that I could have recognized in a thousand. It was Zoe!

I was quite incapable of any remark, and my confusion was further increased when, after a few "Hello's," which I idiotically repeated, her clear, level tones said: "Is that you, Karl? How are you?" How was I? What a question to ask! I wanted to tell her that I was bubbling with joy, that a thousand-kilogramme load had been lifted from my chest, that my blood was coursing through my veins, that I, usually so cool, was trembling with excitement, that I could have kissed the mouthpiece of the humble instrument that linked us together. Yet I was quite incapable of answering her simple question! I can't imagine what I expected her to say, for upon reflection her remark was a very ordinary one, and indeed under the circumstances quite natural, but, as I say, in actual fact I was tongue-tied.

I suppose I must have said something, for I next remember her saying: "Well, you might ask how I am;" and to my horror I realized that she thought I was being rude!

My abject apologies were cut short by her tantalizing laugh, and I understood that the adorable one was teasing me. When at length I made myself believe that I really was talking to this most elusive and delightful woman I wasted no time in suggesting that, late though it was, I might be permitted to go round and see her. She would not permit this, as she said it would create grave scandal, and the Colonel might hear about it upon his return. I pleaded hard and urged my departure in twenty-four hours.

She was firm and reproved me for discussing movements over the telephone. She was right; I was a fool to do so; but Zoe destroys all my caution. However, she said that I might lunch with her next day, and that she had some new music to play to me. I ventured to ask where she had been, but this question was plainly unpleasing to my lady, so I dropped the subject. I blew her a goodnight kiss over the telephone, to which I think I caught an answer, and then she rang off.

Ten minutes had not elapsed, when a messenger entered and informed me that I was wanted at the Commodore's office at once.

A strange feeling of uneasiness and that of impending misfortune overcame me. I felt like a naughty school-boy about to interview the headmaster.

I followed the messenger into the Commodore's office, and found myself alone with the great man. He was seated at a huge roll-top desk, which was the only article of furniture in a room which was to all intents and purposes papered with large scale charts of the east and south coasts of England and of the Channel and North Sea.

The Commodore was sealing an envelope as I came in; he looked up and saw me, then, without taking any further notice of me, he resumed his business with the envelope. I felt that I was in the presence of a personality, and I was, for "Old Man Max" is one of the ten men who count in the Naval Administration. He had a reading lamp on his desk, and I remember noticing that the light shining through its green shade imparted a yellow parchment-like effect to the top of his old bald head. With dainty care he finished sealing the envelope, then, picking up a telephone transmitter, he snapped "Admiralty!" In about a minute he was connected, and to my astonishment I realized that he was talking to the duty captain of the operations department in Berlin.

His words chilled my heart, for he said: "Commodore speaking! *U.39* sails at 2 a.m. for operation F.Q.H.—Repeat."

His words were apparently repeated to his satisfaction, for while I was vainly endeavouring to convince myself that I was unconnected with the sailing of *U.39*, he banged the receiver into place (Old Man Max does everything in bangs) and snapped at me.

"You Lieutenant Von Schenk?"

I admitted I was, and then heard this disgusting news.

"Kranz, 1st Lieutenant *U.39*, reported suddenly ill, Zeebrugge, poisoning—you relieve him. Ship sails in one hour forty minutes from now—my car leaves here in forty minutes and takes you to Zeebrugge. Here are operation orders—inform Von Weissman he acknowledges receipt direct to me on 'phone. That's all."

He handed me the envelope and I suppose I walked outside—at least I found myself in the corridor turning the confounded envelope round and round. For one mad moment I felt like rushing in and saying: "But, sir, you don't understand I'm lunching with Zoe tomorrow!"

Then the mental picture which this idea conjured up made me shake with suppressed laughter and I remembered that war was war and that I had only thirty-five minutes in which to collect such gear as I had handy—most of my sea things being in *U.C.47*—and say goodbye to Zoe.

I ran to my room and made the corridors echo with shouts for my faithful Adolf. The excellent man was soon on the scene, and whilst he stuffed underclothing, towels and other necessary gear into a bag he had purloined from someone's room, I rang up Zoe. I wasted ten minutes getting through, but at last I heard a deliciously sleepy voice murmur, "Who's that?"

I told her, and added that I was off; to my secret joy, an intensely disappointed and long-drawn "Oooh!" came over the wire. So she does care a bit, I thought. Mad ideas of pretending to be suddenly ill crossed my mind—anything to gain twenty-four hours—but the Fatherland is above all such considerations, and after some pleasant talk and many wishes of good luck from the darling girl, with a heavy heart I bade her good-night.

The Old Man's car, which is a sixty horse-power Benz, was waiting at the Mess entrance, and once clear of the sentries we raced down the flat, well-metalled road to Zeebrugge in a very short time. The guard at Bruges barrier had 'phoned us through to the Zeebrugge fortified zone, and we were admitted without delay. In three-quarters of an hour from my interview with old Max I was scrambling across a row of U-boats to reach my new ship, *U.39*.

I went down the after hatch, reported myself to Von Weissman and delivered his orders to him, of which he acknowledged receipt direct to the Commodore according to instructions. Von Weissman is a very different stamp of man to Alten; of medium height, he has sandy-coloured hair, steel-grey eyes and a protruding jaw. He is what he looks, a fine North Prussian, and is, of course, of excellent family, as the Weissmans have been settled in Grinetz for a long period.

He struck me as being about thirty years of age, and on his heart he wore the Cross of the second class. I have heard of him before as being well in the running towards an *ordre pour le mérite*.

An interesting chart is hanging in the wardroom, on which is marked the last resting-place of every ship he has sunk. He puts a coloured dot, the tint of which varies with the tonnage, black up to 2,000, blue from 2,000-5,000, brown 5,000-8,000, green 8,000-11,000, and a red spot with the ship's name for anything over 11,000. He has got about 120,000 tons at present. He opposes the Arnauld de la Perrière school of thought, which pins faith on the gun, and Weissman has done nearly all his work with the good old torpedo.

Altogether, undoubtedly a man to serve with.

The *U.39* was in that buzzing and semi-active condition which to a trained eye is a sure indication that the ship is about to sail. Punctually at five minutes to 2 a.m. Weissman went to the bridge, and at 2 a.m. the wires were slipped and we started on a ten days' trip. As the dim lights on the mole disappeared and the ceaseless fountain of star-shells, mingling with the flashing of guns, rose inland on our port beam my mind travelled overland to the flat at Bruges, and I wondered whether Zoe was lying awake listening to the ceaseless rumble of the Flanders cannon. We went on at full speed, as it was our intention to pass the Dover Straits before dawn. Though our intelligence bureau issues the most alarming reports as to the frightfulness of the defences here I was agreeably surprised at the ease with which we passed. Von Weissman, to whom I had hinted that we might find the passage tricky, rather laughed at my suggestion, and described to me his method, which, at all events, has the merit of simplicity.

He always goes through with the tide, so as to take as short a time as possible, and he always decides on a course and steers it as closely as possible, keeping to the surface unless he sights anything, and diving as soon as anything shows up. Even if he dives he goes on as fast as possible on his course, irrespective of whether he is being bombed or not.

I must say it worked very well last night. We shaped a course to pass five miles west of Gris Nez, and when that light, which for some reason the French had commodiously lit that night, was abeam, we sighted a black object, probably a trawler or destroyer, about half a dozen miles away right ahead. Weissman immediately dived and, without deviating a degree from his course, held on at three-quarters speed on the motors. Some time later the hydrophone watch-keeper reported the sound of propellers in his listeners, and that he judged them to be close at hand, so I imagine we passed very nearly directly underneath whatever it was.

After an hour's submerging we rose, and found dawn breaking over a leaden and choppy sea. Nothing being in sight, we continued on the surface for an hour, charging batteries with the starboard engine (500 amps on each), but at 9 a.m., the clouds lying low and an aerial patrol being frequent hereabouts, we dived and cruised steadily down channel at slow speed, keeping periscope depth. Several times in the course of the forenoon we sighted small destroyers and convoy craft[1] in the distance, all steering westerly. They were probably returning from escorting troopships over to France last night. In every case we went to sixty feet long before they could have seen our "stick."[2] Weissman is evidently as cautious in this matter as he is hardy in others; the more I see of him the more I like him; he is a man of breeding, and it is of value to serve in this boat.

As I write we are on the surface about ten miles east of the Isle of Wight, still steering down channel. To-night at midnight we report our position to Zeebrugge, up till now we have maintained wireless silence for fear of the British and French directional stations picking up our signals and fixing our position.

After supper this evening Von Weissman explained to me the general plan of our operations for the next eight days. Our cruising billet is about 150 miles south-west of the Scillies, at the focal point where trade for Liverpool and Bristol and the up-channel trade diverges. Von Weissman says that this is a plum billet and we should do well.

I feel this is going to be better than those piffling little minelaying trips, and though we shall be away ten days, it will qualify me for four days' leave in Belgium.

* * * * *

There was nearly an awkward moment last night, or, rather, there was an awkward moment, and nearly an awkward accident. I

1: Probably "P" boats.
2: Periscope.

relieved the navigator at midnight (the pilot is an unassuming individual called Siegel) and took on the middle watch. It was blowing about force 4 from the south-west, and a nasty short, lumpy sea was running which caught us just on the port bow. About once every ten seconds she missed her step with the waves and, dipping her nose into it, shovelled up tons of water, which, as the bow lifted, raced aft and, breaking against the gun, flung itself in clouds of spray against the bridge. In a very few minutes every exposed portion of me was streaming with water.

At about 2 a.m. I had turned my back to the sea for a moment, and my thoughts were for an instant in Bruges, when, on facing forward once again I saw a sight which effectually brought me back to earth.

This was the spectacle of two black shapes, evidently steamers, one on either bow, distant, I should estimate, 600 or 700 metres. I had to make a quick decision, and I decided that to fire a torpedo in that sea with any hope of a hit, especially with the boat on surface, was useless; furthermore, that at any moment either of the steamers might sight us from their high bridge and turn and ram.

These thoughts were the work of an instant, and I at once rang the diving bell, and, pushing the look-out before me, in five seconds I was in the conning tower and had the hatch down. I at once proceeded down into the boat, and the first thing that struck my eye was the diving gauge with the needle practically stationary at two metres.

The boat was not going down properly! and for an instant I was rudely shaken, until a cool voice from the wardroom remarked, «Helm hard a-port,» an order that was instantly obeyed, and as she began to turn the moving needle on the depth gauge began its journey round the dial. It was the Captain who had spoken. As soon as he heard the diving alarm he was out of his bunk, and a glance at the gauge he has fitted in the wardroom told him we were not sinking rapidly. In an instant he had put his finger on the trouble, which was that we were almost head on to the sea, with the result that he had given the order as stated above, which, bringing us beam on to the sea, had caused her to dive with ease. He is efficiency itself!

As I explained to him what had happened, the noise of propellers at varying distances from us overhead led him to state his belief that we had run into a convoy homeward bound to Southampton from the Atlantic.

He approved of my actions in every particular, save only in my omission to bring the boat away from the sea as I began to dive.

This morning we are beginning to get the full force of what is evidently going to be a south-westerly gale of some violence. The seas are getting larger as we debouch into the Atlantic. This looks bad for business.

* * * * *

At the moment we are practically hove to on the surface, with the port engine just jogging to keep her head on to sea and the starboard ticking round to give her a long, slow charge of 200 amps.

The wind is force 7-8 and a very big sea is running which makes it entirely impossible to open the conning tower hatch; the engine is getting its air through the special mushroom ventilator, which is apparently not designed to supply both the boat's requirements and those of the engine; the whole ventilator gets covered with sea every now and then, during which period until the baffle drains get the water away no air can get in, so the engine has a good suck at the air in the boat, the result of all this being a slight vacuum in the boat. It is a very unpleasant sensation, and made me very sick. This is really a form of sickness due to the rarefied air.

I had a great surprise when I looked at the barograph this morning as the needle had gone right off the paper at the bottom, and at first glance I thought we had struck a tropical depression of the first magnitude, which, flouting all the laws of meteorology, had somehow found its way to the English Channel; but the engineer explained to me that, as I have already stated, the low atmospheric pressure in the boat was due to the conning-tower hatch being shut down.

I have discovered that Von Weissman is a martyr to sea-sickness—all day he has been lying down as white as a sheet and subsisting on milk tablets and sips of brandy; yet such is the man's inflexibility of will that he forces himself to make a tour of inspection right round the boat every six hours, night and day. It is this will to conquer which has made Germans unconquerable, though "Come the four corners of the world in arms" against us, as the great poet says.

As the dim lights on the mole disappeared, the ceaseless fountain of star shells mingling with the flashing of guns, rose inland on our port beam.

We hit her aft for the second time.

We are, of course, keeping watch from inside the conning tower; it is, at all events, dry, but as to seeing anything one might as well be looking out through a small glass window from inside a breakwater! To bed till 4 a.m.

* * * * *

A most unprofitable day. I grudge every day away from Zoe on which we do nothing. This morning about noon the gale blew itself out, but a heavy confused sea continued to run.

At 2 p.m. we saw a most tantalizing spectacle. A big tank steamer, fully 600 feet long and of probably 17,000 tons burthen hove in sight, escorted by two destroyers. To attack with the gun was impossible, as we could only keep the conning tower open when stern to sea, and in any case the two destroyers prevented any surface work. We tried to get in for an attack, but we had not seen her in time, and the best we could do was to get within 3,000 yards, at which range it would have been absurd to have wasted a torpedo, the chances of hitting being 100 to 1 against, even if the torpedo had run properly in the sea that was on.

I had a good look at her through the foremost periscope in between the waves, and it maddened me to see all that oil, doubtless from Tampico for the Grand Fleet, going safely by. The destroyers were having a bad time of it, crashing into the sea like porpoises, their funnels white with salt, and their bridges enveloped in sheets of water and spray. They little thought that, barely a mile away, amidst the tumbling, crested waves a German eye was watching them!

There is no doubt these damned British have pluck, for it was the last sort of weather in which one would have expected to find destroyers at sea, and yet I suppose they do this throughout the winter.

After all, one would expect them to be tough fellows—they are of Teutonic stock—though by their bearing one might imagine that the Creator made an Englishman and then Adam.

Let's hope we get some decent weather tomorrow. I have just been refreshing my memory by reading of what I wrote in the book, concerning the day in the forest with the adorable girl. There is an exquisite pleasure in transporting the mind into such memories of the past when the body is in such surroundings as the present, if only I could will myself to dream of her!

*****

A fine day in every sense of the word. The weather has been and remains excellent, and I have been present at my first sinking. It was absurdly commonplace. At 10 a.m. this morning a column of smoke crept upwards from the southern horizon.

Von Weissman steered towards it on the surface until two masts and the top of a funnel appeared. We dived and proceeded slowly under water on a southerly course.

Half an hour passed and Von Weissman brought the boat up to periscope depth and had a look. He called to me to come and see, an invitation I accepted with alacrity.

With natural excitement I looked through the periscope and there she was, unconsciously ambling to her doom like a fat sheep.

She was a steamer (British) of about 4,000 tons, slugging home at a steady ten knots, but she was destined to come to her last mooring place ahead of schedule time!

We dipped our periscope and I went forward to the tubes. Five minutes elapsed and the order instrument bell rang, the pointer flicking to "Stand by." I personally removed the firing gear safety pin and put the repeat to "Ready." A breathless pause, then a slight shake and destruction was on its way, whilst I realized by the angle of the boat that Weissman was taking us down a few metres.

That shows his coolness, he didn't even trouble to watch his shot.

Anxiously I watch the second hand of my stop watch. Weissman had told me the range would be about 500 metres—30 seconds—31—32—33—has he missed?—34—35—3—A dull rumble comes through the water and the whole boat shakes. Hurrah! we have hit, and the order "Surface" comes along the voice pipe.

The cheerful voice of the blower is heard, evacuating the tanks; I run to the conning tower and closely follow Weissman up the ladder. At last I am on the bridge. There she is! What a sight!

I feel that I shall never forget what she looked like, though, if all goes well, I shall see many another fine ship go to her grave.

But she was my first; I felt the same sensation when, as a boy, I shot my first roe-deer in the Black Forest, one instant a living thing beautiful to perfection, the next my rifle spoke and a bleeding carcase lay beneath the fine trees. So with this ship. I am a sailor, and to every sailor every ship that floats has, as it were, a soul, a personality, an entity; to carry the analogy further, a merchant craft is like some fat beast of utility, an ox, a cow, or a sheep, whilst a warship is a lion if she is a battleship, a leopard if she is a light cruiser, etc.; in all cases worthy game.

But War has little use for sentimentality! and in my usual wandering manner I see that I have meandered from the point and quite forgotten what she did look like.

What I saw was this:

I saw that the steamer had been hit forward on the starboard side. The upper portion of the stem piece was almost down to the water level, her foremost hold was obviously filling rapidly. Her stern was high out of water, the red ensign of England flapping impotently on the ensign staff. Her propeller, which was still slowly revolving, thrashed the water, and this heightened the impression that I was watching the struggles of a dying animal. The propeller was revolving in spasmodic jerks, due, I imagine, to the fast failing steam only forcing the cranks over their dead centres with an effort.

A boat was being lowered with haste from the two davits abreast the funnel on one side, but when she was full of men and, due to the angle of the ship, well down by the bow, someone inboard let go the foremost fall or else it broke, for the bows of the boat fell downwards and half a dozen figures were projected in grotesque attitudes into the sea. For a few seconds the boat swung backwards and forwards, like a pendulum.

When she came to rest, hanging vertically downwards from the stern, I noticed that a few men were still clinging like flies to her thwarts. Truly, anything is better than the Atlantic in winter. Meanwhile the ship had ceased to sink as far as outward signs went.

I mentioned this to Von Weissman, who was at my side with a slight smile on his face, amused doubtless at the eagerness with which I watched every detail of this, to me, novel tragedy. He answered me that I need not worry, that she was being supported by an air lock somewhere forward, that the water was slowly creeping into her and her boilers would probably soon go.

This remarkable man was absolutely correct.

There was an interval of about five minutes, during which another boat, evidently successfully lowered from the other side, came round her stern, picked up one or two men from the water and also collected the survivors in the hanging boat; then the steamer suddenly sank another two feet, there was a dull rumbling, as of heavy machinery falling from a height, a muffled report, a cloud of steam and smoke, a sucking noise and then a pool in the water, in the middle of which odd bits of wood and other buoyant debris kept on bobbing up. Nothing else!

No! I am wrong, there were two other things: a U-boat, representing the might of Germany, and a whaler with perhaps twenty men in it, representing the plight of England!

As she went I felt hushed and solemn, it was an impressive moment; a slight chuckle came from imperturbable Weissman; he had seen too many go to think much of it, and he gave an order for the helm to be put over, so that we might approach the whaler.

They were horribly overcrowded, and were engaged in trying to sort themselves into some sort of order. We passed by them at 50 yards and Weissman, seizing his megaphone, shouted in English: "Goodbye! steer west for America!" A cold horror gripped my heart. It was an awful moment. I dare not write the thoughts that entered my head.

I turned away my head and faced aft, that he should not see my face; looking back I saw the whaler rocking dangerously in our wash, and then a commotion took place in her stern, from which a huge bearded man arose and, shaking his fist in our direction, shouted something or other before his companions pulled him down.

Von Weissman heard and his lips narrowed in. I held my breath in suspense, but he evidently decided against what he had been about to do, for with the order, "Course north! ten knots," he went below.

I remained on deck watching the rapidly receding whaler through my glasses until she was a mere speck—alone on the ocean, 150 miles from land, Then the navigator came up, and with strangely mixed feelings of exultant joy and depressing sorrow I went below.

Von Weissman was in the wardroom. I watched him unobserved. He was humming a tune to himself and had just completed putting a green dot on the chart. This done he lay back on the settee and closed his eyes—strange, insoluble man!

For long hours I could not forget that whaler; I see it now as I write. I suppose I shall get used to it all. What would Zoe say?

The most wonderful thing about man is that he can stand the strain of his own invention of modern war!

*****

I am rather tired tonight, but must just jot down briefly what has taken place today, as there is never any time in the daylight hours.

Soon after dawn, at about 8 a.m., we sighted a fair-sized steamer of about 3,000 tons, which we sunk, but I cannot say what she looked like, or whether anyone escaped, as we never came to the surface at all, Von Weissman sighting smoke on the western horizon just as he hit her. We accordingly steered in that direction. However, I think she went almost at once as Von Weissman put a dot (black) on the chart as we made towards number 3.

I very much wanted to know whether there were any survivors, but I did not like to ask him at the time and he has been in such an infernal temper ever since that I haven't had a suitable opportunity.

The cause of his rage was as follows:

Steamer number 3 turned out to be a fine fat chap (of the Clan Line, Von Weissman said, when we first sighted her). We moved in to attack and fired our port bow tube. I waited in vain by the tubes for the expected explosion—nothing happened, but after a couple of minutes a snarl came down the voice pipe: "Surface, *gun action stations!*"

I ran aft, and found the Captain white with rage.

"Missed ahead!" he said, with intense feeling, "I'll have to use that confounded gun." In about three minutes the Captain and myself were on the bridge and the crew were at their stations round the gun.

For the first time I saw the ship; she was stern on and apparently painted with black and white stripes. As I examined her through glasses—she was distant about 3,000 yards—I saw a flash aboard her and a few seconds later a projectile moaned overhead and fell about 6,000 yards over. So she is armed, thought I, and she has actually opened fire on us first.

The effect of this unexpected retort on the part of the Englishman was to throw Weissman into a paroxysm of rage.

"Why don't you fire? What the devil are you waiting for?" etc., etc., were some of the remarks he flung at the gun crew.

I did not consider it advisable to mention to him that they were probably waiting his order to fire, and also his orders for range and deflection, as I had imagined that, here as everywhere else, an officer controls the gun-fire. Apparently in this boat it is not so, as Weissman takes so little interest in his gun that he affects to be, or else actually is, ignorant of the elements of gun control.

At any rate, under the lash of his tongue, the gun's crew soon got into action, the gun-layer taking charge. Our first shot was short, very considerably so, as was also the second. Meanwhile the steamer had been keeping up a very creditably controlled rate of fire, straddling us twice, but missing for deflection, as was natural considering that we were bows on to her.

I felt thoroughly in my element listening to the significant wail of the enemy's shell, punctuated by the ear-splitting report of our own gun. Weissman, gripping the rail with both hands, and to my surprise ducking when one went overhead, watched the target with a fixed expression, but made no attempt to control our gun-fire, which was far from creditable, as is inevitable when it is left to the mercy of the inferior intellect of a seaman.

However, at the tenth or eleventh round we hit her in the upper works, as was shown by a bright red and yellow flash near her funnel. This did not check her firing or speed in the least, in fact she seemed to be gaining on us. She also began to zigzag slightly and throw smoke bombs overboard, which were not so effective from her point of view as I had thought they would be.

Matters were thus for some minutes. We had just hit her aft for the second time, though the shooting was so disgustingly bad that I was about to ask whether I might do the duties of control officer, when there was a blinding flash and the air seemed filled with moaning fragments. When I had recovered from my relief from finding that I was personally uninjured, I observed that two of the gun's crew were wounded and one was lying, either killed or seriously wounded, on the casing. We had been hit in the casing, well forward, and, as was subsequently proved when we dived, little material damage was caused to the boat.

This enemy success caused a temporary cessation of fire. The two wounded men were cautiously making their way aft to the conning tower, and I called for a couple of stokers to come up and carry away the third, when Von Weissman suddenly gave the order to dive. The gun's crew at once made a rush for the conning tower, and were down the hatch in a trice, one of the wounded men fainting at the bottom.

I was unaware as to the reason of this order to dive, and thought that perhaps the Captain had sighted a periscope. As I was turning to precede him down the conning tower hatch I distinctly saw the man lying by the gun lift his hand. I felt I could not leave him there, and instinctively cried, "He is still alive!" But Von Weissman, who was urging the crew to hurry down the hatch, pressed the diving alarm as soon as the last sailor was half in the hatch.

I knew that this meant that the boat would be under in 30 to 40 seconds, so I had no alternative but to get down the hatch as quickly as possible.

I did so with reluctance, and I was followed by Von Weissman, who joined me in the upper conning tower.

I forced myself not to look out of the conning tower scuttles during the few seconds that elapsed as the casing slowly went under, until at last nothing but waving green water showed at each little window. I feared that, if I had looked, I would have seen a wounded man, stung into activity by the cold touch of the Atlantic. Perhaps Von Weissman read my thoughts, or else he remembered my remark concerning the man, for he turned to me and in level tones said:

"Have you any doubt that he was dead?"

I hesitated a moment, and he continued:

"By my direction you have no doubt. He *was*!"

How brutal war is, and what a perfect exponent of the art the Captain proves himself to be! To me a life is a life, a particle of the thing divine; to him a life is a unit, and a half-maimed and probably dying seaman is as nothing in the scales when the safety of a U-boat is at stake. The seamen are numbered in their tens of thousands, the U-boats in their tens. The steamer had hit us once, luckily only in the casing, a second hit might well have punctured the pressure hull, and our fate in these waters would have been certain. Therefore, having summed these things up and balanced them in his mind, he dived and the sailor died.

Once below water Von Weissman seemed more his imperturbable self, and unless I am mistaken he is never really happy on the surface, at least when in action. He is a true water mole.

* * * * *

A day full of interest, though once again I have had to force myself to absorb the horrors of War. I imagine that I am now going through the experiences of a new arrival on the Western Front, who feels a desire to shudder at the sight of every corpse.

At 10 a.m. this morning we sighted the topsails of a sailing boat to the southwest. Closing her on the surface, we approached to within about 6,000 metres, when suddenly Von Weissman ordered "Gun Action Stations."

The gun crew came tumbling up, but not quick enough to suit him, for as they were mustering at the gun he gave the order to dive, only, however, taking her down to periscope depth before instantly ordering surface and then "Gun Action Stations" again. This time we opened fire on the ship, which was a Norwegian barque and, being in the barred zone, liable to destruction.

Von Weissman had announced overnight that at the first opportunity he would give "that ——- gun's crew a bellyful of practice," and he certainly did. As soon as the first shot was fired, she backed her topsails, and when our fourth shot struck her, somewhere near the foot of the foremast, her crew could be seen hastily abandoning their ship.

This action on their part had no influence with Von Weissman, who had taken personal charge of the helm, and, with the engines running at three-quarter speed, he was zigzagging about, to make it harder for the gun's crew. Every now and then he flung a gibe at the crew, such as suggesting that they should go back to the High Seas Fleet and learn how to shoot.

The sailing ship was soon on fire, for, considering the circumstances, the shooting was very fair, though had I been controlling it I could have confidently guaranteed better results. When she was blazing nicely fore and aft, Von Weissman ordered the practice to cease, and sent the crew below. He then ordered course south, speed ten knots, and I took over the watch.

An hour and a half later, when the navigator gave me a spell, a black cloud on the northern horizon marked the funeral pyre of another of our victims. When I went below, the Captain had just finished playing with his precious old chart.

* * * * *

We received a message at 2 a.m. last night from Heligoland to return forthwith; it is now 2 a.m. and we are approaching the redoubtable Dover Barrage. We had no trouble coming up channel today, which seems singularly empty, at any rate in mid-channel, where we were.

* * * * *

We got back about three hours ago, and as I was appointed temporary to the boat, Von Weissman kindly allowed me to leave her and come up to Bruges as soon as we got into the shelters at Zeebrugge.

I got up here just, in time for a late dinner. Hunger satisfied, I retired to my room and, needless to say, at once rang up my darling Zoe.

By the mercy of providence she was in, but imagine my sensations when I heard that that accursed swine of a Colonel was also back from the front, and expected in at the flat at any moment, being then, she thought, engaged in his after dinner drinking bouts at the cavalry officers' club. I could only groan.

A laugh at the other end stung me to furious rage, appeased in an instant by her soothing tones as she told me that I should be glad to hear that he was only up from the Somme on a four-days leave, and was returning next morning by the 8 a.m. troop train. Glad! I could have danced for joy. I breathed again.

As the Colonel was expected back at any moment she thought it advisable to terminate the conversation, which was done with obvious reluctance on her part, or so I flatter myself.

He goes tomorrow, so far so good, but what of the intervening period?

Could any more refined torture be imagined than that I, who love her as I love my own soul, should have to sit here, whilst scarcely a mile away, probably at this very moment as I write, that gross brute is privileged to kiss her, to look at her, to—oh! it's unbearable. When I think of that hog, for though I've never seen him, I've seen his photograph, and I know instinctively that he *is* gross, fresh, as she says, from a drinking bout, should at this moment be permitted to raise his pigs' eyes and look into those glorious wells of violet light; when I think that his is the privilege to see those masses of black hair fall in uncontrolled splendour, then I understand to the full the deep pleasures of murder.

I would give anything to destroy this man, and could shake the Englishman by the hand who fires the delivering bullet!

Steady! Steady! What do I write? No! I mean it, every word of it. Yet of all the mysteries, and to me Zoe is a mass of them, surely the strangest of all is contained in the question: Why does she live with him?

She doesn't love him, she's practically told me so. In fact, I know she doesn't. Let me reason it out by logic. She lives with him, whether voluntarily or involuntarily. Suppose it be voluntarily, then her reasons must be (a) Love; (b) Fascination; (c) Some secret reason. If she is living with him involuntarily it must be: (d) He has a hold on her; (e) For financial reasons.

I strike out at once (a) and (e), for in the case of (e) she knows well that I would provide for her, and (a) I refuse to admit, (b) is hardly credible—I eliminate that. I am left with (c) and (d) which might be the same thing. But what hold can he have on her; she can't have a past, she is too young and sweet for that.

I must find out about this before I go to sea again.

*****

Three days ago, I was racking my brains for the solution of a problem, and, as I see from what I wrote, I was somewhat outside myself. In the interval things have taken an amazing turn. I am still bewildered—but I must put it all down from the beginning.

The Colonel left as she said he would, and I went round to lunch with her.

We had a delightful *tête-à-tête*, and after lunch she played the piano. I was feeling in splendid voice and she accompanied me to perfection in Tchaikovsky's "To the Forest," always a favourite of mine. As the last chords died away, Zoe jumped up from the piano and, with eyes dancing with excitement, placed her hands on my shoulders and exclaimed:

"Karl! I have an idea! I shall make a prisoner of you for two or three days."

I laughed heartily and almost told her that she had already made me a prisoner for life, only I can never get those sort of remarks out quick enough.

But when she said, "No! I am not joking, I mean it," I felt there was more meaning in her sentence than I had at first thought. I begged to be enlightened, and she then unfolded her scheme.

She told me for the first time, that in a forest not far from Bruges she had a little summer-house, to which she used to retreat for week-ends in the hot weather when the Colonel was away. He knew nothing of this country house (she was very insistent on that point), so I imagined she paid for it out of her dress allowance or in some other way. The idea that had just struck her was that she had a sudden fancy to go and spend two days there, and I was to go with her.

I was ready to go to Africa with her if my leave permitted, and it so happened that I was due for four days' overseas leave (limited to Belgian territory) so that this fitted in very well, and I told her so.

She was delighted, then, with one of those quick intuitions which women are so clever at, she read the half-formed thought in my mind, and said: "You mustn't think it's not going to be conventional; old Babette will be with us to chaperon me." Old Babette is an aged female whom she calls her maid. I think she is jealous of me.

I agreed at once that of course I quite understood it was to be highly conventional, etc., though I smiled to myself as I visualized my mother's shocked face and uplifted hands had she heard my Zoe's ideas on the conventions.

I was trying to fathom what was at the bottom of it all when she remarked: "Of course, as my prisoner you will have to obey all my orders."

I replied that this was certainly so.

"And one of the first things," she continued, "that happens to a prisoner when he goes through the enemy lines is that he is blindfolded, and in the same way I shan't let you know where you are going."

Seeing a doubtful look in my eyes as I endeavoured to keep pace with the underlying idea, if any, of this truly feminine fancy, she suddenly came up to me and, lifting her eyes to mine, murmured: "Don't you trust me?"

In a moment my passion flared up, and rained hot kisses on her face as she struggled to release herself from my arms.

When I left that night after dinner, and, walking on air, returned to the Mess, it was arranged that I should be at her flat with my suit-case at 6 p.m. the next evening, prepared, to use her own words, "to disappear with me for 48 hours."

She had told me of an address in Bruges which she said would forward on any telegram if I was recalled, and I had to be satisfied with that, for I may as well say here that I never discovered where I went to, and I don't know to this moment in what part of Belgium I spent the last two nights.

I tried to find out at first, but as she obviously attached some importance to keeping the locality of her woodland retreat a secret, probably to circumvent the Colonel, I soon gave up trying to get the secret from her, and contented myself with taking things as they came.

To go on with my account of what happened—which was really so remarkable that I propose writing it out in detail to the best of my memory—at 6 p.m. next day I was naturally at her flat feeling very much as if I was on the threshold of an adventure.

Zoe was excited and the flat was in a turmoil, as apparently she had only just begun to pack her dressing-case.

Soon after six we went down and got into a large Mercedes car which I had noticed standing outside when I arrived. We were soon on our way, and left Bruges by the Eastern barrier; we showed our passes and proceeded into the darkened country-side. We had been running for about a mile when she remarked, "Prisoners will now be blindfolded!" and, to my astonishment, slipped a little black silk bag over my head.

I was so startled I didn't know whether to be angry, or to laugh, or what to do. Eventually I did nothing, and, entering into the spirit of the game, declared that even a wretched prisoner had the right not to be stifled, whereupon she lifted the lower portion of the bag and uncovered my mouth. Shortly afterwards I was electrified to feel a pair of soft lips meet mine, a sensation which was repeated at frequent intervals, and, as I whispered in her ear, under these conditions I was prepared to be taken prisoner into the jaws of hell.

This pleasant journey had lasted for about three-quarters of an hour when my mask was removed and I was informed that I was "inside the enemy lines!" Through the windows of the car I could dimly see that an apparently endless mass of fir trees were rushing past on each side. This state of affairs continued for a kilometre or so, when we branched to the right and soon entered a large clearing in the forest, at one side of which stood the house. Babette, Zoe and myself entered the building, and the car disappeared, presumably back to Bruges.

The house, built of logs, was of two stories; on the ground floor were two living rooms, and the domains of Babette, who amongst her other accomplishments turned out to be not only a most capable valet, but a first-class cook. On the second story there were two large rooms. The whole house was furnished after the manner of a hunting lodge, with stags' heads on the walls, and skins on the floors. In the drawing-room there was a piano and a few etchings of the wild boar by Schaffein.

I dressed for dinner in my "smoking," though under ordinary circumstances I should have considered this rather formal, but I was glad I did, for she appeared in full evening *tenue*. She wore a violet gown, and across her forehead a black satin bandeau with a Z in diamonds upon it. It must have cost two thousand marks, and I wondered with a dull kind of jealousy whether the Colonel had given it to her.

I cannot remember of what we talked during dinner. We have a hundred subjects in common, and we look at so many aspects of the world through the same pair of eyes; I only know that when I have been talking to her for a period—there is no exact measurement of time for me when I am with her—I leave her presence feeling "completed." I feel that a sort of gap within my being has been filled, that a spiritual hunger has been satisfied, that I have got something which I wanted, but for which I could not have formulated the desire in words. I had resolved that on this first night I would bring matters between us to a head and end this delicious but intolerable uncertainty as to how we stood; yet, when old Babette had served us with coffee in the drawing-room, as I call the second living-room, and we were alone together, I could not bring up the subject. Partly because I think she prevented me so doing by that skilful shepherding of the conversation into other paths with an artfulness with which God endows all women, and also partly because I could not screw myself up to the pitch. I could not, or rather would not, put my fate to the touch. I had a presentiment that in reaching for the summit I might fall from the slope. Alas! how true was this foreboding in some senses—but I will keep all things in their right order.

THE TRACK MET OUR RAM.

IN THE FLASH I CAUGHT A GLIMPSE OF HIS CONNING TOWER.

Let it only be recorded that when she kissed me good-night (with the tenderness of a mother) and left me to smoke a final cigar I had said nothing, and I could only wonder at the strange fate that had placed me practically alone with a girl whom I had grown to love with a deep emotion, and who appeared to love me, yet often behaved as if I was her brother.

The next day we were like two children. The snow was deep on the ground, and the fir trees stood like thousands of sentinels in grey uniform round the clearing. Once during the afternoon, as with Zoe's assistance I was furiously chopping wood for the fire, a droning noise made me look up, and thousands of metres overhead a small squadron of aeroplanes, evidently bound for the Western Front, sailed slowly across the sky. I thought how awkward it would be for them if they experienced an engine failure whilst over the forest, though they were up so high that I imagine they could have glided ten kilometres, and as I think (but I am not certain, and I have pledged myself not to try and find out) we were in the Forest of Montellan, which is barely fifteen kilometres broad, I suppose they could have fallen clear of the trees.

As a matter of fact I imagine they would have used our clearing—I'm glad they didn't.

That night after dinner she played to me, first Beethoven and then Chopin. I can see her as I write; she had just finished the 14th Prelude and, resting her chin on her hand, she smiled mysteriously at me.

The hour had come, and, driven by strong impulses, I spoke. I told her that I loved her as I had never thought that a man could love a woman; I told her that I longed to shield her and protect her, and above all things to remove her from the clutches of that bestial Colonel, and as I bent over her and felt my senses swim in the subtleties of her perfume, I begged her passionately to say the word that would give me the right to fight the world on her behalf.

When I had finished she was silent for a long while, and I can remember distinctly that I wondered whether she could hear the thump! thump! thump! of my heart, which to my agitated mind seemed to beat with the strength of a hammer.

At length she spoke; two words came slowly from her lips:

"I cannot."

I was not discouraged. I could see, I could feel, that a tremendous struggle was raging, the outward signs of which were concealed by her averted head.

At length I asked her point-blank whether she loved me. Her silence gave me my answer, and I took her unresisting body into my arms and kissed her to distraction. Oh! these kisses, how bitter they seem to me now, and yet how I long to hold her once again. For, freeing herself from my embrace and speaking almost mechanically, she said:

"Karl! I must tell you. I cannot marry you."

I pleaded, I prayed, I argued, I demanded. It was in vain; I always came up against the immovable "I cannot."

And then I crashed over the precipice towards whose edge I had been blindly going. I had said for the hundredth time, "But you know you love me," when with a sob she abandoned all reserve, and, flinging her arms round my neck, implored me to take her. Then, as I caught my breath, she quickly said, as if frightened that she had gone too far, "But I cannot marry you."

I looked down into those beautiful eyes, and for the first time I understood. For perhaps ten seconds I battled for my soul and the purity of our love; then, tearing my sight from those eyes which would lure an archangel to destruction, I was once more master of my body. As my resolution grew, I hated her for doing this thing that had wrecked in an instant the hopes of months, the ideals on which I had begun to build afresh my life.

She felt the change, and left me.

As she went out by the door she gave me one last look, a look in which love struggled with shame, a look which no man has ever earned the right to receive from any woman.

But I was as a statue of marble, dazed by this calamity.

As the door closed upon her, I started forward—it was too late.

Had she waited another instant—but there, I write of what has happened and not what might have been.

I did not sleep that night, until the dawn began to separate each fir tree from the black mass of the forest. Twice in the night, with shame I confess it, I opened my door and looked down the little passage-way; and twice I closed the door and threw myself upon my bed in an agony of torment. It was ten o'clock when a knock at the door aroused me, and the sunlight through the window-pane was tracing patterns on the floor.

There was a note on the breakfast table, but before I opened it I knew that, save for Babette, I was alone in the house.

The note was brief, unaddressed and unsigned. I have it here before me; I have meant to tear it up but I cannot. It is a weakness to keep it, but I have lost so much in the last few days, that I will not grudge myself some small relic of what has been. The note says:

"I am leaving for Bruges at half-past eight, when the car was ordered to fetch us back. I go alone. Babette will give you breakfast. The car will return for you at eleven o'clock. I rely on your honour in that you will not observe where you have been. Come to me when you want me—till then, farewell."

It was as she said, and I honourably acceded to her request. This afternoon just before lunch I arrived in Bruges, and since tea-time I have tried to write down what has happened since I left the day before yesterday. Oh! how could she do it, how can it be possible that she is a woman like that? I could have sworn that she was not like this—and yet how can I account for her life with the Colonel? There must be some reason, but in Heaven's name, what?

Meanwhile I am to go to her when I want her! And that will be when I can give her my name. But oh! Zoe, I want you now, so badly, oh! so badly!

* * * * *

I saw her once today in the gardens, walking by herself.

* * * * *

I have told Max's secretary that I want to get to sea; to be here in Bruges and not to see her is more than I can bear.

I sail at dawn tomorrow. Shall I see her? No, it is best not.

A frightful noise over the New Year celebrations tonight. Champagne flowing like water in the Mess. I feel the year 1917 opens badly for me.

Weissman also went to sea again for a short trip in the Channel, and has not reported for five days. Perhaps he has despised the Dover Barrage once too often. If this is so, it is a great loss to the service: he was a man of iron resolution in underwater attack.

I feel I ought to despise Zoe, but I can't. I love her too much; after all, am I not perhaps encasing myself in the robe of a Pharisee?

She offered me all she had, save only the one thing I asked, without which I will take nothing. I cannot reconcile her behaviour with her character; why can't she trust me? why can't she be frank with me? I will not believe she is that sort.

I feel I cannot go out again without a *sign*—I may not return, and I will not leave her, perhaps for ever, with this bitterness between us.

* * * * *

At sea in U.C.47 again

Alten as surly as ever. I decided finally to write to Zoe, but found it difficult to know what to say. Eventually I said more than I had intended. I told her frankly that I experienced a shock, but that I had not meant to seem so cold, and that what I had done had been done for both our sakes. I told her that I still loved her, and I implored her once more to leave the Colonel and come to me as my wife. Already I long to know what message awaits me on my return. This will not be for three days. We left at dawn this morning to lay mines off the channel to Harwich harbour; a nest from which submarines, cruisers and destroyers buzz in and out like wasps. It will be ticklish work.

On the bottom

Our mines are still with us, but so are our lives, which is something. We were approaching the appointed spot at 6 a.m. this morning, when without the slightest warning the track of a torpedo was seen streaking towards us about 50 yards on the starboard bow.

Before Alten (who was on the bridge with me) could do more than press the diving alarm, the track met our ram. I breathed again, and was then reminded by an oath from Alten that the boat was diving.

It was evident that we had only been saved by the torpedo running deep under the cut-away part of our bow, otherwise!—well, the tangle of my affairs would have been easily straightened.

Further procedure on the surface was suicidal, and we kept hydrophone patrol, twice hearing the motors of the enemy submarine. At the moment we are on the bottom waiting to come up and charge tonight, and lay our mines at dawn tomorrow.

*****

On the bottom in 28 metres and feeling none too comfortable, as there would appear to be about a dozen destroyers overhead.

Last night, or rather early this morning, I participated in one of the most extraordinary incidents that I have ever heard of.

It was pitch-black dark when I took over at 4 a.m., and a fresh breeze had raised a lumpy sea, which covered the bridge with spray. We were charging 400 amps on each, with the intention of laying one mine directly there was sufficient light to get a fix from some of the buoys which the English stick down all over the place here in the most convenient manner possible. If only one could believe they never shifted them. Alten says it never occurs to an Englishman to do a thing like that, but I'm not so sure. However, we were proceeding along at about five knots, crashing into the sea rather badly, when out of the black beastliness of the night I saw a shape close aboard on the port hand.

As I hesitated for a second as to my course of action, I was astounded to see a large submarine which must have been British, on an opposite course, not more than 25 metres away!

This sounds absurd, but it really wasn't further. I'm not ashamed to confess that I was completely disorganized; it did not seem possible that the enemy was literally alongside me.

I don't know how it struck the officer in the British boat, but I must give him credit for doing something first, for he fired a Very's white light straight at me as the two boats passed. It impinged on the hull, and in the flash I caught a photographic glimpse of his conning tower, on which was painted the letter E, followed by two numbers, of which one was a two I think, and the other a nine.

By this time he was on my port quarter and rapidly disappearing; in a frenzy of rage I managed to get my revolver out, and whilst with the left hand I pressed the diving alarm, with the right hand I emptied the magazine in his direction. When we were down, Alten practically refused to believe me, which made me very pleased that in descending I had trod on a pair of hands which turned out to be his, as he had started up the ladder to the upper conning tower when he first heard the alarm.

I presume our opponent dived as well, but evidently he had put two and two together and used his aerial at some period, for when at dawn we poked a periscope up, a flotilla of destroyers appeared to be looking for something, which "something" was us, unless I am much mistaken; so we bottomed, where we have been ever since. The Hydroplane Operator keeps up a monotonous sing-song to the effect that "Fast running propellers are either receding or approaching." The crew are collected round the mine-tubes as I write, and are singing a lugubrious song, the refrain of which runs:

Death for the Fatherland! Glorious fate,
This is the end that we gladly await.

Why will the seamen always become morbid when possible? And there is not a man amongst them who is not inwardly thinking of some beer-hall in Bruges, though I suppose that like their betters they have their romances of a tenderer kind.

* * * * *

The boat has been rolling about on the bottom in the most sickening manner the whole afternoon. We flooded P and Q to capacity, which gave her 50 tons negative, but it seems to have little effect in steadying her, and it is evident that a really heavy gale is running on top.

* * * * *

Surfaced at 10 p.m.; a very heavy sea running and impossible to do much more than heave to. This weather has one point in its favour and that is that the destroyers are driven in.

It got steadily worse all night, and at midnight we lost our foremost wireless mast overboard; we have now (10 a.m.) been 48 hours without communication. At dawn we could see nothing to fix by; not a buoy in sight, nothing but an expanse of foam-topped short steep waves of dirty neutral-tinted water; how different to the great green and white surges of the broad Atlantic.

Under these circumstances Alten decided to risk it and return without laying our mines; for once in a way I agreed with him, as it is better not to lay a minefield at all than dump one down in some unknown position which one may have to traverse oneself in the course of a month or so. We are now slowly, very slowly, struggling back to Zeebrugge.

A green sea came down the conning tower today, and everything in the boat is damp and smelly and beastly. The propellers race at frequent intervals and the whole boat shudders—I feel miserable.

Alten has started to drink spirits; he began as soon as we decided to go back. He will be incapable by tonight, and it means that I shall have to take her in.

What hell this is, sitting in sodden clothes, with the stench of four days' living assaulting the nostrils, and a motion of the devil; the glass is very low and is slowly rising, so that I suppose it will blow harder soon, though it is about force eight at present.

I wonder what Zoe will have written in reply to my note. When I think of what I rejected and compare it with my beast-like existence here, I can hardly believe that I behaved as I did—what would I not give now to be transported back to the forest! At this rate of progress we shall take another 24 hours. I wonder if I can knock another half-knot out of her without smashing her up.

* * * * *

The extraordinarily violent motion has upset the *Anschutz*.[1] The bearing cone of the stabilizing gyro has cracked, and the master compass began to wander off in circles. I was just resting for an hour or two, wedged up on a wet settee with coats equally wet, when her heavy pitching changed to a wallowing roll, and I heard the pilot, who was on watch, cursing down the voice-pipe, as we had sagged off our course.

I heard the voice of the helmsman querulously maintain that he was steering his course by *Anschutz*, so I got up and gingerly clawed my way into the control room, where I found by comparing *Anschutz* with magnetic that the former had gone to hell, the reason being obvious, as the stabilizer was exerting a strongly biased torque. I stopped the *Anschutz* and asked the pilot to give the helmsman a steady by magnetic.

As we staggered back to our course I heard a thud in the wardroom, and on returning to my settee found that Alten had rolled out of his bunk, where he was lying in a drunken stupor, and that he was face downwards, sprawling on the deck, half his face in the broken half of a dirty dish which had fallen off the table whilst I

1: Gyroscopic compass.

was having tea. As I couldn't let the crew see him like this, I was obliged to struggle and get him back into his bunk. He was like a log and absolutely incapable of rendering me any assistance, though he did open his eyes and mutter once or twice as I lifted him up, trunk first and then his legs. He stank of spirits and I hated touching him. Lord! what a truly hoggish man he is; yet I cannot help envying him his oblivion to these surroundings.

* * * * *

Arrived in, this afternoon.

Alten quite slept off his drink, and was offensively sarcastic as I worked on the forepart with wires, getting her into the shelters alongside the mole.

I hastened up to Bruges, and in the Mess heard several items of news and found two letters. The first, in a well-known handwriting, I opened eagerly, but received a chill of disappointment when I read its single line.

I am here when you want me.—Z.

So she thinks to break my resolution!

No! I am stronger than she, and, now that I know she loves me, I can and will bend her to my will. Even now, at this distance of time, I can hardly understand my conduct the other day. I must have been given the strength of ten. I feel that I could not do it again; had she hesitated a second longer at the door—well, I can hardly say what I would have done.

It is my duty to do so, for her sake and my own. But I know my weakness, and in this fact lies my strength. Cost what it may, I shall not permit myself to go near her until she yields.

The second letter gave me a great surprise. It was from Rosa. She has passed some examination, and is coming *here* of all places as a Red Cross nurse. She says she is looking forward to going round a U-boat! She assumes a good deal, I must say, still, I suppose I must be polite to her; but why the deuce does she sign herself "Yours, Rosa?" She's not mine, and I don't want her; it seems funny to me that I once thought of her vaguely in that sort of way. Now, I feel rather disturbed that she is coming here, though I don't quite see why I should worry, and yet I wonder if it is a coincidence her coming to Bruges?

I'm almost inclined to think it isn't. After all, every girl wants to get married, and without conceit my family, circumstances and, in the privacy of the pages of this journal I may add, my personal appearances, are such as would appeal to most girls—except Zoe, apparently!

I'll have to be on my guard against Miss Rosa.

I heard today that I am likely to be appointed to the periscope school in a few weeks' time, and meanwhile I am to be attached as supernumerary to the operations division on old Max's staff.

* * * * *

The work here is most interesting. I feel glad that I am one of the spiders weaving the web for Britain's destruction.

The impasse with Zoe still continues, and my peace of mind has been still further disturbed by the actual arrival of Rosa. She rang me up within twelve hours of her arrival, and, of course, I was obliged to call. That was the day before yesterday. Rosa is at the No. 3 Hospital here, and was horribly effusive. Some people would, I suppose, call her good-looking, but to me, with my mind's-eye in perpetual contemplation of my darling Zoe, Rosa looked like a turnip. Her first movement after the preliminary greetings was to offer me a cigarette! I then noticed that her fingers were stained with nicotine, unpleasant in a man, disgusting in a woman.

Her nose was shiny and greasy—horrible. After a little talk she volunteered the statement that yesterday was her afternoon off, and she was simply longing to have tea in the gardens.

I endeavoured to make some feeble excuse on the grounds of the weather being unsuitable, but I am no good at these social lies, and I was eventually obliged to promise to take her there. I was the more annoyed in that her main object was obviously to be seen walking with a U-boat officer.

Accordingly, yesterday, I found myself walking about with her at my side. My feelings can better be imagined than described when I suddenly saw Zoe, accompanied by Babette, in the distance. I hastily altered course, and pray she didn't see me.

In the course of the afternoon Rosa had the impertinence to say that at Frankfurt they were saying that I was interested in a beautiful widow at Bruges, and could she (Rosa) write and say I was heart-whole, or else what the girl was like. I'm afraid that I lost my temper a little, and I told Rosa she could write to all the busybodies at home and tell them from me to go to the devil.

These women in the home circle, and especially aunts, are always the same; firstly, they badger one to get married, and then if they think one is contemplating such a step they are all agog to find out whether she is suitable!

* * * * *

Three more boats, two of which are U.C.'s, are overdue. It is distinctly unpleasant not knowing how or where they go, though the U.B. boat (Friederich Althofen) made her incoming position the day before yesterday as off Dungeness, so it looks as if the barrage at Dover which got Weissman has got Althofen as well. I wonder what new devilry they have put down there.

How one wishes that in 1914, instead of seeking the capture of Paris, we had realized the importance of the Channel Ports to England, and struck for them!

It would not have been necessary to strike even in September, 1914. We could have walked into them. Dunkirk, at all events, should have been ours; however, we must do the best with things as they are, not that I would consider it too late even now to make a big push for the French coast.

It would seem, as a matter of fact, that all the pushing is to be at the other end of the line, in the Verdun sector, from the rumours I hear, though I should have thought once bitten twice shy in that quarter.

* * * * *

Saw Zoe again in the distance, and I think she saw me; at all events she turned round and walked away.

This girl whom I cannot, and would not if I could, obliterate from my thoughts, is causing me much worry.

She shows no sign of giving in, and I for one intend to be adamant. I shall defeat her in time. The male intellect is always ultimately victorious, other things being equal. I was reading Schopenhauer on the subject last night. What a brain that man had, though I confess his analysis of the female mentality is so terribly and truthfully cruel that it jars on certain of my feelings.

Zoe's resolution in this conflict, this sex war one might call it, only adds to her charm in my eyes; she is, I feel, a worthy mate for me, both intellectually and physically, and she shall be mine—I have decided it.

Met Rosa today at old Max's house, where I went to pay a duty call.

Her Excellency is as forbidding a specimen of her sex as any I have ever met. She quite frightened me, and in the home circle the old man seemed quite subdued.

I escorted Rosa home, and on the way to her hospital she gave me a great surprise, as after much evasive talk she suddenly came out with the news that she was engaged to Heinrich Baumer, of U.C.23. I was quite taken aback, and will frankly confess that not so very long ago I imagined, evidently erroneously, that she was disposed to let her affections become engaged in another quarter. However, I was really very glad to hear this news, and congratulated her with genuine feeling.

The knowledge that she was a promised woman quite altered my feelings towards her, and before I quite meant to, I had told her a considerable amount about Zoe. It gave me much relief to be able to unburden myself, and confide my difficulties elsewhere than in the pages of this journal.

I have asked the girl to tea tomorrow.

*****

A vile air raid last night. British machines, of course. They seemed determined to get over the town, and from 1 a.m. to 3 a.m. relays of machines (of which not *one* was shot down) attacked us. The din was tremendous, and all sleep was out of the question.

Morning revealed surprisingly little damage, as is often the case in these big raids, whereas a few bombs from a chance machine often work havoc. I was down at 50 B.C. aerodrome this morning, and heard that as soon as the moon suits we are going to make Dunkirk sit up as retaliation for last night's efforts. There were also rumours of big attacks impending on London as soon as the new type of Gothas are delivered. That will shake the smug security of those cursed islanders.

Rosa came to tea, and afterwards I told her more about Zoe,

and as I expect any day to be appointed to the periscope school at Kiel, I asked Rosa to try and effect an introduction to Zoe, and do what she could for me. Rosa gave me the impression that she was somewhat surprised that I should have had any difficulty with Zoe (of course I had not told her of the shooting-box scene). Rosa evidently thinks any woman ought to be honoured....

Perhaps I was not so far wrong in my surmises as to Rosa's previous inclinations—I wonder; at any rate she will undoubtedly make Baumer a good wife, and she will probably be very fruitful and grow still fatter and housewifely. She is of a type of woman appointed by God in his foresight as breeders. Zoe, my adorable one, will probably not take kindly to babies.

* * * * *

I am ordered to report myself at Kiel by next Monday.

I am terribly tempted to ring up Zoe on the telephone before I leave: it seems dreadful to leave her without a word; but at the same time I feel that she would interpret this as a sign of weakness on my part—as indeed it would be. I must be firm, for strength of mind pays with women, even more than with men.

At Kiel

I left Bruges without a word either to or from my obstinate darling. It is torture being away from her. I had thought that when I was here and not exposed to the temptation of going round and seeing her, that it would be easier; it is not. I long to write, and how I wonder whether she is feeling it as I do.

I have read somewhere that a woman's passion once aroused is more ungovernable than a man's. That her whole being cries aloud for me cannot be doubted, and if the above statement is true what inflexibility of will she must be showing—it almost makes me fear—but no, I will defeat her in this strange contest, and she shall be my wife.

The work here is strenuous, and the grass does not grow under one's feet. The course for commanding officers lasts four weeks, and terminates in an exceedingly practical but rather fearsome test—*i.e.*, they have six steamers here camouflaged after the English fashion with dazzle painting, and these six steamers, protected by launches and harbour defence craft, steam across Kiel Bay in the manner of a convoy. The officer being examined has to attack this group of ships in one of the instructional submarines, and in three attacks he must score at least two hits, or else, in theory, he is returned to general service in the Fleet.

Fortunately at the moment I hear that owing to recent losses they are distinctly on the short side where submarine officers are concerned, so they'll probably make it easy when I do my test.

* * * * *

I see I have written nothing here for a fortnight; this is due to two causes: Firstly, I have been so extraordinarily busy, and, secondly, I have been most depressed through a letter I received from Fritz. It contained two items of bad news.

In the first place, I heard for the first time of the tragedy of Heinrich Baumer's boat, and to my astonishment Fritz tells me that Rosa and another girl were in her when she was lost!

It appears that she was to go out for a couple of hours' diving off the port as a matter of routine after her two months' overhaul. She went out at 10 a.m., and was sighted from the signal station at the end of the mole at 11.30, when almost immediately afterwards there was an explosion and she disappeared. Motor-boats were quickly on the scene, but only debris came to the surface. Divers were sent down, and reported that she was in ten metres of water completely shattered. It is assumed, for lack of other explanation, that she struck a chance drifting mine which was moving down the coast on the tide.

Meanwhile Rosa and another sister were missing from the hospital, and after forty-eight hours someone put two and two together and started investigations. It has been ascertained that Baumer motored down from Bruges after breakfast, and that in the car were two figures taken to be sailors, as they were muffled up in oilskins. This fact was noted by the control sentries, as, though the day was showery, it was not raining hard. Other scraps of evidence unite in showing that these were the two girls who had apparently induced Baumer to take them out for a dive as a treat.

What a tragedy! However, it must have been quite instantaneous. Poor Rosa, with all her vanities about war work, to think that the war would claim her like that![1]

Fritz added that old Max is almost off his head with rage over the whole business, and it is difficult to say whether he is more angry over Baumer and the boat being lost, or over the fact that Baumer being dead he is unable to administer those "disciplinary actions" in which he delights.

* * * * *

Great excitement here, as the day after tomorrow His Imperial Majesty the Kaiser and Hindenburg are due to pay Kiel a surprise visit. We are to be inspected and addressed. Tremendous preparations are going on.

* * * * *

His Majesty, accompanied by the great Field-Marshal, inspected us this morning, and made a fine speech, of which we have been given printed copies. I shall frame mine and hang it in my boat, if I get a command.

I transcribe it:

Officers and men of the U-boat service:

In the midst of the anxious moments in which we live I have determined to make time to come and witness in my own person the labours of those on whom I and the Fatherland rely. Fresh from the great battles on the West which are gnawing at the vitals of our hereditary enemies, I come to those whose glorious mission it will be to strike relentlessly at our most deadly and cunning enemy—cursed Britain. God is on our side and will protect you at sea for, in the striking at the nation which openly boasts that it aims at starving our women and children, you are engaged on a mission of undoubted holiness.

You must sink and destroy even as of old the Israelites smote and destroyed the alien races.

To the officers I would particularly say, my person is your

1: It is known that a boat with women on board was lost whilst exercising off Zeebrugge in the Spring of 1917. This would appear to be the boat in question.

honour, and I am your supreme chief. From my hands you will receive honour, and from my hands will proceed just punishment for the unhappy ones who fail in their duty.

To the men I would say, trust and obey your officers as you would your God. Officers and men! In you, your Kaiser and Fatherland place their trust—let neither be disappointed!

After his address, His Majesty graciously spoke a few words to individuals, of whom I had the signal honour of being one. I felt that I was in the presence of an Emperor. His gestures, his eyes, his voice, impressed me as belonging to a man born to command and to fill high places. The Field-Marshal never opened his mouth. I understand from his A.D.C. that he rarely speaks in public.

* * * * *

The colonel is *killed*! When I think about it, I am so excited I can hardly write!

I heard the great news last night, quite by accident. I was sitting in the Mess after dinner, and picked up *Die Woche*, and glancing at the pictures, I suddenly saw the portrait of Colonel Stein, of the Brandenburgers, killed on the 7th instant near Ypres. I recognized the ugly and bloated face immediately from the photograph of him which she had once shown me.

My first impulse was to send her a wire, but, on thinking matters over, I decided that it would be difficult to put all my thoughts into the curt sentences of a telegram, and, further, that as all wires are doubtless examined at the Main Post Office at Bruges, it might lead to trouble, so I wrote her a letter.

This, in a way, has been an exhibition of weakness on my part, as I had promised myself that I would not take the first step in reopening communication; but I feel that the fortunate death of Stein has completely altered the case. I told her in the letter that I realized that I had made mistakes, but that if she still loved me with half the strength that I loved her, then a telegram to me would make me the happiest of men.

I wrote that yesterday, but have had no wire. Perhaps, like me, she distrusts telegrams and prefers letters.

* * * * *

A long letter from Zoe: an accursed fetter—an abominable letter—a damnable letter; she still refuses to marry me. I leave for Bruges tonight on forty-eight hours' special leave.

Kiel, 17th

I hate Zoe, she has broken my heart.

After her preposterous letter of the 14th, I decided that in a matter which so closely affected my happiness no stone ought to remain unturned to ensure a satisfactory solution of the problem, so I determined to have a personal interview. I arrived at Bruges after tea and went at once to the flat.

I tackled her immediately on the subject of her letter, and told her that naturally I understood that a decent interval must elapse before we married; but, granted this fact, I told her that I failed to see what prevented our marriage.

A most unpleasant and harrowing scene ensued, the details of which form such painful recollections that I really cannot write them down here, though in the passage of months I have acquired the habit of writing in the pages of this journal with the same freedom as I would talk to that wife whom I had hoped to possess. She maintained an obstinate silence when I urged her to give me at least some tangible reason as to why she would not marry me. She contented herself and maddened me by reflecting in a kind of monotone: "I love you, Karl! and am yours, but I cannot marry you."

I could have beaten her till she was senseless, but I had enough sense to realize that with Zoe, whose resolution, considering she is a woman, amazes me, force is not the best method. As I continued to press her (time was important: had I not journeyed far to see her?), those glorious eyes of hers, which I love and whose power I dread, filled with tears. I was a brute! I was heartless! I was inconsiderate! I could not love her! I was cruel! And I know not what other accusation crushed me down. Broken-hearted and dispirited, I told her to choose there and then.

She collapsed on to a sofa in a storm of tears, and after a severe mental struggle I took the only possible course, and leaving the room—left her for ever. I have resumed my service life determined to cast her out from my mind.

I will not deceive myself: it will be hard. Love and Logic are deadly enemies, but Logic must and shall prevail. Though I have seen her for the last time, I cannot escape the net of fascination which the girl has thrown over me. Perhaps in the course of time I shall slowly emerge and free myself from its entanglements. At present I hate her for this blow she has dealt me, and yet, O Zoe! my darling, how I long to be with you!

* * * * *

To-day I went through my final test for qualification as U-boat commander.

At 9 a.m. I proceeded to sea in command of the *U.11*, one of the instructional boats here. We proceeded out into Kiel Bay. On board and watching my every movement was a committee consisting of a commander and two lieutenant-commanders.

On arrival at the entrance lightship, I was ordered to attack a convoy of camouflaged ships which were just visible about fifteen kilometres away off the Spit Bank. I had a very shrewd idea as to the course they would steer, and on coming up for my final observation I found myself in an excellent position, 1,000 metres on the bow of the leading ship. The rest was easy. I gave the leader the two bow torpedoes, and, turning sixteen points, fired my stern tube at the third ship of the line. Two hits were obtained, and I returned to harbour well pleased with myself. There is not the slightest chance of having failed to qualify.

* * * * *

My confidence in myself was not misplaced; I heard today that I am on the command list, and anticipate in a few days being appointed to a boat. I wonder which craft I shall get?

* * * * *

I met the A.D.C. to the Chief of the Staff at the school, at the gardens, and in conversation with him discovered that he had heard that three boats were being detached from the Flanders flotilla for an unknown destination. This has given me an idea, for I feel that I can never return to Bruges, and I was rather dreading being appointed to one of the boats there. I have dropped a line to Fritz Regels, who is on old Max's staff, and told him that I do not wish to return to Bruges, and I further hinted that I understood a detached squadron was proceeding somewhere, and, as far as I was concerned, the further the better, if I could get into it.

I have tried the night life at this place at the Mascotte and Trocadero,¹ in order to forget, but it is a poor consolation.

* * * * *

A letter from Fritz, saying that he has an idea that Korting's boat would suit me, though he could not of course give me further details in a letter; however, he informs me positively that I shall not be at Bruges.

On the strength of this I have wired to Fritz, and asked him to try and fix up an exchange between me and Korting, provided the latter is agreeable and the people in Max's office have no objection. I have a recollection that Korting's boat is one of the U.40—U.60 class, which would suit me admirably, and, as for destination, I care not where it is, provided only that it be far from Bruges.

At sea

I have quite neglected my poor old journal for several weeks. But I have passed through an extraordinarily busy period.

It was approved that I should relieve Korting, whose boat, the *U.59*, I discovered to be refitting at Wilhelmshaven. I was very pleased not to go back to Bruges, though as we steam steadily north at this moment I cannot escape a sense of deep disappointment that upon my return from this trip I shall not enjoy as of old the fascination of Zoe. But I shall have plenty of time to get accustomed to this idea, for this is no ordinary trip.

We are bound for the North Cape and Murman Coast, where we remain until well into the cold weather—at any rate, for three months. Our mission is to work off that fogbound and desolate coast, and attack the constant stream of traffic between England and Archangel. There are two other boats besides ourselves on the job, but we shall all be working far apart.

Our first billet is off the North Cape. In order to save time, we are to be provisioned once a month in one of the fjords. I don't

---

1: Two well-known cabarets at Kiel.

imagine the Admiralty will have any difficulty in getting supplies up to us, as at the moment we are off the Lofotens, and we actually have not had to dive since we left the Bight!

There seems to be nothing on the sea except ourselves. Where is the much vaunted and impenetrable web of blockade which the English are supposed to have spread around us? And yet many raw materials are getting very short with us. I see that in this boat they have replaced several copper pipes with steel ones during her refit, and this will lead to trouble unless we are careful—steel pipes corrode so badly that I never feel ready to trust them for pressure work.

The truth about the blockade is that it is largely a paper blockade, yet not ineffective for all that. Unfortunately for us, the damned English and their hangers-on control the cables of the world, and hence all the markets, and I don't suppose, to take the case of copper, that a single pound of it is mined from the Rio Tinto without the British Board of Trade knowing all about it. The neutral firms simply dare not risk getting put on to the British Black List; it means ruination for them. And then all these dollar-grabbing Yankees, enjoying all the advantages of war without any of its dangers—they make me sick.

This seems a most profitable job. I have only been up seven days, but I've bagged four steamers, all by gun-fire, and all fat ships, brimful of stuff for the Russians. My practice has been to make the North Cape every day or two to fix position, as the currents are the most abnormal in these parts, and I should say that the *Sailing Directions Pilotage Handbook* and tidal charts were compiled by a gentleman at a desk who had never visited these latitudes.

At the moment I am standing well out to sea, as the immediate vicinity of the North Cape has become rather unhealthy.

Yesterday afternoon (I had sunk number four in the morning, and the crew were still pulling for the coast) four British trawlers turned up. These damned little craft seem to turn up wherever one goes. I longed to have a bang at them with my gun, but, apart from the uncertainty as to what they carried in the way of armament, I have strict orders to avoid all that sort of thing, so I dived and steamed slowly west, came up at dusk and proceeded to charge up my batteries.

These U.60's are excellent boats, and I am very lucky to get one so soon. I suppose Korting, being a married man, wants to stay near his wife. I cannot write that word without painful memories of Zoe and idle thoughts of what might have been. Well, perhaps it is for the best. I am not sure that a member of the U-boat service has the right to get married in war-time, for unless he is of exceptional mentality it must affect his outlook under certain circumstances, though I think I should have been an exception here. Then the anxiety to the woman must be enormous; as every trip comes round a voice must cry within her, this may be the last. The contrast between the times in harbour and the trips is so violent, so shattering and clear cut.

With a soldier's wife, she merely knows that he is at the front; with us, at 8 p.m. one may be kissing one's wife in Bruges, and at 6 a.m. creeping with nerves on edge through the unknown dangers of the Dover Barrage—but I have strayed from what I meant to write about—my first command and her crew.

The quarters in this class are immensely superior to the U.C.-boats. Here I have a little cabin to myself, with a knee-hole table in it. My First Lieutenant, the Navigator and the Engineer have bunks in a room together, and then we have a small officers' mess.

On this job up here, as we are not to return to Germany for supplies, and, consequently, I should say we may have to live on what we can get out of steamers, I don't propose to use my torpedoes unless I meet a warship or an exceptionally large steamer.

The gun's the thing, as Arnauld de la Perrière has proved in the Mediterranean; but half the fellows won't follow his example, simply because they don't realize that it's no use employing the gun unless it is used accurately, and good shooting only comes after long drill.

I have impressed this fact on my gun crew, and particularly the two gun-layers, and I make Voigtman (my young First Lieutenant) take the crew through their loading drill twice a day, together with practice of rapid manning of the gun after a "surface" or rapid abandonment of the gun should the diving alarms sound in the middle of practice. I have also impressed on Voigtman that I consider that he is the gun control officer, and that I expect him to make the efficient working of the gun his main consideration.

As regards the crew, they are the usual mixed crowd that one gets

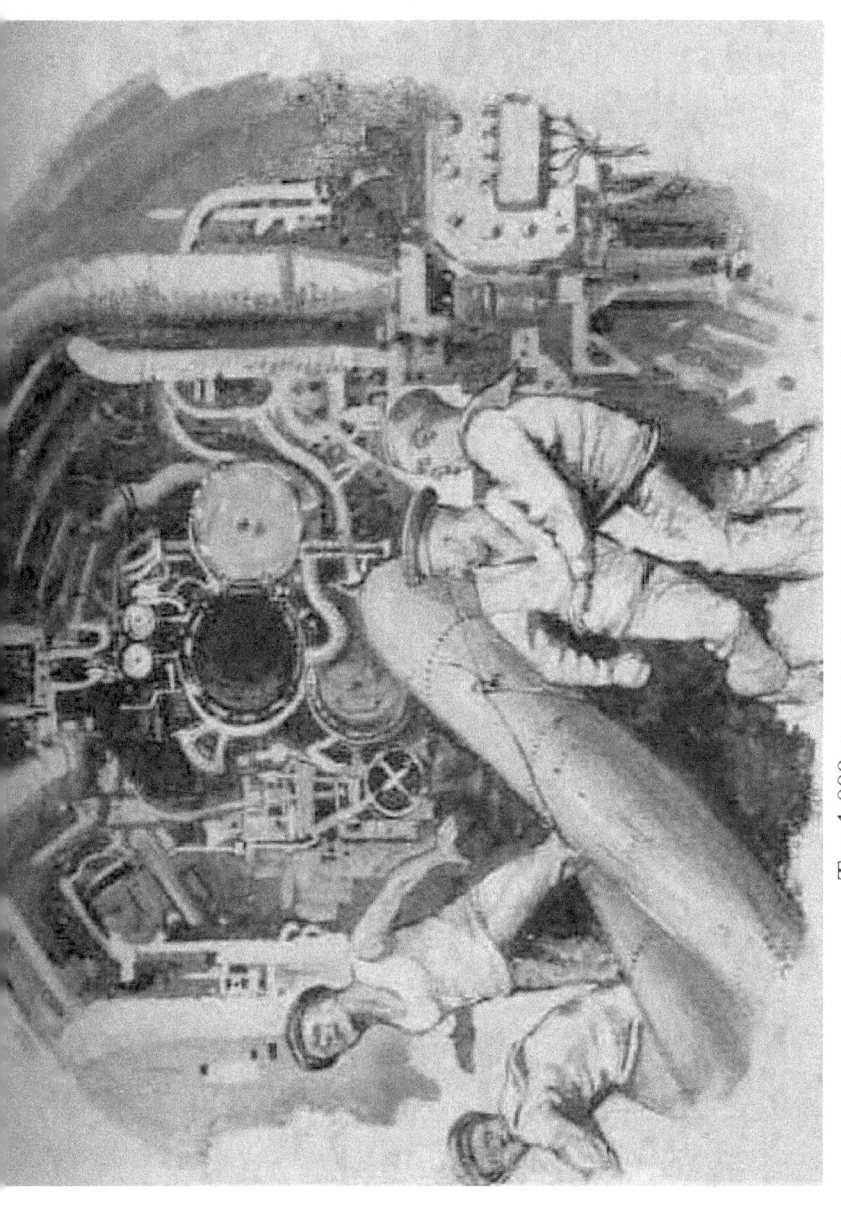

The 1,000 kilograms of metal crashed down.

GOOD-BYE! STEER WEST FOR AMERICA!

IT IS A SNUG ANCHORAGE AND HERE I INTEND TO REMAIN.

nowadays: half of them are old sailors, the others recruits and new arrivals from the Fleet. My main business at the moment is to get the youngsters into shape, and for this purpose I have been doing a number of crash dives. It also gives me an opportunity of getting used to the boat's peculiarities under water. She seems to have a tendency to become tail-heavy, but this may be due to bad trimming.

Voigtman has been in *U.B. 43* for nine months, and seems a capable officer. Socially, I don't think he can boast of much descent, but he has no airs, and treats me with pleasing respect, apart from service considerations.

* * * * *

A very awkward accident took place this morning, which resulted in severe injury to Johann Wiener, my second coxswain.

A party of men under his direction were engaged in shifting the stern torpedo from its tube, in order to replace it with a spare torpedo, as I never allow any of my torpedoes to stay in the tube for more than a week at a time owing to corrosion. The torpedo which had been in the tube had been launched back and was on the floor plates.

The spare torpedo, destined for the vacant tube, was hanging overhead, when without any warning the hook on the lifting band fractured, and the 1,000 kilograms mass of metal crashed down.

Wonderful to relate, no one was killed, but two men were badly bruised, and Wiener has been very seriously injured. He was standing astride the spare torpedo, and his right leg was extremely badly crushed, mostly below the knee.

Unfortunately it took about ten minutes to release him from his position of terrible agony. I should have expected him to faint, but he did not. His face went dead white, and he began to sweat freely, but otherwise endured his ordeal with praiseworthy fortitude.

I am now confronted with a perplexing situation. I cannot take him back to Germany; I cannot even leave my station and proceed south to any of the Norwegian ports. If I could find a neutral steamer with a doctor on board, I would tranship him to her; but the chances of this God-send materializing are a thousand to one in these latitudes. If I sighted a hospital ship I would close her, but as far as I know at present there are no hospital ships running up here. The chances of outside assistance may therefore be reckoned as nil. Wiener's hope of life depends on me, and I cannot make up my mind to take the step which sooner or later must be taken—that is to say, amputation.

It is a curious fact, but true, nevertheless, that although, as a result of the war, men's lives, considered in quantity, seem of little importance, when it comes to the individual case, a personal contact, a man's life assumes all its pre-war importance.

I feel acutely my responsibility in this matter. I see from his papers that he is a married man with a family; this seems to make it worse. I feel that a whole chain of people depend on me.

*****

Since I wrote the above words this morning, Wiener has taken a decided turn for the worse.

I have been reading the "Medical Handbook," with reference to the remarks on amputation, gangrene, etc., and I have also been examining his leg. The poor devil is in great pain, and there is no doubt that mortification has set in, as was indeed inevitable. I have decided that he must have his last chance, and that at 8 p.m. tonight I will endeavour to amputate.

Midnight

I have done it—only partially successful.

*****

Last night, in accordance with my decision, I operated on Wiener. Voigtman assisted me. It was a terrible business, but I think it desirable to record the details whilst they are fresh in my memory, as a Court of Inquiry may be held later on. Voigtman and I spent the whole afternoon in the study of such meagre details on the subject as are available in the "Medical Handbook." We selected our knives and a saw and sterilized them; we also disinfected our hands.

At 7.45 I dived the boat to sixty metres, at which depth the boat was steady. We had done our best with the wardroom-table, and upon this the patient was placed. I decided to amputate about four inches above the knee, where the flesh still seemed sound. I considered it impracticable to administer an anaesthetic, owing to my absolute inexperience in this matter.

Three men held the patient down, as with a firm incision I began the work. The sawing through the bone was an agonizing procedure, and I needed all my resolution to complete the task. Up to this stage all had gone as well as could be expected, when I suddenly went through the last piece of bone and cut deep into the flesh on the other side. An instantaneous gush of blood took place, and I realized that I had unexpectedly severed the *popliteal* artery, before Voigtman, who was tying the veins, was ready to deal with it.

I endeavoured to staunch the deadly flow by nipping the vein between my thumb and forefinger, whilst Voigtman hastily tried to tie it. Thinking it was tied, I released it, and alas! the flow at once started again; once more I seized the vein, and once again Voigtman tried to tie it. Useless—we could not stop the blood. He would undoubtedly have bled to death before our eyes, had not Voigtman cauterized the place with an electric soldering-iron which was handy.

Much shaken, I completed the amputation, and we dressed the stump as well as we could.

At the moment of writing he is still alive, but as white as snow; he must have lost litres of blood through that artery.

9 P.M

Wiener died two hours ago. I should say the immediate cause of death was shock and loss of blood. I did my best.

*****

We have been out on this extended patrol area seven days, but not a wisp of smoke greets our eyes.

Nothing but sea, sea, sea. Oh, how monotonous it is! I cannot make out where the shipping has got to. Tomorrow I am going to close the North Cape again. I think everything must be going inside me. I am too far out here.

*****

The North Cape bears due east. Nothing afloat in sight. Where the devil can all the shipping be? In ten days' time I am due to meet my supply ship; meanwhile I think I'll have to take another cast out, of three hundred miles or so.

* * * * *

Nothing in sight, nothing, nothing.

The barometer falling fast and we are in for a gale. I have decided to make the coast again, as I don't want to fail to turn up punctually at the rendezvous.

* * * * *

In the Standarak-Landholm Fjord

Thank heavens—Heavens! we have had a time. We were still two hundred and fifty miles from the coast when we were caught by the gale. And a gale up here is a gale, and no second thoughts about it. To say it blew with the force of ten thousand devils is to understate the case. The sea came on to us in huge foaming rollers like waves of attacking infantry intent on overwhelming us.

We struggled east at about three knots. But she stuck it magnificently. Low scudding clouds obscured the sky and came like a procession of ghosts from the north-east. Sun observations were impossible for two reasons. Firstly, no one could get on deck; secondly, there was no visible sun. This lasted for three days, at the end of which time we had only the vaguest idea as to where we were.

The gale then blew out, but, contrary to all expectations, was succeeded by a most abominable fog, thick and white like cotton-wool. These were hardly ideal conditions under which to close a rocky and unknown coast, but it had to be done. The trouble was that it was entirely useless taking soundings, as the twenty-metre depth-line on the chart went right up to the land. We crept slowly eastwards, till, when by dead reckoning we were ten miles inside the coast, the Navigator accidentally leant on the whistle lever; this action on his part probably saved the ship, as an immediate echo answered the blast. In an instant we were going full-speed astern. We altered course sixteen points and proceeded ten miles westerly, where we lay on and off the coast all night, cursing the fog.

Next day it lifted, and we spent the whole time trying to find the entrance to the S. Landholm Fjord. The coast appeared to bear no resemblance to the chart whatsoever.

The cliffs stand up to a height of several hundred metres, with occasional clefts where a stream runs down. There are no trees, houses, animals, or any signs of life, except sea birds, of which there are myriads. The Engineer declares he saw a reindeer, but five other people on deck failed to see any signs of the beast.

After hours of nosing about, during which my heart was in my mouth, as I quite expected to fetch up on a pinnacle rock, items which are officially described in the Handbook as being "very numerous," we rounded a bluff and got into a place which seems to answer the description of S. Landholm. At any rate, it is a snug anchorage, and here I intend to remain for a few days, and hope for my store-ship to turn up.

I've posted a daylight look-out on top of the bluff; it would be very awkward to be caught unawares in this place, which is only about 150 metres wide in places.

I'm taking advantage of the rest to give the crew some exercises and execute various minor repairs to the Diesels.

* * * * *

Yesterday we fought what must be one of the most remarkable single-ship actions of the war.

At 9 a.m. the look-out on the cliffs reported smoke to the northward.

I got the anchor up and made ready to push off, but still kept the look-out ashore. At 9.30 he reported a destroyer in sight, which seemed serious if she chose to look into my particular nook.

At any rate, I thought, I wouldn't be caught like a rat, so I got my look-out on board—a matter of ten minutes—and then proceeded out, trimmed down and ready for diving.

When I drew clear of the entrance I saw the enemy distant about a thousand metres. I at once recognized her as being one of the oldest type of Russian torpedo boats afloat. When I established this fact, a devil entered into my mind, and did a most foolhardy act.

I decided that I would not retreat beneath the sea, but that I would fight her as one service ship to another.

When I make up my mind, I do so in no uncertain manner—indecision is abhorrent to me—and I sharply ordered, "Gun's Crew—Action."

I can still see the comical look of wonderment which passed over my First Lieutenant's face, but he knows me, and did not hesitate an instant. We drilled like a battleship, and in sixty-five seconds—I timed it as a matter of interest—from my order we fired the first shot. It fell short.

Extraordinary to relate, the torpedo boat, without firing a gun, put her helm hard over, and started to steam away at her full speed, which I suppose was about seventeen knots.

I actually began to chase her—a submarine chasing a torpedo boat! It was ludicrous.

With broad smiles on their faces, my good gun's crew rapidly fired the gun, and we had the satisfaction of striking her once, near her after funnel, but it did no vital damage, as a few minutes afterwards she drew out of range! What a pack of incompetent cowards!

They never fired a shot at us. I suppose half of them were drunk or else in a state of semi-mutiny, for one hears strange tales of affairs in Russia these days.

The whole incident was quite humorous, but I realized that I had hardly been wise, as without doubt the English will hear of this, and these trawlers of theirs will turn up, and I'm certainly not going to try any heroics with John Bull, who is as tough a fighter as we are.

Meanwhile, what of the supply ship, for I'm supposed to meet her here, and it's already twenty-four hours since yesterday's epoch-making battle and I expect the English any moment.

*****

My doubts were removed for me since I received special orders at noon by high-power wireless from Nordreich, and on decoding them found that, for some reason or other, we are ordered to proceed to Muckle Flugga Cape, and thence down the coast of Shetlands to the Fair Island Channel, where we are directed to cruise till further orders. Special warning is included as to encountering friendly submarines.

It appears to me that a special concentration of U-boats is being ordered round about the Orkneys, and that some big scheme is on hand.

We are now steering south-westerly to make Muckle Flugga, which I hope to do in four days' time if the weather holds.

These Northern waters have proved very barren of shipping in the last few weeks, and this fact, coupled with the approaching winter weather, which must be fiendish in these latitudes, makes me quite ready to exchange the Archangel billet for the work round the Orkneys and Shetlands, though this is damnable enough in the winter, in all conscience.

There is only one fly in the ointment, and that is that this premature return to North Sea waters might conceivably mean a visit to Zeebrugge, though this class are not likely to be sent there.

Though it is many weeks since I left Zoe, I have not been able to forget her. I continually wonder what she is doing, and often when I am not on my guard she wanders into my thoughts.

Whilst I am up here, it does not matter much, except that it causes me unhappiness, but if I found myself at Bruges it would be very hard. However, I don't suppose I shall ever see her again.

* * * * *

Sighted Muckle Flugga this morning, and shaped course for Fair Island.

* * * * *

Oh! what a hell I have passed through. I can hardly realize that I am alive, but I am, though whether I shall be tomorrow morning is doubtful—it all depends on the weather, and who would willingly stake their life on North Sea weather at this time of the year?

Curses on the man who sent us to the Fair Island Channel. Where the devil is our Intelligence Service? If we make Flanders I have a story to tell that will open their eyes, blind bats that they are, luxuriating in the comfort of their fat staff jobs ashore.

The Fair Island Channel is an English death-trap; it stinks with death. By cursed luck we arrived there just as the English were trying one of their new devices, and it is the devil. Exactly what the system is, I don't quite know, and I hope never again to have to investigate it.

For forty-seven, hours we have been hunted like a rat, and now, with the pressure hull leaking in three places, and the boat half full of chlorine, we are struggling back on the surface, practically incapable of diving at least for more than ten minutes at a time. Even on the surface, with all the fans working, one must wear a gas mask to penetrate the fore compartment. Oh! these English, what devils they are!

Here is what happened:

Fair Island was away on our port beam when we sighted a large English trawler, which I suspected of being a patrol. To be on the safe side, I dived and proceeded at twenty metres for about an hour.

At 5 p.m. (approximately) I came up to periscope depth to have a look round, but quickly dived again as I discovered a trawler, steering on the same course as myself, about a thousand metres astern of me. This was the more disconcerting, as in the short time at my disposal it seemed to me that she was remarkably similar to the craft I had seen in the afternoon, and yet this hardly seemed likely, as I did not think she could have sighted me then.

On diving, I altered course ninety degrees, and proceeded for half an hour at full speed, then altered another ninety degrees, in the same direction as the previous alteration, and diving to thirty metres I proceeded at dead slow. By midnight I had been diving so much that I decided to get a charge on the batteries before dawn; I also wanted to be up at 1 a.m. to make my position report.

I surfaced after a good look round through the right periscope, which, as usual, revealed nothing. I had hardly got on the bridge, when a flash of flame stabbed the night on the starboard beam and a shell moaned just overhead.

I crash-dived at once, but could not get under before the enemy fired a second shot at us, which fortunately missed us. As we dived I ordered the helm hard a starboard, to counteract the expected depth-charge attack. We must have been a hundred and fifty metres from the first charge and a little below it, five others followed in rapid succession, but were further away, and we suffered no damage beyond a couple of broken lights. The situation was now extremely unpleasant. I did not dare venture to the surface, and thus missed my 1 a.m. signal from Headquarters. I wanted a charge badly, and so proceeded at the lowest possible speed. At regular intervals our enemy dropped one depth-charge somewhere astern of us, but these reports always seemed the same distance away.

At dawn I very cautiously came up to periscope depth, and had a look. To my consternation I discovered our relentless pursuer about 1,500 metres away on the port quarter. In some extraordinary manner he had tracked us during the night.

I dived and altered course through ninety degrees to south.

At 9 a.m. a tremendous explosion shook the boat from stem to stern, smashing several lights, and giving her a big inclination up by the bow.

As I was only at twenty metres I feared the boat would break surface, and our enemy was evidently very nearly right over us. I at once ordered hard to dive, and went down to the great depth of ninety-five metres.

A series of shattering explosions somewhere above us showed that we were marked down, and we were only saved from destruction by our great depth, the English charges being set apparently to about thirty metres.

At noon the situation was critical in the extreme. My battery density was down to 1,150, the few lamps that I had burning were glowing with a faint, dull red appearance, which eloquently told of the falling voltage and the dying struggles of the battery.

The motors with all fields out were just going round. The faces of the crew, pallid with exhaustion, seemed of an ivory whiteness in the dusky gloom of the boat, which never resembled a gigantic and fantastically ornamental coffin so closely as she did at that time.

The air was fetid. I struck a match; it went out in my fingers. The slightest effort was an agony. I bent down to take off my sea-boots, and cold sweat dropped off my forehead, and my pulse rose with a kind of jerk to a rapid beating, like a hammer.

I left one sea-boot on.

At 1 p.m. a deputation of the crew came aft, and in whispered voices implored me to surface the boat and make a last effort on the surface. A muffled report, as our implacable enemy dropped a depth-charge somewhere astern of us, added point to the conversation, and showed me that our appearance on the surface could have but one end.

At 3 p.m. the second coxswain, who was working the hydroplanes, fell off his stool in a dead faint.

At 3.30 p.m. the supreme crisis was reached: two more men fainted, and I realized that if I did not surface at once I might find the crew incapable of starting the Diesels.

At the order "Surface," a feeble cheer came from the men.

We surfaced, and I dragged myself-up to the conning tower. Luckily we started the Diesels with ease, and in a few minutes gusts of beautiful air were circulating through the boat.

Meanwhile, what of the enemy? I had half expected a shell as soon as we came up, and it was with great anxiety that I looked round. We had been slightly favoured by fortune in that the only thing in sight was a trawler away on the port beam. It was our hunter.

I trimmed right down, hoping to avoid being seen, as it was essential to stay on the surface and get some amperes into the battery. I also altered course away from him.

It was about 5 p.m. that I saw two trawlers ahead, one on each bow. By this time the boat's crew had quite recovered, but I did not wish to dive, as the battery was still pitiably low. I gradually altered course to north-east, but after half an hour's run I almost ran on top of a group of patrols in the dusk.

I crash-dived, and they must have seen me go down, as a few minutes later the boat was violently shaken by a depth-charge.

We were at twenty metres, still diving at the time. I consulted the chart, but could find no bottoming ground within fifty miles, a distance which was quite beyond my powers.

At 11 p.m. I simply had to come up again and get a charge on the batteries.

From 7 p.m. to 10 p.m., at regular half-hourly intervals, a depth-charge had gone off somewhere within a radius of two miles of me. Needless to say, I was only crawling along at about one knot and altering course frequently. What was so terrible was the patent fact that the patrols in this area had evidently got some device which enabled them to keep in continual touch with me to a certain extent.

These monotonous and regular depth-charges seemed to say: "We know, Oh! U-boat, that we are somewhere near you, and here is a depth-charge just to tell you that we haven't lost you yet."[1]

As an hour had elapsed since the last depth-charge, I felt fairly happy at coming up, and on making the surface I was delighted to

---

1: Karl was quite right; it is evident that he had the misfortune to encounter one of our new hydrophone-hunting groups, just started In the Fair Island Channel. The incident of the depth-charges every half-hour was known as "Tickling up." Probably the patrol only heard faint noises from him.

find a pitch-black night and a considerable sea. From 10 p.m. to 1 a.m. I actually had three hours of peace, and in this period I managed to cram a considerable amount of stuff into the batteries. The densities were rising nicely and all seemed well, when I did what I now see was a very foolish thing.

I made my 1 a.m. wireless report to Nordreich, in which I requested orders at 3 a.m. and reported my position, together with the fact that I had been badly hunted.

In twenty-five minutes they were on me again! I had most idiotically assumed that the English had no directional wireless in these parts. They have. They've got everything that they have ever tried up there; it was concentrated in that infernal Fair Island Channel.

I was only saved by seeing a destroyer coming straight at me, silhouetted against, the low-lying crescent of a new moon. When I dived she was about six hundred metres away. As I have confessed to doing a foolish thing, I give myself the pleasure of recording a cleverer move on my part. I anticipated depth-charge attack as a matter of course, but instead of going down to twenty-five metres, I kept her at twelve.

The depth-charges came all right, seven smashing explosions, but, as I had calculated, they were set to go off at about thirty metres, and so were well below me.

The boat was thrown bodily up by one, and I think the top of the conning tower must have broken surface, but there was little danger of this being seen in the prevailing water conditions.

* * * * *

I have just had to stop recording my experiences of the past forty-eight hours, as the Navigator, who is on watch, sent down a message to say that smoke was in sight.

The next hour was full of anxiety, but by hauling off to port we managed to lose it. I then had a little food, and I will now conclude my account before trying again to get some sleep.

THE ACCOUNT CONTINUED

All my hopes of getting up again that night, both for the purpose of charging and of getting the 3 a.m. signal, were doomed to be disappointed, as the hydrophone operator kept on reporting the noise of destroyers overhead. Occasional distant thuds seemed to indicate a never-ending supply of depth-charges, but they were about four or five miles from me. Perhaps some other unfortunate devil was going through the fires of hell.

At daylight on the second day my position was still miserable. The battery was getting low again, the sea had gone down, and when I put my periscope up at 9 a.m. the horizon seemed to be ringed with patrols. I felt as if I was in an invisible net, and though I endeavoured to conceal my apprehension from the crew, I could see from the listless way they went about their duties that they realized that once again we were near the end of our resources.

All the forenoon we crept along at thirty metres, until the tension was broken at 1 p.m. by a furious depth-charge attack. In some extraordinary way they had located me again and closed in upon me. The first charges were some little distance off, and as they got closer a feeling of desperation overcame me, and I seriously contemplated ending the agony by surfacing and fighting to the last with my gun.

Curiously enough, the procedure that I adopted was the exact opposite. I decided to dive deep. I went down to 114 metres. At this exceptional depth, three rivets in the pressure hull began to leak, and jets of water with the rigidity of bars of iron shot into the boat. I held on for five minutes, which was sufficient to save me from the depth-charge attack, though two which went off almost above me broke some lamps. I then came up to twenty metres and slowly crawled on. Throughout the long afternoon, though we were not directly attacked again, I heard depth-charges on several occasions sufficiently close to me to demonstrate that these implacable and tireless devils had an idea of the area I was in.

By a supreme effort, working one motor at the only speed it would go, *viz.*, "Dead slow," I managed to squeeze out the battery until I estimated it must be dusk.

There was only one thing to do—I surfaced. It was not as dark as I had hoped, and I saw a fairly large sloop-like vessel, about eight thousand metres away, on the port beam. She must have seen me simultaneously, as the flash of a gun darted from her, the shell falling short.

I couldn't dive; there seemed only one thing to do: fight and then die. I ordered the gun's crew up, and the unequal duel began. We were going full speed on the diesels, and my course was east by north. A good deal of water and spray was flying over the gun, and my crew had little hope of doing much accurate shooting, but I have often found that when one is being fired at there is nothing so comforting as the sound of one's own gun.

Our enemy was armed with two large guns, fifteen centimetres or over, but had no speed, a discovery which raised my hopes again. It was soon evident that, provided we were not heading for another patrol, if we could survive ten minutes' shelling, we should be saved for the time being by the fading light, which was evidently causing our enemy increasing difficulties, as his shots alternated between very short and very much over.

I was actually congratulating the Navigator on our escape, and I had just told the gun's crew to cease firing at the blurred outlines on the port quarter from which the random shells still came, when there was a sheet of yellow flame and a jar which threw me against the signalman. The latter had been standing near the conning-tower hatch, and unfortunately I knocked him off his balance, and he fell with a thud into the upper conning tower. He had the good fortune to escape with a couple of ribs broken, but when I recovered myself and got to my feet, far worse consequences met my eyes.

By the worst of ill-luck, a shell which must have been fired practically at random had hit the gun just below the port trunnion.

The result of the explosion was very severe. Four of the seven men at the gun had been blown overboard, the breech worker was uninjured, though from the way he swayed about it was evident that he was dazed, and I expected to see him fall over the side at any moment. The remaining two men were as dead as horse-flesh.

The material damage was even more serious. The gun had been practically thrown out of its cradle, but in the main the trunnion blocks had held firm, and the whole pedestal had been carried over to starboard.

The really terrible effects of this injury were not apparent at first sight, but I soon realized them, for an hour later (we had shaken off the sloop) I saw red flame on the horizon, which plainly indicated flaming at the funnel from some destroyer doubtless looking for us at high speed.

I dived, intending to surface again as soon as possible. With this intention in my head, I did not go below the upper conning tower. We had barely got to ten metres, when loud cries from below and the disquieting noise of rushing water told me that something was wrong. I blew all tanks, surfaced, left the First Lieutenant on watch and went below.

There were five centimetres of water on the battery boards, and I understood at once that we could never dive again.

For the pedestal of the gun, in being forced over, had strained the longitudinal seam of the pressure hull, to which it is bolted, and a shower of water had come through as soon as we got under.

It might have been hoped that this was enough, but no! our cup was not yet full. Chlorine gas suddenly began to fill the fore-end. The salt water running down into the battery tanks had found acid, and though I ordered quantities of soda to be put down into the tank, it became, and still is at the moment of writing, impossible to move forward of the conning tower without putting on a gas mask and oxygen helmet. So we are helpless, and at the mercy of any little trawler, or even the weather.

We have no gun; we cannot dive. The English must know that they have hit us, and every hour I expect to see the hull of a destroyer climb over the horizon astern. We are fortunate in two respects: in that for the time being the weather seems to promise well, and our Diesels are thoroughly sound.

We are ordered to Zeebrugge—I could have wished elsewhere for many reasons, but it does not matter, as I cannot believe we are intended to escape.

I feel I would almost welcome an enemy ship, it would soon be over; but this uncertainty and anxiety drags on for hour after hour—and now I cannot sleep, though I haven't slept properly for over seventy hours. I am so worn out that my body screams for sleep, but it is denied to me, and so, lest I go mad, I write; it is better to do this, though my eyes ache and the letters seem to wriggle, than to stand up on the bridge looking for the smoke of our enemies, or to lie in my bunk and count the revolutions of the Diesels; thousands of thousands of thudding beats, one after the other, relentless hammer strokes.

I have endured much.

Note by Etienne

A break occurs in Karl von Schenk's diary at this juncture. Fortunately the main outlines of the story are preserved owing to Zoe's long letter, which was in a small packet inside the cover of the second notebook. Zoe's letter will be reproduced in this book in its proper chronological position, but in order to save the reader the trouble of reading the book from the letter back to this point, a brief summary of what took place is given here. The entries in his diary which follow the words "I have endured much," are very meagre for a period which seems to have been about a month in length. There is no further mention of the latter stages of Karl's passage in the wrecked boat to Zeebrugge, so it is presumed that he made that port without further adventure. He was evidently on the verge of a nervous breakdown, and appears to have been suffering from very severe insomnia. He had been hunted for two days, during which he was perpetually on the verge of destruction, and the cumulative effect of such an experience is bound to leave its mark on the strongest man. When he got back to Zeebrugge he must have been at the end of his tether, and whether by chance or design it was when Karl was, as he would have said, "at a low mental ebb" that Zoe made her last and successful attack upon his resolution not to see her again unless she consented to marry him. It is plain from her letter that when he left her after the stormy interview in which he vowed never to see her again, Zoe did not lose hope. She seems to have kept herself *au courant* with his movements, and actually to have known when he was expected in.

We know that she had many friends amongst the officers, and it is probable that from one of these she was able to get information about Karl's movements.

Bruges was probably a hot-bed of U-boat gossip, and, not unlike the conditions at certain other Naval ports during the war, the ladies were often too well informed. At any rate it appears that Zoe rushed to see Karl directly he arrived at Bruges, and found him a mental and physical wreck, suffering from acute insomnia.

With the impetuous vigour which evidently guided most of her actions, she took complete charge of Karl, and, as he was due for four days' leave, she whisked him off to the forest.

Karl may have protested, but was probably in no state to wish to do so. At her shooting-box in the forest Zoe achieved her desire, and the stubborn struggle between the lovers ended in victory for the woman. There is an entry in Karl's diary which may refer to this period; he simply says, "Slept at last! Oh, what a joy!"

If this entry was written in the forest, it seemed as if Karl had been unable to sleep until Zoe carried him off to the forest peace of her shooting-box and surrounded him with the atmosphere of her tender sympathy.

There is no evidence of the light in which Karl viewed his defeat, when, having regained his strength, he was able to take stock of the changed situation. It is reasonable to suppose that his silence upon this matter in the pages of his diary is evidence that he was ashamed of what he must have considered a great act of weakness on his part.

At all events he realized that he had crossed the Rubicon and that he had better acquiesce in the *fait accompli*.

He seems to have been in harbour for about six weeks, during which he lived with Zoe, and the lovers enjoyed a brief spell of happiness before Karl set out on his next trip.

Karl seems to have found those six weeks very pleasant ones, though his diary merely contains brief references, such as: "A. day in the country with Z."; "Z. and I went to the Cavalry dance," and other trivial entries—of his thoughts there is not a word.

About the end of 1917 Karl's boat was repaired, and he left for the Atlantic; and once more resumed full entries in his diary.

Karl's Diary resumed

Sailed at 9 p.m. last night, and we are now seventeen miles off Beachy Head. The Straits of Dover were frightful; the glare of the acetylene flares on the barrage showed for miles. Seen from a distance it gave me the impression of the gates of hell, through which we had to pass.

I dived, ten miles away, and went through with the tide at a depth of forty metres.

Two hours and three quarters of suspense, and at dawn we came up, having passed safely through the great death-trap. At the moment there is nothing in sight, except a little smoke on the horizon. I am going to dive again till dusk.

2 A.M

We are thrashing down the Channel with a south-westerly wind right ahead. My instructions are to work for two days between the Lizard and Kinsale Head, and then proceed far out in the Atlantic, where the convoys are supposed to meet the destroyers.

That Fair Island Channel experience was enough for a lifetime. Death, quick, short and sudden, this I am ready for. But torture, slow, long and drawn-out, is not in the bargain which in this year of grace every civilized man and half the savages of the world seem to have had to make with the god Mars.

As I sit in this steel, cigar-shaped mass of machinery, the question rings incessantly in my ears: "To what object is all this war directed, when analysed from the point of view of the individual?"

It does not satisfy any longing of mine. I have not got a lust for battle: no one who fights has a lust for battle. Editors of newspapers and people on General Staffs, possibly also Cabinet Ministers, have lusts for battles, as long as they arrange the battle and talk about it afterwards—curse them!

The only thing I want is to be with Zoe. I want to live and spend long years with her, enjoying life—this life of which I have spent half already, and now perhaps it will be taken from me by some other man: some Englishman who doesn't really want to take my life, reckoned as an individual.

Around me in the darkness are the patrol boats, manned by the Englishmen who are seeking my life. Seeking it, not to gratify their private emotions, but because we are all in the whirlpool of War and cannot escape.

Like an avalanche, it seems to gather strength and speed as it rolls on, this War of Nations. The world must be mad! I cannot see how it can ever stop. England will never be defeated at sea. We shall conquer on land—then what?

An inconclusive peace.

Even if we smash this island Empire and gain the dominion of the world, how will it advantage me? I can see no way in which I can gain. It would be said, if any one should read this: *Gott*! what a selfish point of view—he thinks only of his personal gain, not of his country.

But, confound it all, I reply, answer me this:

Do I exist for my country, or does my country exist for me?

For example, does man live for the sake of the Church, or was the Church created for man?

Does not my country exist for my benefit?

Surely it is so.

Then again, I am risking my all, my life; I live in danger, apprehension and great discomfort; I do all these things, and yet if as a reasonable man I ponder what advantage I am to gain from all these sacrifices I am adjudged selfish.

It is all madness; I cannot fathom the meaning of these things.

* * * * *

In position on the Bristol line of approach

The weather is bad.

At twenty metres

Once again Death has stretched forth his bony fingers to catch me by the throat, and only by a chance have I wriggled free.

Yesterday afternoon at 5 p.m. we sighted a small steamer flying Spanish colours and steering for Cardiff. The weather was choppy, but not too bad, and I decided to exercise the gun's crew, though I did not think there would be much doing, as the Spaniards soon give in.

I opened fire at six thousand metres, and pitched a shell ahead of her and ran up the signal to heave-to. The wretched little craft paid no attention, and continued on her lumbering course. I suspected the presence of an Englishman on her bridge, and determined to hit.

This we did with our sixth shot, and she stopped dead and wallowed in the trough, with clouds of steam pouring out of her engine-room; we had evidently got the engine-room.

As we closed her, it was evident that a tremendous panic was taking place on board. The port sea boat was being launched, but one fall broke and the occupants fell into the water. My Navigator begged me to give her another, which I did, and hit her right aft. Two boatloads of gesticulating individuals now appeared from the shelter of her lee side and began pulling wildly away from the ship.

The Navigator, whose eyes were dancing with excitement, was very keen to play with them by spraying the water with machine-gun bullets; but it seemed to me to be waste of ammunition, and I would not permit it.

Meanwhile we had approached to within about four hundred metres of her port bow. I was debating whether to accelerate her sinking, when I noticed that a fire had broken out aft, and I became possessed with a childish curiosity to see the fire being put out as she sank. It was a kind of contest between the elements.

As I watched her, I was startled to hear three or four reports from the region of the fire.

"Ammunition!" shouted the pilot, with wide-opened eyes.

In an instant I pressed the diving alarm as I realized our deadly peril. Fool that I had been, she was a decoy-ship. They must have realized on board that I had seen through their disguise, for as we began to move forward, under the motors, a trap-door near her bows fell down, the white ensign was broken at the fore, and a 4-inch gun opened fire from the embrasure that was revealed on her side.

We were fortunate in that our conning tower was already right ahead of the enemy, and as I dropped down into the conning tower, I saw that as she could not turn we were safe.

A few shells plunged harmlessly into the water near our stern, and then we were under.

We came up to a periscope depth, and I surveyed her from a position off her stern. She was sinking fast, but I felt so furious at being nearly trapped that I could not resist giving her a torpedo; detonation was complete, and a mass of wreckage shot into the air as the hull of the ship disappeared. As to the two boats, I left them to make the best course to land that they could.

As they were fifty miles off the shore when I left them and

it blew force six a few hours afterwards, I rather think they have joined the list of "Missing." We are now steering due west to our second position.

* * * * *

Received orders last night to return to base forthwith on the north about route.[1]

I have shaped course to pass fifty miles north of Muckle Flugga; no more Fair Island Channel for me.

* * * * *

Statlandlet in sight, with the Norwegian coast looking very lovely under the snow—we never saw a ship from north of the Shetlands to this place, when we saw a light cruiser of the town class steaming south-west at high speed.

She had probably been on patrol off this place, where the Inner and Outer Leads join up and ships have to leave the three-mile limit.

She was well away from me, and an attack would have been useless. I did not shed any tears; I have lost much of the fire-eating ideas which filled my mind when I first joined this service.

* * * * *

We are due off the mole at 8 p.m. tonight, and my heart leaps with joy at the thought of seeing my Zoe; already I can almost imagine her lovely arms round my neck, her face raised to mine, and all the other wonderful things that make her so glorious in my eyes.

Note by Etienne

Before quoting the next entry in Karl's journal it is necessary to explain the situation which confronted him when he arrived in Zeebrugge. In his absence, his beloved Zoe had been arrested as an Allied Agent, and she was tried for espionage within a day or two of his arrival. There is no record of how he heard the news, and the blow he sustained was probably so terrible that whilst there was yet

---

1: This means into the North Sea round Scotland.

hope he felt no desire to write; but, as will be seen, there came a time when he turned to his journal as the last friend that remained to him. It is a curious fact that, with the exception of an entry at the beginning of this journal, Karl makes little mention of his mother and home at Frankfurt. Though he does not say so, it seems possible that his mother had heard of his entanglement with Zoe, and a barrier had risen between them; this suggestion gains strength from the fact that in his blackest moments of despair he never seems to consider the question of turning to Frankfurt for sympathy. Interest is naturally aroused as to the details of Zoe's trial. The available material consists solely of the long letter she wrote to him from Bruges jail. It may be that one day the German archives of the period of occupation will reveal further details. Information on the subject is possibly at the disposal of the British Intelligence Service, but this would be kept secret. All we know on the matter is derived from the letter, which has been preserved inside the second volume of Karl's diary.

There seems no doubt that she was caught red-handed, but to say more would be to anticipate her own words.

It was a matter of some difficulty to know where best to introduce Zoe's letter, but with a view to securing as much continuity of thought in the story as possible it has been decided to quote it at this juncture, although he did not receive it until after he had made the entry in the journal which will be quoted directly after the letter.

I would like to appeal to any reader who may happen to be engaged in administrative or reconstructive work in Belgium, to communicate with me, care of Messrs. Hutchinson, should he handle any papers dealing with Zoe's trial.

Zoe's Letter

My Best Beloved,

When you get this letter cease to sorrow for what will have happened, for I shall be at rest, and in peace at last, freed from a world in which I have known bitter sorrow and, until you came into my life, but little joy.

For these past months I am grateful to God, if such a being exists and regulates the conduct of a world gone mad.

For in a few hours I am to die.

It is harder for you than for me; one moment of agony I suffered, a moment that seemed to last a century, when, amidst the sea of faces that swam in a confused mass before me at the trial, I saw your eyes and the torture that you were suffering. When I saw your eyes I knew that the President had said I must die. I am glad that I was told this by you, the only one amongst all these men who loved me. I suppose the President spoke; I never heard him, but I saw your eyes and I knew.

My darling, it was cruel of you to come, cruel to me and cruel to yourself, but I loved you for being there; it showed me that up till the last you would stand by me, and until you read this you cannot know all the facts. That to you, as to the others, I must have seemed a woman spy and that nevertheless you stood by me, is to me a recollection of unsurpassable sweetness, compared with which all other thoughts of you fade into insignificance.

Know now, oh, well beloved, that I was not unworthy of your love.

I have a story to tell you, and I have such a little time left that I must write quickly. The priest who has been with me comes again an hour before the dawn, and he has promised to deliver these my last words of love into your hands.

My real name is Zoe Xenia Olga Sbeiliez, and I was born twenty-nine years ago at my father's country house at Inkovano, near Koniesfol. I am Polish; at least, my father was, and my mother comes from the Don country. There was a day when my father's ancestors were Princes in Poland. Poor Poland was torn by the vultures of Europe, just as your countrymen, my Karl, are tearing poor Belgium and France, and so my family lost estates year by year, and my grandfather is buried somewhere in the dreary steppes of Siberia because he dared to be a Polish patriot.

My father bowed before the storm, and under my mother's influence he never became mixed up with politics. Thus he lived on his estates at Inkovano, and nursed them for my

A TRAPDOOR NEAR HER BOWS FELL DOWN, THE WHITE ENSIGN WAS BROKEN AT THE FORE, AND A 4-INCH GUN OPENED FIRE FROM THE EMBRASURE THAT WAS REVEALED ON HER SIDE.

I SIGHTED TWO CONVOYS, BUT THERE WERE DESTROYERS THERE. . . .

younger brother, Alexandrovitch, the child of his old age. Alex would be nineteen now, had he lived. The estates were large as these things go in Western Europe, but they were but a garden as compared with the lands held by my great-grandfather, Boris Sbeiliez.

My father had a dream, and he dreamed this dream from the day Alex was born to the day they both died in each other's arms.

My father dreamt that one day the Tsars would soften their heart to Poland, and raise her up from the dust to a place amongst the nations, and my father dreamt that Alexandrovitch Sbeiliez would become a leader of Poland, as his ancestors had been before him. And so my father nursed his estates and pinched and saved, in preparation for the day when his beautiful dream should come true.

My poor idealistic father never realized, oh, my Karl, that when one wants a thing one must fight—to the death. Alex was the apple of his eye, but I was much loved by my mother; perhaps she dreamed a dream about me—I know not, but she determined that I should have all that was necessary. Paris, Berlin, Munich, Dresden, and a season in London, then I came home at twenty-one, perfectly educated according to the world, beautiful according to men, and dressed according to Paris. But I was only to find out how little I knew. My mother and I used to take a house in Warsaw for the season, and I met many notable men and women. In these days I, also, thought I could do something for Poland, but after two or three seasons I found that I, too, was only dreaming idle dreams. Oh! my beloved, beware of dreaming idle dreams.

Listen! I once met the Prime Minister of all Russia at a reception. I captivated him, and thought, now! now! I shall do something.

I sat next to him at dinner; I talked of Poland—and I knew my subject—I talked brilliantly; he listened, he hung on my words, and he, the Prime Minister of all Russia, the Tsar's right-hand man, asked me to drive with him next day in his sledge. I, an almost unknown Polish girl!

When I accepted, I was in the seventh heaven of delight.

Next day he called and we set forth; at a deserted spot in the woods near Warsaw he tried to kiss me—I struck him in the face with the butt of his own whip.

That was why he had hung on my words, that was why he had taken me for my drive; it was my Polish body that interested *him*—not Poland.

The Prime Minister of Russia was confined to his room for two days, "owing to an indisposition." How I laughed when I saw the bulletin in the paper, signed by two doctors, but it taught me a lesson; I never dreamt idle dreams again.

No, I am wrong, my beloved. I dreamt an idle dream, a lovely dream about you and I. An after-the-war dream, if this war should ever end, but like other dreams it has ended—in dreams.

But I must hurry, for my little watch tells me that one hour of my five has gone, and I have much to say.

I could have married, and married brilliantly, but Poland held me back. I did not know what I could do for my country, it all seemed so hopeless, and yet I felt that perhaps one day ... and I felt I ought to be single when that day came.

It was not easy, my Karl, sometimes it was hard; one man there was, Sergius was his Christian name; he loved me madly, and sometimes I thought—but no matter, he is dead now, killed at Tannenberg, and I—well, I will tell you more of my story.

When the war broke out and clouded over that last beautiful summer in 1914 (I wonder will there ever be another like it in your lifetime, my Karl? No, I don't think it can ever be quite the same after all this!), we were all in the country. Alex was back from his school in Petrograd, and my father kept him at home for the autumn term.

How well I remember the excitement, the mobilization, the blessing of the colours, the wave of patriotism which swept over the country; even I, under the influence of the specious proclamations that were issued broadcast by the Government, with their promises of reform, and redress for Poland after the war was over, felt more Russian than Polish. Lies! Lies! Lies! that was what the Government promises were, my Karl.

Under the stress of war the rottenness of that great white sepulchre, Russia, feared the revival of the Polish spirit; it might have been awkward, and so they lied with their tongues in their cheeks, and we simple Poles believed them; the peasantry flocked to their depots, little knowing whom they fought, but the proclamations which were read to them told them they fought for Poland, and we women worked and prayed for the success of Russian arms.

Then the tide of war swept westward, and all day long and every day the troops, and the guns and the motor-cars and the wagons rolled through the village to the west.

Guarded hints in the papers seemed to say that all was not well in France, but France was so far away, and all the time the Russians were going west through our village. Mighty Russia was putting forth her strength, and the Austrian debacle was in full swing; these were great days, my Karl, for a Russian!

Then one day the long columns of men and all the traffic seemed to hesitate in the sluggish westward flow, and then it stopped, and then it began to go east. The weeks went on, and one day, very, very faintly, there was a rumbling like a distant thunderstorm. It was the guns! The front was coming back.

Have you ever seen forest fires, my Karl? We had them every autumn in our woods. If you have, then you know how all the small animals and the birds, the rabbits and the foxes, and perhaps a wolf or two, and the deer, and the thrushes and the linnets come out from the shelter of the trees, fleeing blindly from the great peril, anxious only to save their lives. So it was when the front came back. Herds of *moujiks*, the old men, the women, the children, the poor little babies, struggled blindly eastwards through the village.

Pushing their miserable household gods on handcarts, or staggering along with loads on their backs, and weary children dragging at their arms, the human tide flowed eastwards, round our house, begged perhaps a drink of water, and then wandered feverishly onwards.

They knew not in ninety-nine cases out of a hundred where they were going; their only destination was summed up in the words, "Away from the Front"—away from the ominous rumbling which began to get louder, away from that western horizon which was beginning to have a lurid glow at nights, like a sunset prolonged to dawn.

Then, as the Germans advanced more and more, the character of the tide changed, the civilian element was outnumbered by the military. Companies, battalions, brigades, sometimes in good order, sometimes in no order, marched through the village. They would often halt for a short time, and the officers would come up to the house, where my mother and I gave them what we could. My father lived amongst his books and accounts, and bemoaned the extravagance of the war. Then there were the deserters, the stragglers, the walking wounded, the—but you know, my Karl, what an army in retreat means.

I must proceed with my story, for time moves relentlessly on. One day a desperately wounded officer, a young Lieutenant of the Guard, a boy of twenty-five, was taken out of a motor ambulance to die.

The ambulance had stopped opposite our gates, and lying on his stretcher he had seen our garden, my garden. He knew he was to die, and he had begged with tears in his eyes to the doctor that he might be left in the garden.

Who could refuse him?

He died within two hours, amongst our flowers, with Alex and I at his side.

Before he died, he begged us, implored us, almost ordered us, to move east before it was too late.

We repeated his arguments to my father, but the latter was obdurate, and he swore that a regiment of angels would not move him from his ancestral home. So we made up our minds to stay.

Things got worse and worse, and one day shells fell in the grounds and we hid in the cellars. That night all our servants ran away, and my father cursed them for cowards. Next day in the early morning we heard machine guns fire outside the village, and then all was still.

At six o'clock Alex, white-faced, came running into the

house. He had been down to the gates and he had seen the enemy. They were drunk, he said, and going down the street firing the houses and shooting the people as they came out. It seemed impossible and yet it was true. It was growing dark, when we heard shouts and saw lights, and from the top of the house I saw a crowd of singing and shouting soldiers, with pine torches, half running, half walking up the drive.

They massed in a body opposite the house. Paralysed with terror, I looked down on the scene, and shuddered to see that every second man seemed to have a bottle. One of them fired a shot at the house, and next I remember a flood of light on the drive, and, in the circle of light, my father standing with hand raised. What my father intended can never be known, for, as he paused and faced the mob, a solitary shot rang out, and he fell in a huddled heap.

As he fell, a boyish voice from the door shouted "Murderers!" It was Alex. With his little pistol I had given him for a birthday present in his hand, he ran forward and, standing over my father's body, head thrown back, he pointed his pistol at the mob and fired twice. A man dropped, there was a flash of steel, the crowd surged forward, and—and, oh! my Karl, they had murdered my beloved brother, my darling Alex.

The next moment they were in the house. I escaped from my window on to the roof of the dairy, and from there down a water-pipe, across the yard to an old hay-loft. For a long time they ran in and out of the house, like ants, looting and pillaging; then there was a great shout, and for some time not a soul came out of the house. I guessed they had got into the cellars. At about midnight I saw that the house was on fire. In a few minutes it was an inferno and the drunken soldiers came pouring out, firing their rifles in all directions.

I had found a piece of rope in the loft. One end I placed on a hook and the other round my neck. I was close to the upper doors of the loft, with a drop to the courtyard, and thus I stayed, for I feared that some soldier, more sober than the rest, might explore the outhouses and find me. I was watching this unearthly spectacle, and never, my best beloved, did I conceive that man could become lower than the beasts, but before my eyes it was so, when I noticed that the great gates at the southern end of the courtyard were opening. As they opened I saw that beyond them were drawn up a line of men. An officer gave an order, and two machine guns were placed in position in the gate entrance; round the guns lay their crews, and the seething mass of revellers saw nothing. I felt that a fearful tragedy was impending, and as I held my breath with anxiety the officer gave a short, sharp movement with his hand and a hideous rattle rose above all noises. The pandemonium that ensued was indescribable. Some ran helplessly into the burning house, others ran round and round in circles, others tried to get into the dairy; one man got upon its roof and fell back dead as soon as his head appeared above the outer wall. The place was surrounded. It was horrible. A few tried to rush for the gate, they melted away like snow before the sun, as their bodies met the pitiless stream of bullets. I suppose two hundred men were killed in as many seconds. The machine guns ceased fire. Ambulance parties came into the yard, collected the dead and living, and within half an hour there was not a soul save myself in the place. Discipline had received its oblation of men's lives.

As an example, it was one of the most wonderful things I have ever known in your wonderful army, my Karl, but it was terrible—terribly cruel.

I never knew what became of my mother, though I feel she is dead—murdered, perhaps, like my father and my darling Alex, or perhaps she hid somewhere in the house and remained petrified with terror till the flames came. Next morning I left my hiding-place and walked about. Not a German was to be seen, but in the wood was a huge newly-made grave. It was all open warfare then, and this flying column, which was miles in advance of the main body, had moved on. The house was a smoking mass of ruins, but the farm buildings had been spared, and I let out all the poor animals and turned them into the woods, so that they might have their chance.

All day I searched for my father and brother, but not a sign was to be seen, and at dusk I stood alone, faint and broken, amongst the ruins of my ancestors' home. As I looked at this scene of desolation and I contrasted what had been my life twenty-four hours before and what it was then, something seemed to snap in my brain, and for the first time I cried. Oh! the blessed relief of those tears, my Karl, for I was a poor weak, helpless girl, and alone with death and bitterness all round me. Late that night I hid once more in my hay-loft and next morning I left Inkovano for ever. Before I left, I made a vow. It is because of this vow, my beloved, that I am to die. For I vowed by the body of our Saviour and the murdered bodies of my family that, whilst life was in me and the war was maintained, for so long would I work unceasingly for the Allies against Germany. As the war ran its fiery course, I have seen more and more that the Allies are the only ones who will do anything for Poland, my beloved country, so have I been strengthened in my vow.

I struck south on my feet, as a poor girl—I, the daughter of a princely family of Poland! No hardships were too great for me, provided I could reach Allied territory. I travelled from village to village as a singing girl, and once I was driven away with stones by villagers set upon me by a fanatical priest. I came by Cracow, and across the Carpathians, helped to pass the lines by a Hungarian Lieutenant—but I tricked him of his reward; I was not ready for that sacrifice. Then across the Hungarian plains to Buda-Pesth, where I remained three weeks, singing in a third-rate café, to make some money for my next stage. But I had to leave too soon—the old story!—this time it was the proprietor's son. What beasts men are, my Karl! And yet to me you are above all other men, a prince amongst your fellows, and never did I love you so distractedly as that first night at the shooting-box, when I read the scorn in your eyes as you rejected me. I have no shame in telling you this. Am I not already in the grave? And then I must be silent and can only await your coming. After many struggles, wearisome to relate, I came to Hermanstadt, and there, whilst pushing my trade as a dancer, came into touch with a Hungarian band of smugglers, working across the mountain passes between Eastern Hungary and Romania. I did certain work for these men, and in return crossed with them one bitter night in a thunderstorm into Romania. At Bucharest I got a good engagement, and when I had saved a thousand marks, I bought a passport for five hundred, and came to Serbia, then staggering beneath the great Austrian offensive.

Once again I was in the horrors of a retreat, but I escaped, reaching Valona, and crossed to Brindisi, by the aid of a French officer to whom I told my story and who believed me. His name is Pierre Lemansour, and he lives at Bordeaux. If fortune places him in your power, be kind to him, my Karl, for your Zoe's sake.

I came to Rome; and thence to Paris. I stayed here three weeks, singing in a cabaret. Whilst here I tried to advance my plans in vain! What could I, a poor girl, do for the Allies? The Embassy laughed at me, all except one young attaché who tried to make love to me.

Then I thought of England—England, and her cold, hard islanders, phlegmatic in movements, slow to hate, slow to move, but once roused—ah! they never let go, these islanders!

One of their poets has said: "The mills of God grind slowly, but they grind exceeding small."

That, my Karl, is like England.

They are your most terrible enemies, and you know it.

Do not be angry with me when you read this.

For me it is Poland, for you Germany.

Where I am going in a few hours there is no Poland, no Germany, no England, no war. And perhaps, perhaps, no love.

You and I, Karl, have loved, too well, perchance, but our love was above even the love of countries.

God made the love of men and women, then men and women created their countries.

I see the future before me, Karl, and I foresee that the struggle will be at the end of all things, between England and Germany. One will be in the dust.

Thus, I crossed to England and was swallowed up in the great city of London. England has always had a corner of her calculating heart for the small nations, and in London there is a Polish organization. I applied there, and one day I was taken to

the Foreign Office, and found myself alone with a great Englishman. His name was—No, I promised, and it will not matter to you, for though he gave me my chance, I have no love for him, and he will never be in your power. Even as I write these words, he has probably taken a list from a locked safe and neatly ruled a red line through the name Zoe Sbeiliez. I tell you they know everything, these Englishmen. I told him my story, and then he asked me whether I was prepared to do all things for the Allies. I told him I was. He then said that I could go as agent for a back area in Belgium, and my centre would be Bruges. I agreed, and asked him innocently enough how I was to live in Bruges. He looked up from his desk and said:
"You will be given facilities to cross the Belgium-Holland frontier, as a German singer."
"And then?" I asked.
"You will go to Bruges and make friends with an Army officer; he must be high up on the staff."
I guessed what he meant, but hoped against hope, and I said: "How?"
I can still see his fish-like face, hair brushed back with scrupulous care, as without a shadow of emotion he looked up, puffed his pipe, and said in matter-of-fact tones:
"You have a pretty face and an excellent figure. Need I say more?" I could have struck him in the face. I was speechless, my mind a whirl of conflicting emotions. I was roused by the level tones again.
"Is it too much—for Poland?"
Oh! the cunning of the man; he knew my weakness. Mechanically, I agreed. Certain details were settled, and he pressed a bell. Within five minutes I was walking back to my lodgings.
Thanks to a marvellous organization, which your police will never discover, my Karl, within *three weeks* I was singing on the Bruges music-hall stage, and accepted without question as being what I was not, a German artist from Dantzig. The men were soon round me, but I had no use for youngsters with money. I wanted a man with information. At last I found my man—the Colonel. He was on the Headquarters staff of the 11th Army, the army of occupation in Belgium,

when I first met him. Subsequently he went back to regimental work; but by the time he was killed (and to realize what a release that meant for me, you would have had to have lived with him) I had established regular sources of information concerning which I will say no more. Let your country's agents find them if they can. This must I say for the Colonel: he was a brute and a drunkard, but in his own gross way he loved me, and he licked my boots at my desire, but I had to pay the price. You are a man, and with all your loving sympathy you can but dimly realize what this costs a woman. To me it was a dual sacrifice of honour and life, but it was for Poland, and the memories of my parents and Alex steeled me and strengthened my resolution, and so, and so, my Karl, I paid the price.

My special work was on the military side, and consisted in making quarterly reports on the general dispositions of large bodies of troops, the massing of corps for spring offensives, and big pushes and hammer blows.

Then you came into my life! When the Colonel used to go away it was my habit to mix in the *demi-mondaine* society of Bruges, to try and live a few hours in which I could forget—oh! don't think the worst! *That* sort of thing had no attraction for me. I didn't seek oblivion in that direction! I had never even kissed anyone in Bruges until I kissed you that first night we met at dinner—I was attracted to you from the very first; the Colonel was due back in a few days, and I suddenly felt mad, and kissed you. I suppose you put me down as one of the usual kind, out to sell myself at a price varying between a good dinner and the rent of a flat! You will now know that I had already mortgaged my body to Poland.

Then a few days later you will remember we went down for that wonderful day in the forest, and for the first time, Karl, I began to see that I was really caring for you, and a faint realization of the dangers and impossibilities towards which we were drifting crossed my mind.

Do you remember how silent I was on the drive back? In a fashion, my Karl, I could foresee dimly a little of what was going to happen. I had a presentiment that the end would be disaster, but I thrust the idea away from me. Then came the day, just before one of your trips—oh! the agony, my darling, of those days, each an age in length, when you were at sea—when you told me at the flat that you loved me.

How I longed to throw my arms round your neck and abandon myself to your embraces, but I was still strong enough in those days to hold back for both our sakes.

Each time we were together I loved you more and more, and each time when you had gone I seemed to see with clearer vision the fatal and inevitable ending.

But I refused to give up the first real happiness that had been mine in my short and stormy life, and so I clung desperately to my idle dream.

I prayed, I prayed for hours, Karl, that the war might end, for I felt that in this lay our only hope—but what are one woman's prayers, a sinful woman's prayers, to the Creator of all things, and the war ground on in its endless agony just as it does tonight—Karl! Karl! will this torture ever end?

But I must hurry, there is still much to tell you, and Time goes on relentlessly just like the war; it is only life that ends. Then came the days I took you to the shooting-box for the first time, and that night I broke down and, unashamed, offered you myself. Think not too badly of your Zoe, my Karl; when a woman loves as I do, what is convention? A nothing, a straw on the waters of life. I wanted you for my own, passionately and desperately, for I feared that any moment the end might come, and to die without having felt your arms around me would have added a thousand tortures to death. Though I could have welcomed death with joy when I saw the look of sorrowful contempt which you cast upon me that night. Heavens above! but you were strong, my Karl. I am not ugly, and yet you resisted, and I hated and loved you at the same time—oh! I know that sounds impossible, but it isn't for a woman. I slept little that night and, feeling that I could not look you in the face in the morning, I left for Bruges before you got up.

I felt that I could trust you not to try and find out the secret of the shooting-box.

What a relief it is to be able to tell you everything frankly, and how I hated the perpetual game of deception which I had to play.

I used to rack my brains for answers to your perpetual question, "Why won't you marry me?" It was a desperate risk taking you down to the forest, but you loved me so much that you never questioned the reasons I gave you for my secrecy. I can tell you now, Karl, that in the early days when I used to disappear from Bruges, it was to the shooting-box that I went.

But I will write more of that later.

Did you suffer the same agony as I did before you left for Kiel, and your pride would not allow you to come to me? You understand now, my darling, why I could never marry you, and when the Colonel was killed it became harder than ever. Once during that terrible interview before you went up the Russian coast, I nearly gave way and promised to marry you. But how could I? I had sworn my vow, and even tonight, though I stand in the shadow of death, I do not regret my vow.

It is inconceivable that I could have married you and carried on my work—a spy on my husband's country—and if I ever thought of trying to do this impossible thing, a vision which has partially come true always restrained me.

I saw a submarine officer disgraced and perhaps sentenced to death, because his wife had been convicted as a spy!

No! it was impossible.

But if I could not marry you, I still wanted your love.

Then you went up the Russian coast, and I heard of your return in a submarine terribly wrecked. I guessed what you must have gone through, and determined to see you, but when I entered your room and saw you lying open-eyed on your bed, with no one but a clumsy soldier to nurse you, I could have wept. You know the rest; you can perhaps hardly remember how I led you to my car and took you down to the forest. Oh, Karl, are you angry with me for what happened? Do you sometimes think that I took an unfair advantage of your weakness? Please! Please forgive me, you were so helpless, and I loved you so.

Then came those unforgettable weeks whilst your boat was being repaired, weeks which opened to me the door of the paradise I was never to enter. Oh! Karl, I pray that all those memories may remain sweet and unclouded all your life. Think of those days when you think of your Zoe. Alas! they came to an end too soon, and you left for the Atlantic. When you came back all was over; I had been caught at last.

The evidence at the trial was clear enough. I have no complaints. I was fairly caught. You remember the big open space in front of the shooting-box? I do not mind saying now that five times have I been taken up from there in an English aeroplane, and landed there again after two days. Each time I took over a full report on military affairs. Not a word of naval news, my Karl; you will remember I never tried to find out U-boat information. I even warned you to be cautious. Well, they caught me as I landed; the English boy who had flown me back tried hard to save me, but it only cost him his own life.

My first thought was of you, and there is not a jot of evidence against you, save only your friendship for me. Remember this fact, if they persecute you. Admit nothing, believe nothing they tell you, deny everything; they have no evidence; but they are certain to try and trap you.

It was noble of you, Karl, to engage Monsieur Labordin in my defence, but it was useless and may do you harm.

I also know of your efforts with the Governor. I hoped nothing from him, but what you did has made me ready to die; I tremble lest you are compromised.

If only I could feel absolutely certain that I have not dragged you down in my ruin I should face the rifles with a smile. For my sake be careful, Karl.

When it is all over, cause a few little flowers to cover my resting-place, if this is permitted for a spy. Order them, do not place them yourself; you *must not* be compromised.

I have told my story, and the end is very near. What else is there to say?

Mere words are empty husks when I try to express my thoughts of you.

Do not sorrow for your Zoe, to whom you have given such happiness.

I am not afraid to die and cross into the unknown, which, however terrible it is, cannot be much worse than this awful war.

Karl! Karl! how I long to kiss you and feel your strong arms crushing the breath from this body of mine which has caused so much sorrow.

Oh, Mother Mary, support me in this hour of trial.

I cannot leave you!

May the Saints guard you and keep you through all the perils of war, and grant that we meet again in the perfect peace of eternity.

For ever, Your devoted and adoring

Zoe

Karl's Diary resumed

She is dead!

They have killed her, my Zoe, my adorable darling, and I am still alive—under close arrest. Perhaps they will shoot me too, in their insatiable thirst for blood. Oh! if they would! Perhaps, my Zoe, if I could only die and leave this useless world behind, I might find you in the mysterious regions where your spirit now dwells.

Oh! is it well with you, Zoe? Give me a sign—a little sign—that all is well. I have knelt in prayer and asked for a sign, but nothing comes—all is a blank, forbidding and mysterious. Is God angry with us, my Zoe, that we sinned before Him? Surely, surely He understands. He must have mercy on me if He is going to make me go on living. If this is my punishment, I can bear it; I will live without you happily if only I may know that all is well with you.

*****

Your letter, Zoe! Can you read these words as I write; can you sense my thoughts? Speak! Ah! I thought I heard your voice, and it was only the laughter of a woman in the street. Your letter has filled me with joy and sorrow. I read and re-read the wonderful words in which you say you loved me from the beginning, but when you plead that I shall not turn in loathing from your memory—with these words you smash me to the ground.

Most glorious woman, I never loved you so well and so passionately as the day you stood at the trial, ringed round with the wolves, the clever lawyers, the stolid witnesses, the ponderous books, the cynical air of religious solemnity with which the machinery of the law thinly cloaks its lust for blood—for a life.

Even when my ears heard the sentence, I could not believe it would be carried out. The firing party, the chair, the bandage. Oh, God! spare me these awful thoughts. To think of your breasts lacerated by the——Oh! this is unendurable! Stop, madman that I am!

* * * * *

I am calmer now; I have read your letter again and rescued the journal from the grate into which I flung it.

The fire was out; I am not sorry; my journal is all I have left, and in its pages are enshrined small, feeble word-pictures of paradise on earth. To read them is to catch an echo of the music we both loved so well. Music! you were all music to me, my Zoe. Your voice, your movements, your caresses all seemed to me to speak of music.

I ask myself, I shall always ask myself until the last hour, whether all that could be done to save you was done. I tried to telegraph to the Kaiser for you, Zoe, but the wire never got further than Bruges post office; they stopped it, and put me under arrest. It was only open arrest, my darling, and on that last awful night I forced them to let me see the Governor. I, Karl Von Schenk, knelt at his feet and begged for your life. He simply said, "You are mad." I left the Palace under close arrest.

Was ever woman's nobleness of character so exemplified as in your life? Be comforted, Zoe, that in all my black sorrow I cling desperately to my pride in your strength. I long to shout abroad what you did and why you would never marry me, to tell all the gaping world that when you died a martyr to duty was killed. I am so unworthy of what you did for me, my darling, and it tortures me with mental rendings to think that whilst I prided myself in my strength of mind, I was dragging you through the fires of hell. When I think of those six weeks we had together, my brain says, "And they might have been months had you not spurned her in the forest." Oh, Zoe! if the priests say truth and all things are now revealed to you, forgive me for this act of mine. Come to me in spirit and give me mental peace.

... WHEN THERE WAS A BLINDING FLASH AND THE AIR SEEMED FILLED WITH MOANING FRAGMENTS.

WHEN I PUT UP MY PERISCOPE AT 9 A.M. THE HORIZON SEEMED TO BE RINGED WITH PATROLS.

As I write like this, as if it was a letter that you might read, I am comforted a little; I rely utterly on the hope, which I struggle to change into belief, that you can read this and know my thoughts.

For when I think that had things been otherwise you might have been leaning over my chair at this moment, and running your cool fingers through my stiff hair; when I think of this, my darling, the full realization comes to me of the gulf which must divide us for some uncertain period, and the lines of this page run mistily before my eyes.

Zoe, my Zoe, strange things have happened in this war; wives declare they have seen their husbands, mothers have felt the presence of their sons; if the powers permit, come to me once again, I implore you, and give me strength to live my life alone.

* * * * *

Examined before the Court of Inquiry today. Fools! can't they realize that I don't care if they do shoot me?

In the Mess, people avoid me. What do I care? Not one of them is worthy to stand on the same soil that holds her beloved body. They have buried her in the Castle grounds. In accordance with her wishes, I have arranged for flowers. Perhaps one day when all this is over I may be able to live here and tend the place where she sleeps, free at last from all her cares.

* * * * *

At the Court of Inquiry they tried to cross-examine me on our life together. Dolts! what do they aim at proving? That I loved you? I hardly listened. When they finished the evidence, the President asked me if I had anything to say! Anything to say! I felt like telling them they were cogs in the most monstrous machine for manufacturing sorrow and destruction that mankind had ever devised. I could have shaken my fist in their solemn faces and shouted "Beasts! you murdered her! You destroyed that most wonderful woman who lowered herself to love me."

Actually there was a long silence, and then the Vice-President, Captain Fruhlingsohn, said, "Speak; we wish you well."

It was the first touch of sympathy, the only sign of humanity I had received in all these awful days, and it touched my stubborn heart and the longed-for tears flowed at last.

I murmured: "Gentlemen, I am no traitor; but I loved her as my own soul."

"Dissolve the Court. Remove the prisoner." Like the clash of iron gates, officialdom came into its own again.

* * * * *

So I am not to be shot! Not even imprisoned! "Don't fall in love with enemy agents again!"—that summarized their verdict.

Ha! Ha! Ha! It is all horribly funny. The real reason is that they need me. I am a trained and skilful slaughterer on the seas; I am an essential part of the great machine. And they haven't got any spares! I was in the Mess yesterday when the English papers we get from Amsterdam arrived. Oh! a pretty surprise awaited the first man who opened *The Times*. These English had published the names of 150 U-boat commanders they had caught. There they all were. Christian names and all complete. The only thing missing was a blank space in which to fill in our names when the time comes.

Dinner was a silent meal last night, and next morning some rat of a Belgian had posted the list on the gatepost of the Mess. The machine has offered five hundred marks for his apprehension—how foolish; as if by shooting him they would take any names off the long list.

* * * * *

I am to sail at dawn tomorrow. I shall not be sorry to get away for a space from this place with its mingled memories of delight and death.

* * * * *

Back again, and I haven't written a word for three weeks.

My billet last trip was off Finisterre. I sighted two convoys, but there were destroyers there; they are so black and swift I don't go near them.

I don't want to die in a U-boat. It's not worth while. It is easy to avoid these convoys. I dive and make a great fuss of attacking, then I steer divergently. Nobody knows where the enemy is except me; I am the only one who looks through the periscope—I take good care of that. And then how I curse and swear when I announce that the convoy has altered course, and there is no chance of getting in to attack. None of them are so disappointed as I am!

The mines get on my nerves, there is no way of dodging them, and Lord! how they sprout on the Flanders coast.

I am to go out in six days. It is very little rest. I believe they want to kill me. But I won't die! Not I.

I went to her grave yesterday for the first time. I had thought I should weep, but I did not; in fact it left me quite unmoved. I feel she's not really dead; she comes to me sometimes, always at night when I am alone and when we are at sea. There's nothing very tangible, but I catch an echo of her voice in the surge of the sea along the casing, or the sound of the breeze as it plays along the aerial. And so I will not die until she calls me, for up to the present her messages have told me to live and endure.

* * * * *

A very awkward incident took place last night. We were off the Naze and saw a steamer some distance away.

We dived to attack. When we were about a mile away I had a look at her, and something about her put me off. I half thought she was a decoy ship, and I privately determined I would not attack. I steered a course which brought me well on her quarter, and as soon as I saw that it was impossible to get into position to fire I increased speed on the engines and shook the whole boat in efforts which were ostensibly directed to getting her into position. At length I eased speed and bitterly exclaimed that my luck was out.

The First Lieutenant suggested that we should give her gunfire, but I pointed out that I had good reason to suspect her of being a wolf in sheep's clothing, and as he had not seen her he could hardly question my judgment. I was going forward, when I accidentally overheard the Navigator and the Engineer talking in the wardroom. I listened.

The Engineer said: "The Captain doesn't seem to have the luck he used to command."

"Or else he has lost skill!" replied Ebert. "We never fired a torpedo at all last trip, and it looks as if we are following that precedent this time."

I had heard enough, and, without their realizing my presence, I returned to the control room. I considered the situation, and came to the conclusion that they suspected nothing, but it was evident that their minds were running on lines of thought which might be dangerous. I looked at my watch and saw that there was still two hours of daylight left, and then decided to play a trick on them all. I relieved the First Lieutenant at the periscope, and when a decent interval of about half an hour had elapsed I saw a ship. This vessel of my imagination, a veritable Flying Dutchman in fact, I proceeded to attack, and, after about twenty minutes of frequent alterations of speed and course, I electrified the boat by bringing the bow tubes to the ready.

The usual delay was most artistically arranged, and then I fired. With secret amusement I watched the two expensive weapons of war rushing along, but destined to sink ingloriously in the ocean, instead of burying themselves in the vitals of a ship. An oath from myself and an order to take the boat to twenty metres.

With gloomy countenance I curtly remarked: "The port torpedo broke surface and then dived underneath her, the starboard one missed astern."

So far all had gone well, but ten minutes later I nearly made a fatal error. We had been diving for several hours, the atmosphere was bad, and as it was dusk I decided to come up, ventilate, and put a charge on the batteries. I gave the necessary orders, and was on my way up the conning tower to open the outer hatch. The coxswain had just announced that the boat was on the surface, when a terrible thought paralysed me, and I clung helplessly to the ladder trying to think out the situation.

It had just occurred to me that as soon as the officers and crew came on deck they would naturally look for the steamer we had recently fired at; this ship in the time interval which had elapsed would still be in sight.

As I came down, the First Lieutenant was at the periscope, looking round the horizon. Quickly I thrust the youth from the eyepiece, and, as calmly as I could, said: "I thought I heard propellers."

Half an hour later we surfaced for the night. I have been wondering ever since whether they suspect, for the three of them were talking in the wardroom after dinner and stopped suddenly when I came in.

I must be careful in future.

* * * * *

I was sent for this morning by the Commodore's office, and handed my appointment as Senior Lieutenant at the barracks Wilhelmshafen.

No explanation, though I suspected something of the sort was coming, as three days after we got in from my last trip I was examined by the medical board attached to the flotilla.

So I am to leave the U-boat service, and leave it under a cloud! It is a sad come-down from Captain of a U-boat to Lieutenant in barracks, a job reserved for the medically unfit for sea service.

Am I sorry? No, I think I am glad. Life here at Bruges is one long painful episode. No one speaks to me in the Mess. I am left severely alone with my memories. The night before last I found a revolver in my room, and attached to it was a piece of paper bearing the words: "From a friend."

Perhaps at Wilhelmshafen it will be different, and yet, when I went down to the boat at noon and collected my personal affairs and stepped over her side for the last time, I could not check a feeling of great sadness. We had endured much together, my boat and I, and the parting was hard.

At Barracks

As I suspected when I was appointed here, my job is deadly to a degree, and my main duty is to sign leave passes.

Our great effort in France has failed, and now the Allies react furiously. The great war machine is strained to its utmost capacity; can it endure the load?

Our proper move is to paralyse the Allied offensive by striking with all our naval weight at his cross-channel communications. The U-boat war is too slow, and time is not on our side, whilst a hammer blow down the Channel might do great things. But we have no naval imagination, and who am I, that I should advance an opinion?

A discredited Lieutenant in barracks—that's all.

Worse and worse—there are rumours of troubles in the Fleet taking place under certain conditions.

It is the beginning of the end!

Last night the High Seas Fleet were ordered to weigh at 8 a.m. this morning.

A mutiny broke out in the *König* and quickly spread. By 9 a.m. half a dozen ships were flying the red flag, and today Wilhelmshafen is being administered by the Council of Soldiers and Sailors.

There has been little disorder; the men have been unanimous in declaring that they would not go to sea for a last useless massacre, a last oblation on the bloodstained altars of war.

Can they be blamed? Of what use would such sacrifice be?

Yet to an officer it is all very sad and disheartening.

I have seen enough to sicken me of the whole German system of making war, and yet if the call came I know I would gladly go forth and die when *tout est perdu fors l'honneur*. Such instincts are bred deep into the men of families such as mine.

We approach the culmination of events. To-day Germany has called for an armistice. It has been inevitable since our Allies began falling away from us like rotten print.

The terms will doubtless be hard.

* * * * *

Heavens above! but the terms are crushing!

All the U-boats to be surrendered, the High Seas Fleet interned; why not say "surrendered" straight out, it will come to that, unless we blow them up in German ports.

The end of Kaiserdom has come; we are virtually a republic; it is all like a dream.

* * * * *

We have signed, and the last shot of the world-war has been fired.

Here everything is confusion; the saner elements are trying to keep order, the roughs are going round the dockyard and ships, looting freely.

"Better we should steal them than the English," and "There is no Government, so all is free," are two of their cries.

There has been a little shooting in the streets, and it is not safe for officers to move about in uniform, though, on the whole, I have experienced little difficulty.

I was summoned today before the Local Council, which is run by a man who was a Petty Officer of signals in the *König*. He recognized me and looked away.

I was instructed to take *U.122* over to Harwich for surrender to the English.

I made no difficulty; some one has got to do it, and I verily believe I am indifferent to all emotions.

We sail in convoy on the day after tomorrow; that is to say, if the crew condescend to fuel the boat in time. Three looters were executed today in the dockyard and this has had a steadying effect on the worst elements.

* * * * *

I went on board *122* today, and on showing my authority which was signed by the Council (which has now become the Council of Soldiers, Sailors and Workmen), the crew of the boat held a meeting at which I was not invited to be present.

At its conclusion the coxswain came up to me and informed me that a resolution had been carried by seventeen votes to ten, to the effect that I was to be obeyed as Captain of the boat.

I begged him to convey to the crew my gratification, and expressed the hope that I should give satisfaction.

I am afraid the sarcasm was quite lost on them.

* * * * *

We are within sixty miles of Harwich and I expect to sight the English cruisers any moment.

I wrote some days ago that I was incapable of any emotion.

I was wrong, as I have been so often during the last two years.

In fact, I have come to the conclusion that I am no psychologist—I don't believe we Germans are any good at psychology, and that's the root reason why we've failed.

I do feel emotion—it's terrible; the shame—the humiliation is unbearable.

I wonder how the English will behave? What a day of triumph for them.

The signalman has just come down and reported British cruisers right ahead; it will soon be over. I must go up on deck and exercise my functions as elected Captain of *U.122*, and representative of Germany in defeat. One last effort is demanded, and then——

Note by Etienne

This is the last sentence in the diary. It is probable that he suddenly had to hurry on deck and in the subsequent confusion forgot to rescue his diary from the locker in which he had thrust it.

ALSO FROM LEONAUR
AVAILABLE IN SOFTCOVER OR HARDCOVER WITH DUST JACKET

DOING OUR 'BIT' by *Ian Hay*—Two Classic Accounts of the Men of Kitchener's 'New Army' During the Great War including *The First 100,000* & *All In It*.

AN EYE IN THE STORM by *Arthur Ruhl*—An American War Correspondent's Experiences of the First World War from the Western Front to Gallipoli and Beyond.

STAND & FALL by *Joe Cassells*—A Soldier's Recollections of the 'Contemptible Little Army' and the Retreat from Mons to the Marne, 1914.

RIFLEMAN MACGILL'S WAR by *Patrick MacGill*—A Soldier of the London Irish During the Great War in Europe including *The Amateur Army, The Red Horizon* & *The Great Push*.

WITH THE GUNS by *C. A. Rose & Hugh Dalton*—Two First Hand Accounts of British Gunners at War in Europe During World War 1- Three Years in France with the Guns and With the British Guns in Italy.

EAGLES OVER THE TRENCHES by *James R. McConnell & William B. Perry*—Two First Hand Accounts of the American Escadrille at War in the Air During World War 1-Flying For France: With the American Escadrille at Verdun and Our Pilots in the Air.

THE BUSH WAR DOCTOR by *Robert V. Dolbey*—The Experiences of a British Army Doctor During the East African Campaign of the First World War.

THE 9TH—THE KING'S (LIVERPOOL REGIMENT) IN THE GREAT WAR 1914 - 1918 by *Enos H. G. Roberts*—Like many large cities, Liverpool raised a number of battalions in the Great War. Notable among them were the Pals, the Liverpool Irish and Scottish, but this book concerns the wartime history of the 9th Battalion – The Kings.

THE GAMBARDIER by *Mark Severn*—The experiences of a battery of Heavy artillery on the Western Front during the First World War.

FROM MESSINES TO THIRD YPRES by *Thomas Floyd*—A personal account of the First World War on the Western front by a 2/5th Lancashire Fusilier.

THE IRISH GUARDS IN THE GREAT WAR - VOLUME 1 by *Rudyard Kipling*—Edited and Compiled from Their Diaries and Papers Volume 1 The First Battalion.

THE IRISH GUARDS IN THE GREAT WAR - VOLUME 2 by *Rudyard Kipling*—Edited and Compiled from Their Diaries and Papers Volume 2 The Second Battalion.

AVAILABLE ONLINE AT
www.leonaur.com
AND OTHER GOOD BOOK STORES

ALSO FROM LEONAUR
AVAILABLE IN SOFTCOVER OR HARDCOVER WITH DUST JACKET

ARMOURED CARS IN EDEN by *K. Roosevelt*—An American President's son serving in Rolls Royce armoured cars with the British in Mesopotamia & with the American Artillery in France during the First World War.

CHASSEUR OF 1914 by *Marcel Dupont*—Experiences of the twilight of the French Light Cavalry by a young officer during the early battles of the great war in Europe.

TROOP HORSE & TRENCH by *R.A. Lloyd*—The experiences of a British Lifeguardsman of the household cavalry fighting on the western front during the First World War 1914-18.

THE LONG PATROL by *George Berrie*—A Novel of Light Horsemen from Gallipoli to the Palestine campaign of the First World War.

THE EAST AFRICAN MOUNTED RIFLES by *C.J. Wilson*—Experiences of the campaign in the East African bush during the First World War

THE FIGHTING CAMELIERS by *Frank Reid*—The exploits of the Imperial Camel Corps in the desert and Palestine campaigns of the First World War.

WITH THE IMPERIAL CAMEL CORPS IN THE GREAT WAR by *Geoffrey Inchbald*—The story of a serving officer with the British 2nd battalion against the Senussi and during the Palestine campaign.

STEEL CHARIOTS IN THE DESERT by *S.C.Rolls*—The first world war experiences of a Rolls Royce armoured car driver with the Duke of Westminster in Libya and in Arabia with T.E. Lawrence.

INFANTRY BRIGADE: 1914 by *Edward Gleichen*—The Diary of a Commander of the 15th Infantry Brigade, 5th Division, British Army, During the Retreat from Mons

HEARTS & DRAGONS by *Charles R. M. F. Crutwell*—The first world war experiences of a Rolls Royce armoured car driver with the DuThe 4th Royal Berkshire Regiment in France and Italy During the Great War, 1914-1918.

TIGERS ALONG THE TIGRIS by *E. J. Thompson*—The Leicestershire Regiment in Mesopotamia During the First World War.

DESPATCH RIDER by *W. H. L. Watson*—The Experiences of a British Army Motorcycle Despatch Rider During the Opening Battles of the Great War in Europe.

AVAILABLE ONLINE AT
www.leonaur.com
AND OTHER GOOD BOOK STORES

ALSO FROM LEONAUR

AVAILABLE IN SOFTCOVER OR HARDCOVER WITH DUST JACKET

WELLINGTON AND THE PYRENEES CAMPAIGN VOLUME I: FROM VITORIA TO THE BIDASSOA by *F. C. Beatson*—The final phase of the campaign in the Iberian Peninsula.

WELLINGTON AND THE INVASION OF FRANCE VOLUME II: THE BIDASSOA TO THE BATTLE OF THE NIVELLE by *F. C. Beatson*—The second of Beatson's series on the fall of Revolutionary France published by Leonaur, the reader is once again taken into the centre of Wellington's strategic and tactical genius.

WELLINGTON AND THE FALL OF FRANCE VOLUME III: THE GAVES AND THE BATTLE OF ORTHEZ by *F. C. Beatson*—This final chapter of F. C. Beatson's brilliant trilogy shows the 'captain of the age' at his most inspired and makes all three books essential additions to any Peninsular War library.

NAVAL BATTLES OF THE NAPOLEONIC WARS by *W. H. Fitchett*—Cape St. Vincent, the Nile, Cadiz, Copenhagen, Trafalgar & Others

SERGEANT GUILLEMARD: THE MAN WHO SHOT NELSON? by *Robert Guillemard*—A Soldier of the Infantry of the French Army of Napoleon on Campaign Throughout Europe

WITH THE GUARDS ACROSS THE PYRENEES by *Robert Batty*—The Experiences of a British Officer of Wellington's Army During the Battles for the Fall of Napoleonic France, 1813.

A STAFF OFFICER IN THE PENINSULA by *E. W. Buckham*—An Officer of the British Staff Corps Cavalry During the Peninsula Campaign of the Napoleonic Wars

THE LEIPZIG CAMPAIGN: 1813—NAPOLEON AND THE "BATTLE OF THE NATIONS" by *F. N. Maude*—Colonel Maude's analysis of Napoleon's campaign of 1813.

BUGEAUD: A PACK WITH A BATON by *Thomas Robert Bugeaud*—The Early Campaigns of a Soldier of Napoleon's Army Who Would Become a Marshal of France.

TWO LEONAUR ORIGINALS

SERGEANT NICOL by *Daniel Nicol*—The Experiences of a Gordon Highlander During the Napoleonic Wars in Egypt, the Peninsula and France.

WATERLOO RECOLLECTIONS by *Frederick Llewellyn*—Rare First Hand Accounts, Letters, Reports and Retellings from the Campaign of 1815.

www.ingramcontent.com/pod-product-compliance
Lightning Source LLC
Chambersburg PA
CBHW031620160426
43196CB00006B/215